Children's Literature in the Classroom:

Weaving Charlotte's Web

Edited By:

Janet Hickman
Bernice E. Cullinan

Christopher-Gordon Publishers, Inc.
480 Washington Street
Norwood, MA 02062

ISBN 0-926-84200-5

Printed in the United States of America

10 9 8 7 6 5   94 93 92 91

Permissions and

Credit Lines

Text

Chapter 2, p. 16

From *In Coal Country* by Judith Hendershot. Copyright © 1987 by Judith Hendershot.
Reprinted by permission of Alfred A. Knopf, Inc.

Chapter 5, pp. 58-59

Web on Natalie Babbitt and her works by Esther Slauson. Reprinted with permission.

Chapter 9, pp. 99-108

From *Lotus Seeds: Children, Pictures, and Books* by Marcia Brown. Copyright © 1986
by Marcia Brown. Reprinted by permission of Charles Scribner's Sons

Chapter 10, p. 109

''Invitation'' from *Where the Sidewalk Ends* by Shel Silverstein. Copyright © 1974
by Evil Eye Music, Inc. Reprinted by permission of Harper & Row, Publishers, Inc.

pp. 111, 112

Excerpts from *Sweetwater* by Laurence Yep. Text copyright © 1973 by Laurence Yep.
Reprinted by permission of Harper & Row, Publishers, Inc.

p. 115

Excerpts from *Charlotte's Web* by E.B. White. Copyright © 1952 by E.B. White. Text
copyright renewed by E.B. White.

Chapter 15, pp. 157-160

Copyright © 1989 by Maureen Mollie Hunter McIlwraith.

Chapter 16

p. 165

From *One at Time* by David McCord. Copyright © 1980 by David McCord. Reprinted
by permission.

p. 166

Excerpts from p. 78 of *Dogs & Dragons, Trees & Dreams* by Karla Kuskin. Reprinted
by permission of Harper & Row, Publishers, Inc.

Illustrations

Table of

Contents

Preface   ix

Acknowledgements   xi

Prologue: Charlotte S. Huck — Weaving a Web of Love for Literature   xiii
  Bernice E. Cullinan and Janet Hickman

Part I
Beginnings: Understanding the Uses of
Literature in the Classroom

Introduction to Part I   2

Chapter 1:   A Point of View on Literature and Learning   3
  Janet Hickman and Bernice E. Cullinan

Chapter 2:   Selecting Children's Books: "The Rarest Kind of Best"   13
  Betty Marion Brett

Chapter 3:   Changing Conceptions of Early Literacy Learning   25
  Moira McKenzie and Gay Su Pinnell

Chapter 4:   "Please Don't Stop There!": The Power of Reading Aloud   39
              Barbara Friedberg and Elizabeth Strong

Chapter 5:   Literature: A Foundation and Source for
              Learning to Write   49
              C. Ann Terry

Chapter 6:   Using Literature Across the Curriculum   61
              Barbara Chatton

Part II
Strands: Celebrating Books and Authors
in Four Genres

Introduction to Part II   72

Picture Books

Chapter 7:   Picture Books for All the Ages   75
              Barbara Kiefer

Chapter 8:   Teachers Using Picture Books   89
              Marilyn Reed

Chapter 9:   My Goals as an Illustrator   99
              Marcia Brown

Fantasy

Chapter 10:   Dreams and Wishes: Fantasy Literature for Children   109
              Dan Woolsey

Chapter 11:   Fantasy in the Classroom   121
              Virginia Stelk

Chapter 12:   Fantasy is What Fantasy Does   129
              Madeleine L'Engle

Historical Fiction

Chapter 13:   A Gift of Time: Children's Historical Fiction   135
              Linda Levstik

Chapter 14:   Teachers Using Historical Fiction   147
              Lillian Webb

Chapter 15:   Living Close to History   157
              Mollie Hunter

Poetry

Chapter 16: Knowing Poetry: Choosing Poetry for Children   161
             Rebecca L. Thomas

Chapter 17: Poetry in the School: Bringing Children and Poetry
             Together   173
             Amy McClure, Peggy Harrison and Peg Reed

Chapter 18: A Bouquet of Poems about Poetry for Charlotte   189
             Eve Merriam

Part III
Patterns: Developing Literature-Based Programs

Introduction to Part III   198

Chapter 19: Moving Toward a Literature-Based Program   199
             Joan I. Glazer

Chapter 20: A Literature Program: Getting It Together,
             Keeping It Going   209
             Susan Hepler

Chapter 21: Administrative Support for Literature-Based
             Reading Programs   221
             Steven R. DeLapp

Chapter 22: Librarians and Teachers Working Together   231
             Diane Driessen

Chapter 23: Enriching Your Literature Resources   239
             Barbara Peterson

Epilogue: No Wider then the Heart is Wide
             Charlotte S. Huck   251

References: Children's Books   263

The Contributors

Betty Marion Brett, Memorial University of Newfoundland
Marcia Brown, three-time winner of the Caldecott Medal
Barbara Chatton, The University of Wyoming
Bernice E. Cullinan, New York University
Steven R. DeLapp, principal, Wickliffe Informal Alternative
    Elementary School, Upper Arlington, OH
Diane Driessen, school librarian, Wickliffe Informal Alternative
    Elementary School, Upper Arlington, OH
Barbara Friedberg, teacher, Martin Luther King, Jr. Laboratory
    School, Evanston, IL
Joan I. Glazer, Rhode Island College
Peggy Harrison and Peg Reed, teachers, formerly of Ridgemont
    Elementary School, Mount Victory, OH
Susan Hepler, educational consultant, Alexandria, VA
Janet Hickman, The Ohio State University
Mollie Hunter, Britain's Carnegie Medal winner
Barbara Kiefer, The University of Oregon
Madeleine L'Engle, Newbery Medal winner
Linda Levstik, The University of Kentucky
Eve Merriam, winner of the Award for Excellence in Poetry for
    Children given by the NCTE
Amy McClure, Ohio Wesleyan University
Moira McKenzie, formerly Warden at the Center for Language in
    Primary Education, London, England
Barbara Peterson, The Ohio State University
Gay Su Pinnell, The Ohio State University
Marilyn Reed, former co-ordinator, Informal Classroom Program,
    Upper Arlington Schools, OH
Virginia Stelk, teacher, Lakeland-Copper Beech Middle School, Shrub
    Oak, NY
Elizabeth Strong, primary education co-ordinator, Avalon
    Consolidated School Board, St. John's Newfoundland
C. Ann Terry, Baylor University
Rebecca L. Thomas, elementary library media specialist, Boulevard
    Elementary School, Shaker Heights, OH
Lillian Webb, teacher, Worthington Hills Elementary School,
    Worthington, OH
Dan Woolsey, Seattle Pacific University

Preface

Those who come under the guidance of a remarkable teacher learn a great deal about their subject, themselves, and the teacher. In this book we the contributors share some of the knowledge and insights derived from experiences as students of Charlotte Huck. A master teacher sends her students out to grow and extend the knowledge taught them. You will find here the voices of former students who reflect Charlotte's love of children's literature and who have continued to learn about the use of literature in schools. This book is a way of actively continuing to spread Charlotte Huck's teachings and philosophy about the qualities of literature for children and the role of books in the classroom.

The idea for this book was born in the mind of Susanne Canavan, an astute editor and promoter of literature for children. When she proposed the idea of a Festschrift for Charlotte Huck, we, too, saw the value of such a book, wished that we had thought of it ourselves, and immediately began to plan. We knew that we wanted to draw upon many of Charlotte's former students, and given the tremendous number of outstanding students who have come under her influence, we had a wealth of possibilities from which to draw. We regret that we could not call upon all of the talented people who studied with Charlotte Huck, but a single book could not contain them all. We knew

Charlotte's favorite genres, her research and writing interests, and her strong convictions about how children can learn to love books. These elements form the content of the book.

Through lively discussions, the book began to take shape. It fell logically into three parts, with a prologue and an epilogue serving as book ends for the central chapters. The prologue introduces the woman and her work through a vignette of her personal and professional life. Part I contains a discussion of her philosophy, perspectives on literary quality, early literacy, reading aloud, literature as a foundation and source for children's writing, and literature across the curriculum. Part II deals with four selected genres in which Charlotte has had a special interest: picture books, fantasy, historical fiction, and poetry. We did not attempt in this book to provide a comprehensive view of literature since Charlotte has done that with Janet Hickman and Susan Hepler in *Children's Literature in the Elementary School.* Within each of the four chosen genres, different voices speak. University professors provide an overview of the genres; teachers describe how they use the genres effectively in the classroom; and finally, authors offer personal perspectives on their work in the genres.

Part III includes discussions of how literature becomes a part of the school curriculum. There are chapters on moving toward a literature-based program, getting a literature-based program going, administrative support for literature-based programs, librarians and teachers working together, and ways for teachers to enrich their literature resources. Each chapter contains discussions of outstanding books for children. While not intended as an exhaustive list, the books cited represent some of the best literature for children. Professional references are listed at the end of each chapter. A comprehensive bibliography of all children's books cited appears at the end of the book.

This book is intended for teachers, librarians, administrators, and others who want to make literature a central part of children's lives. These are the same groups, plus children's authors, that we have drawn upon to contribute to the book. We believe that this book, written by the students and friends of a master teacher, will enrich the study of literature for children at the graduate, undergraduate, preservice, and in-service levels of education.

J.H.
B.C.

Acknowledgements

The publisher and editors of *Children's Literature in the Classroom: Weaving Charlotte's Web* would like to thank the publishers for their cooperation and assistance with this project. Their time and generosity are much appreciated.

Prologue

Charlotte S. Huck—

Weaving a Web of

Love for Literature

Bernice E. Cullinan and Janet Hickman

She sits in a comfortable study lined with children's books and reminders of books — an original watercolor by Barbara Cooney from *Ox-Cart Man*, a storyteller doll from the Southwest, a woodblock used in printing Evaline Ness's *Tom Tit Tot*. There is a quilted square above the fireplace and a basket of needlework, more quilting, within close reach. On an antique table, graced with a huge piggyback plant in a copper pot, lie a notebook filled with details of family genealogy and a folder from the last vestry meeting at church, both awaiting attention. At the moment she is reading one of the professional journals from the low fireside table, which also holds a book on wellness and nutrition, a treatise on Jung, and several volumes of poetry. The doorbell interrupts the woman's solitude, and Bridie, a well-groomed Sheltie, barks to announce a visitor. The woman is Charlotte Huck, and her visitor will immediately sense the warmth of her home and the force of the lively personality that fills it.

Remarkable achievers often have remarkable human qualities, and Charlotte is no exception. One should not be misled by the relative serenity of her surroundings for here is a woman of passionate conviction and fierce energy, as busy in retirement as she was in a long career.

As teacher, writer, researcher, and speaker, she has encouraged thousands upon thousands of adults to bring literature and the joys of reading to an untold number of children. She is most widely known, perhaps, as the senior author of *Children's Literature in the Elementary School,* now in its fourth edition, and for developing a graduate level program in children's literature at The Ohio State University. Others may think of her as past president of the National Council of Teachers of English, as a former chair of the American Library Association's Caldecott Medal Committee, or as an Arbuthnot Award winner for the outstanding teacher of children's literature presented by the International Reading Association.

Children's Literature in the Classroom: Weaving Charlotte's Web, prepared in her honor, concerns itself with the prevailing theme of her professional life: children's literature and its role in the classroom. The starting point is Charlotte's own work, and to understand it, we need to look at some of the influences that brought her to literature.

Shaping the Focus of a Lifework

Charlotte and her twin, Virginia, grew up in Kenilworth, Illinois, with three older sisters — Mary, Marsha, and Lucy. Books were a natural part of their childhood. Their mother and father both read to them frequently. The large upstairs hall contained two five-foot bookcases filled with children's books. Charlotte, called Chip by her family, and Ginny were inseparable; they shared books as they shared life and developed an abiding love of literature.

Each year the family packed a station wagon with clothes, food, and pets to head for a summer cabin beside a lake in the Wisconsin woods. Taking along enough food and clothing for five girls caused the station wagon to bulge, but each child was allowed to bring her favorite books. Perhaps it was on the screened porch in the Wisconsin cabin that Charlotte first discovered *The Secret Garden, Little Women,* or *Winnie the Pooh,* read on rainy days when she could not go swimming, hiking, or horseback riding.

New Trier High School in Winnetka provided alternative courses of study and many opportunities to know literature. Charlotte and Ginny were a part of the Eight-Year Study that waived college boards in order to offer a more creative curriculum than was then in vogue. The Huck twins, followed by the study through their year at Wellesley and graduation from Northwestern University, demonstrated that students could be successful in college when given wider choices than the rigid classical high school curriculum of the time.

After college graduation, Charlotte and Ginny went off to their first teaching assignment together. At Price School in City of Ladue, Missouri, Charlotte taught the middle grades, and Ginny taught kindergarten. Later, Charlotte taught at the Halsey School in Lake Forest, Illinois, and then at Joseph Sears School in Kenilworth, Illinois. During her seven years as both a primary and middle grade teacher, Charlotte was exploring the power of literature in the classroom and testing ideas that would shape her professional convictions and philosophy.

A masters' degree, an instructorship, and a Ph.D. degree from Northwestern University continued her apprenticeship as a researcher and scholar in literature. Two important relationships were developed during her years at Northwestern: one through her studies with mentor Harold Shane and the other through her friendship with a classmate, Doris Young.

The roots of Charlotte's love for literature sink deep into those Wisconsin woods and in her early experiences as a reader. Perhaps being a twin added a special dimension because she always had Ginny to discuss books they read in common. Books became a central part of the real life and imaginative world they shared. No sooner would one finish a book and want to talk about it than it would be passed to the other twin's eager hands. That unexpressible joy of sharing life and reading continued until Ginny's death in 1980.

Professing the Power of Literature

Charlotte joined the faculty of The Ohio State University in 1955, where there was only a single undergraduate course offered in children's literature; it did not take Charlotte long to generate enthusiasm for new courses. She had a vision of what an elementary school classroom should be like, and it focused upon literature. A former professor, Harold Shane, urged Charlotte Huck and Doris Young to put some of their creative ideas about literature into writing. One day over lunch, Doris and Charlotte sketched a rough outline for a book on a convenient paper napkin. That book, *Children's Literature in the Elementary School,* first published in 1961, is now in its fourth edition with Susan Hepler and Janet Hickman as coauthors. What started as roughly sketched notes on a paper napkin became the major, leading professional text in children's literature.

Charlotte Huck's vision of literature as the heart of the school curriculum began to change the nature of student interest and course offerings in the College of Education at Ohio State. Wherever she spoke at professional meetings, people came up to her to ask how they could study with her. Graduate students began clustering at Ohio State to study, and the course offerings in children's literature have grown accordingly. A children's literature master's program includes courses in specific areas of children's literature, such as the Roots of Fantasy, the History of Children's Literature, Poetry, Informational Books, and the Art of the Picture Book. The doctoral program builds upon these courses with seminars in research in children's literature, narrative theory, and readers' response.

From her earliest days at Ohio State, Charlotte organized conferences on children's literature. For conference speakers, she chose the outstanding authors and illustrators that teachers and librarians wanted to know. Following early conferences she would invite all the staff and speakers to her home for a postconference reception with food and camaraderie for all. People have been known to volunteer to work at a conference just to get an invitation to Charlotte's postconference soiree. Well known authors such as Eve Merriam, Madeleine L'Engle, Katherine Paterson, Mollie Hunter, and many others have been happy to return for repeat performances. The conferences have now become the well-established Children's Literature Festival, directed by colleagues Dr. Janet Hickman and Dr. Rudine Sims Bishop. Held annually in late January or early February, the conference attracts an overflow audience each year.

Another of the ways in which Charlotte envisioned sharing the power of literature with teachers was through a small publication that would review new children's books and give special attention to their classroom possibilities. Since its first issue in 1976 with Janet Hickman as coeditor, *The WEB* (Wonderfully Exciting Books) has featured contributions by teachers, school librarians, and graduate students who frequently try new books with children before reviewing them. What made *The WEB* truly distinctive, however, was the acronym's literal meaning: Charlotte insisted that every issue should include a "Web of Possibilities" — a chart of interconnected book titles, questions, and activity ideas with a common center such as a content theme, a single book, a genre, or an author. What began as a resource for local teachers is now a publication with nearly 4,000 subscribers throughout the United States, Canada, and beyond.

A Teacher's Teacher

Charlotte Huck is a remarkable teacher. She invites students into an active role of searching with her for the meaning of a text, the connections to poetry, the allusions in a line. There are no passive observers in her classes. Charlotte has camped out with EPIC students to demonstrate how informational books, novels, and outdoor activity can work together. She brings bags of books into every class from which she draws examples to illustrate her points; students borrow books from her to try to see what she sees. She juxtaposes groups of titles for comparisons that reveal universal themes. She demonstrates how readers' theatre, drama, debate, chart making, recounting of a character's changes, and the joy of hearing words read aloud can stimulate a love of literature in classrooms.

Charlotte treats her graduate students as fellow professionals. She regards them with respect and assumes that they are capable of all that she asks of them. Students live up to her expectations for she has created unique experiences where her students are eager to teach and return to share with her what they have learned. This is a happy regenerative process: Charlotte teaches her students, and they, in turn, invigorate and illuminate her teaching.

Susan Hepler says, "I look on my graduate school days and, later, my days as a colleague with Charlotte as some of the most fulfilling because I felt that I was growing continually. Charlotte was and has always been well-informed both in the field of children's literature and in research. She was able to feed our growing enthusiasm for reading with new books, but she was also able to provide a framework for us on which to hang our learnings. It is to Charlotte's credit that she never merely inspires teachers for the moment. She kindles a desire in us to learn more, to do more with what we know, to make a difference, no matter how small. Thousands of teachers attest to this, and countless children have benefited from this.''

One of Charlotte Huck's most memorable speeches (See p. 252) was titled with a line from a poem, ''No wider than the heart is wide.'' She exemplifies the meaning of the phrase in her life and teaching, illuminating a part of her nature that the outside world does not know. Over the years she invited a series of struggling doctoral students to share her home. It is a storybook cottage located on a quiet street near a wooded ravine. The upstairs of this story-and-a-half house has a bedroom, bath, and little study, which students termed ''the attic.'' As the group grew, one by one, they began to call themselves ''The Attic Rats.'' These individuals, partially by natural talent but largely by Charlotte's nurturing, became leaders in children's literature in various parts of the world.

Charlotte's love of good books is contagious and her concern for students genuine. These qualities have been passed along to the numerous students she nurtured during her career. Her graduates span the globe — from Saudi Arabia to Australia to England to Canada, as well as to many states including Hawaii to Maine and Michigan to Texas. In this volume, a representative few have been invited to address some of the special areas she guided them in developing. Her former students are a widely scattered group who work in diverse ways, yet all of them are handing down the magic of literature once worked upon them by a remarkable teacher.

A Researcher and a Scholar

From the beginning of her career as a professor, Charlotte Huck distinguished herself as a scholar and researcher. One of her early studies, the Critical Reading Project, launched directions in reading and literature that continue today. Charlotte worked with colleagues Willavene Wolf and Martha L. King to develop a comprehensive three-year study to see if they could improve children's critical reading abilities. They searched for consensus on a definition of critical reading, developed materials, trained teachers, and conducted the experimental program in twenty-four central Ohio classrooms. Major findings of the study showed that critical reading abilities were enhanced through direct instruction and the wide use of literature in the curriculum.

The Experienced Teacher Fellowship Program on Developmental Reading, undertaken with colleague Martha L. King, was an attempt to improve reading programs by working with experienced teachers in both a university and a clinical setting. The program not only shaped the future direction of teacher education programs at Ohio State, but the model was adopted by other universities across the nation. This experimental program led to a program based on the British Primary School, the EPIC program, where literature was used throughout an integrated curriculum including reading, language arts, social studies, science, and math. The program spread as teachers became excited about introducing literature to children when they saw the positive effects it had on learning in all areas. Experienced teachers who had participated in the program took EPIC undergraduates as student teachers, thereby passing along the benefits of their own experience and knowledge in a theoretically consistent program.

The most recent study, the Ohio Reading Recovery Program, continues today. This program, aimed at identifying first grade children who have difficulty learning to read, provides help long before ineffective habits are ingrained. Teams of teachers trained in this project have spread across the state so that nearly every child in Ohio who needs this intensive program has access to it. Reading Recovery staff also train faculty from other universities and school systems to implement the program in their areas. Charlotte serves as a consultant to this project, now directed by Dr. Gay Su Pinnell.

A Worker in Professional Organizations

Students of Charlotte Huck's soon find that part of their education comes from a broader arena than The Ohio State University campus. Gentle hints such as ''Well, you ARE going to NCTE, aren't you?'' make it apparent that indeed they should go. Charlotte Huck served at nearly every level of NCTE. She chaired the Elementary Section, served as a member of the Editorial Board and the Literature Commission, and cochaired Commission III at the York, England, International Conference. She served on the Executive Committee as president elect, program chair, president, and past president. She was one of the initiators and members of the NCTE/International Reading Association Committee: Impact of Child Development Research on Curriculum and Instruction and was elected as a member of the trustees of the NCTE Research Foundation. She was awarded the NCTE Distinguished Service Award in 1987.

It was a natural marriage of interests that led Charlotte Huck into the work of the American Library Association. Her interests in children's literature and her penchant for excellence drew her toward the work of the Newbery and Caldecott committees. She was a member of the Newbery-Caldecott Book Award Committee, chair of the May Hill Arbuthnot Honorary Lecture Committee, and elected chair of the Caldecott Committee.

Charlotte Huck has also given of her time and energy to support the efforts of the International Reading Association. She served as a Regional Team Leader for the IRA/Children's Book Council "Children's Choices" project and also as a member of the Editorial Advisory Board for the IRA *Dictionary of Reading*. She was a frequent keynote speaker at IRA conferences and contributed to numerous publications. Charlotte Huck was awarded the prestigious Arbuthnot Award for a distinguished professor of children's literature by IRA in 1988. She was also elected to the IRA Reading Hall of Fame in the same year.

Retirement Activity

It is obvious to Charlotte Huck's many friends that retirement merely represents a slight change in schedule. She continues to teach classes at local schools that reach out for her guidance. She serves as a consultant on the Reading Recovery Project, which is still growing. She speaks at national and international meetings, continues to write, and serves her church. She takes quilting classes, reads more books, and savors poetry as she plans a move to California, close to Ginny's daughters, Char and Jeannie. Retirement does bring the promise of time for new endeavors, however. As a start, she has written her version of a favorite folktale, *Princess Furball*, which is to be illustrated by Anita Lobel and published by Greenwillow.

Children's Literature in the Classroom: Weaving Charlotte's Web is an acknowledgment of the esteem in which its contributors, editors, and publisher hold Charlotte Huck. It is a tribute to the links she has made, teacher to student, literature to life, one professional to another; an intricate fabric of pleasure in books, passion for teaching, and personal support. Royalties derived from the sale of this book will be contributed to the Charlotte S. Huck Professorship in Children's Literature at The Ohio State University, the first endowed Children's Literature Professorship in the United States.

Part I

Beginnings: Understanding the Uses of Literature in the Classroom

Introduction

What is the basis for a philosophy that guides the selection and use of high quality children's literature in every aspect of a school curriculum? Janet Hickman and Bernice Cullinan address that question in two ways: first, in the prologue, by tracing the tapestry of a teacher's life that formed some of the strong patterns; and second, in Part I, by surveying major beliefs that emerged in her work. While the prologue provides a brief personal glimpse into Charlotte Huck's early interests, Chapter 1 traces basic views on literature and learning that are major threads in her work. It also serves to introduce principles discussed in greater detail by other contributors.

In one of the lead chapters, Betty Brett succinctly describes the experiences that led to the development of her belief in the necessity of searching for quality in children's books. She explains that she now uses a three-pronged approach that is work centered, child centered, and issues centered. Next, Moira McKenzie and Gay Su Pinnell show the effects of early encounters with literature in the development of literacy in young children. Barbara Friedberg and Elizabeth Strong next present a convincing argument for the power of reading aloud in helping children negotiate meanings for words and experiences in their lives. Following upon the case for reading aloud, Ann Terry describes literature as a foundation and source for learning to write. Through examples from children's writing, she shows how students become intuitively aware of form, structure of events, patterns of language and other conventions of literary discourse. She also describes Joan Aiken's development as a writer and presents a menu of literary experiences related to Natalie Babbitt's books. To conclude the section, Barbara Chatton delineates the functions of literature as it is used in conjunction with social studies, science, math, art, and music. She shows how literature raises questions, avoids fragmentation, makes connections, enhances problem solving, fosters critical thinking, and expands horizons. The chapters in Part I add to an understanding of the basic premises underlying the role of literature in a child's education.

1

A Point of View

on Literature

and Learning

Janet Hickman and Bernice E. Cullinan

Why do some teachers make time to read aloud every day or turn to literature rather than textbooks as a base for reading instruction? What makes them seek out a children's book to provide encouragement for a student writer or go to the library shelf to support lessons in history or science? Such classroom practices rest on a base of interconnected ideas — beliefs about the aesthetic and personal values of literature; theories on the nature of narrative and reader response; research evidence for the educational impact of children's books; and some basic assumptions about how children (and teachers) learn. The following pages provide an overview of this philosophical base for children's literature in the classroom. In general, these are the beliefs that underlie most of the writings in this volume since they have been major precepts in Charlotte Huck's teaching over the years.

The Inherent Values of Literature

> Reading and discussing. . . books is one way of humanizing our children. I am not so naive as to think literature will save the world, but I do believe it is one of the things that makes this world worth saving. (Huck, 1982, p. 316)

The first and best reasons for using literature stem from its aesthetic and personal values. Good children's books are a form of art and like all art have an infinite capacity to delight and move us, to touch the emotions and perceptions that make us truly human.

Literature provides for children personal satisfactions that are not a natural part of most other school subjects because literature is the one area that deals not just with facts but with feelings. Children love to laugh at the gentle predicaments of Arnold Lobel's Frog and Toad or share the surprise when *The Very Hungry Caterpillar* by Eric Carle emerges, transformed, from its fat cocoon. They are pleased to find some of their own enthusiasm for food in Arnold Adoff's *Eats: Poems* or to discover the visual delights of picture books like *Mufaro's Beautiful Daughters* by John Steptoe. Even sad stories bring their own kind of cathartic satisfaction. Countless young people have wept at the ending of Wilson Rawls' novel *Where the Red Fern Grows* and then asked for "another book just as good." It is this capacity to produce personal enjoyment that is the key to the power of literature in the classroom and in children's lives. Fostering that enjoyment is one of the most important things a teacher can do.

Literature also widens a child's world by providing a chance to participate through story in new experiences, meet new people, go new places, and see new things. Most children will probably never go "owling" except through the pages of Jane Yolen's *Owl Moon*, with the illustrations of John Schoenherr to draw them into the cold and quiet of a winter night. Readers in Georgia or Idaho can easily visit New York's Metropolitan Museum of Art through E.L. Konigsburg's story of two sophisticated runaways in *From the Mixed-Up Files of Mrs. Basil E. Frankweiler.*

Certainly literature provides bridges across centuries and cultures. Beautiful presentations of Native American tales in the work of Paul Goble or in a book like *The Mud Pony* by Caron Lee Cohen and Shonto Begay help children make connections with the world view of specific peoples in an earlier time. Such diverse books as Elizabeth George Speare's *The Witch of Blackbird Pond,* Mildred Taylor's *Roll of Thunder, Hear My Cry,* and Bette Bao Lord's *In the Year of the Boar and Jackie Robinson* demonstrate the universality of human feeling within the rich and sometimes painful variety of human experience.

Because literature gives children glimpses of so many different lives and ways of living, it allows for developing insights about oneself and others that might go undiscovered in the course of a single life. In Katherine Paterson's *Bridge to Terabithia,* children learn something of a grief they may never face; in Scott O'Dell's *Island of the Blue Dolphins,* they plumb depths of courage that their own lives may not require.

Literature also develops the imagination. Myths and fairy tales put children in touch with the huge store of symbols that constitutes our common human heritage; they give us new material with which to think and dream. The imagined worlds of fantasy allow children to explore strong emotion, as they do through Max in Maurice Sendak's *Where the Wild Things Are,* or to speculate about the unknown in stories like Jill Paton Walsh's *The Green Book.*

In a larger sense it is not just fantasy but all literature that is imaginative. Literary works of all genres encourage the imagination and nourish the thinking process. Theories about the nature of narrative and the reader's response help to explain why this is so.

Barbara Hardy (1978) has called narrative "a primary act of mind." It gives form to dreams and daydreams, plans, and ideas. Children in particular think in terms of story (Moffett, 1968) since they have not yet developed skill in other forms of discourse that are common to adults. Stories in print affirm and enrich children's personal narratives by supplying devices of order and meaning like the repetition that brings emphasis and suspense to the story of "The Three Bears" or the symbolic assurance of "plenty of chocolate cake" at the end of *A Baby Sister for Frances* by the Hobans.

In his book of essays, *Actual Minds, Possible Worlds,* Jerome Bruner (1986) argues that one of the contributions of literature is its power for generating hypotheses, for cultivating multiple perspectives or possible worlds. It is the nature of literature, he says, to

". . . render [the] world newly strange, rescue it from obviousness, fill it with gaps. . ." (Bruner, p. 24). Those gaps, as critic Wolfgang Iser (1974) and others have explained, enable the reader to bring characters, scenes, and events to life in the imagination. It is the business of the reader or listener to bridge the gaps, to imagine the possibilities, to create his or her own completed story. If the experience of literature makes readers more skillful predictors and speculators, more flexible thinkers who consider alternatives more easily, that is surely a plus for literature.

All these benefits inherent in literature ought automatically to secure a prominent place in the classroom for children's books. Yet many teachers who first used literature because of its artistry and power have continued to do so for another good reason: Literature helps children learn.

Literature and Learning

> For today we have proof of the impact of literature on children's reading and writing. What you and I have always known intuitively, what literate parents have always known as the natural way to interest children in books, has been proven to be correct. (Huck, 1986, p. 14)

The growing number of teachers who use literature in the classroom can testify to its value in teaching reading and writing. We also have rapidly accumulating research evidence to support claims for the educational value of children's books. The benefits are clearest in the case of young children, perhaps because much of the research has focused on that age group.

Sharing literature with children has a significant effect on language development. One well-known study by Ninio and Bruner (1973) describes how a picture book was the means for a parent to teach her toddler new words as they developed a routine for pointing, questioning, and labeling the pictures together. Hearing stories and having the opportunity to discuss them turned out to be a potent stimulus for young children's language development in an early study by Cazden (1965). Chomsky (1972) found that prior exposure to works of literature as measured by an inventory of story knowledge had a high correlation to several measures of linguistic development in a group of children ages six to ten. Recent research (Nagy, Herman, & Anderson, 1985) indicates that children in grade three and above learn the meanings of about 3,000 new words each year and that most of these are probably acquired in the context of children's independent reading. Most parents and teachers can also furnish convincing anecdotal evidence about the impact of literature on language. For example, one child of four called her brother "obstreperous" after hearing the word in a book by William Steig, and a boy complimented a classmate by saying, "You talk just like a book!"

Experience with stories is critical preparation for learning to read. The Commission on Reading (Anderson, 1984) advises that "The single most important activity for building the knowledge required for eventual success in reading is reading aloud to children" (p. 23). Gordon Wells (1986) makes the same point and supports it with compelling detail in his report of a longitudinal study in Bristol, England. His observations of children at home and later in the primary school showed that the best indicator of school achievement was their early experience of listening to stories. A study by Cohen (1968) involved reading aloud and simple follow-up activities with seven year olds who had little prior knowledge of stories; her experimental group showed significant gains in reading comprehension and reading vocabulary. A related study at New York University (Cullinan, Jaggar, & Strickland, 1974) confirmed that hearing stories did produce gains in language and reading, but that the greatest gains occurred when children also discussed and worked with the stories they heard.

At all levels, experience with literature helps children build the sense of story they need to be able to recognize the conventions and patterns of language they will meet in their reading. The more we know of stories, the better able we are to predict and adjust our expectations about characters and events in new stories. Skill and confidence come with practice—the kind of practice that comes from being read to or from reading alone. Recent research (Allington, 1984; Fielding, Wilson & Anderson, 1986) indicates that the amount of time children spend in silent, independent reading, both in and out of school, is significantly related to their progress in reading achievement. Teachers can be quick to assure doubting parents or administrators that a child curled up with a good book is not wasting time, but doing important work.

Another major educational value of literature is its influence on children's writing. Some effects are obvious. Children quickly pick up conventional beginnings and endings like "Once upon a time" and "happily ever after" or borrow names and situations from stories, sometimes unconsciously. The impact of literature, however, goes further. Separate studies by DeFord (1981) and Eckhoff (1983) found that the stories children wrote reflected characteristics of the materials used for their reading instruction; those who read basal texts produced simple, repetitious stories while those who read literary texts used more complex sentences and a wider range of forms. In Glenda Bissex's (1980) case study of her son's developing literacy, it is clear that Paul's varied writing productions are modeled on the large number of print sources familiar to him, including favorite children's books. Teachers and researchers (Smith, 1982; Tierney & Pearson, 1983; Calkins, 1986) continue to give increased attention to the connections between reading and writing and to value the contribution of good children's books.

Literature also supports learning in all the content areas. Fiction can introduce important concepts in the social studies or science curriculum, or in both, as the books of Jean Craighead George often do. Her novel *Water Sky* encompasses information about animal behavior and the environment as well as themes of cultural change in the story of an Inuit community's search for a whale. Jo Carr (1982) reminds us of the contribution of informational books that reflect both scholarship and passionate enthusiasm for their subject. Such writers are both teachers and artists, creating a literature of fact that makes a topic memorable as well as understandable. The use of fiction and nonfiction literature in the content areas can also be effective in encouraging critical thinking. Different books present various points of view and different ways of organizing or selecting information, making it a practical necessity for readers to compare, evaluate, and make choices.

There is plenty of evidence that literature provides a rich, supportive context for the development of new knowledge and for literacy learning. Having a classroom full of children's books does not guarantee, however, that children will be better writers and readers. Most of the evidence that supports the use of children's literature in teaching points to methods and approaches as well as materials.

A Response-centered Point of View

> It is important to help children discover the ways authors create meaning, rather than to superimpose an adult concept of literary analysis. (Huck, 1977, p. 367)

Claiming the full benefits of literature for children means that teachers must recognize and allow for basic characteristics of children as learners. They must also understand and be sensitive to children's responses to literature.

Most important of all, children are active learners. Piaget's motto, "To learn is to invent," tells us that children do not need to be crammed with knowledge *about* literature. Instead, they need opportunities to work *with* literature—to discuss, discover, consider, represent, and reread — in order to make their own meanings. Theories of response to literature affirm that reading and responding are in themselves active processes. Readers (and those who listen to stories) are busy as they predict, reflect, interpret, and make connections. Louise Rosenblatt (1938, 1978) explains response as an exploration of meaning or as a transaction between the reader and the text. The words on the page are cues from the author, but the reader has to contribute much in the way of personal knowledge, associations, and feelings. Rosenblatt's ideas about nurturing students in their explorations of literature are now guiding a third generation of teachers.

It is also important to realize that although children's discoveries about literature may be different from those made by adult critics, they are no less legitimate. James Britton's (1968) far-reaching advice is to help children redefine and develop the responses that come naturally to them, encouraging them toward an increasing sense of literary form. This sense of pattern or frame of reference for literature grows as children become familiar with more books and stories of various kinds, but it also depends upon children's own growth and experience in the real world. We know from research (Applebee, 1978; Hickman, 1986) that some kinds of interpretations and approaches to response are more characteristic of one age level than another. It is helpful for teachers to think of the more naive responses as age-appropriate rather than as mistakes that have to be corrected. However, we also know that in the context of good discussions children often reveal an "innate critical faculty" (Chambers, 1985), and this cautions us not to set our expectations too low. A response-centered point of view urges teachers to help children see meaning and value in literature but at their own pace and in their own way. Pushing children into formalized analysis has many dangers; only by inviting them into literature itself can we lead them to the best it has to offer.

The Importance of the Teacher

> If the future of our country depends on developing a "nation of readers," then each classroom must become a small community of children and teachers who know the value of books and discover the joy of reading. (Huck, 1987, p. viii)

> [There are] connections. . . between helping students and helping teachers grow in the process of becoming all that they can be. (Huck, 1980)

Not too many decades ago, children learned how to read at school, but they became real readers at home. Now that the prevalence of television and the pace of contemporary life have changed the pattern of family reading, the classroom has become the place for children of school age to read, to talk about books, and to learn to love literature. The teacher is the one who makes it happen.

An enthusiastic teacher who reads and enjoys books, shares favorites, asks for recommendations, and joins the class in solving legitimate questions about their common reading becomes a point of focus for students, some of whom may have no other model for fully literate behavior. Teachers need to be fellow readers as well as caring, expert guides. In order to fill both roles, teachers themselves need to be regular participants in the experience of literature, discovering new books, considering new ways of looking at familiar stories, and making new connections. It may be impossible to keep up with the yearly output of new children's books, but it is essential to stay involved in literature learning.

Teachers as well as children benefit from being part of a community of learners, whether in their own classrooms or with their peers, for many ideas can be developed only through talk, and many hesitant responses grow only because someone else is there to offer support. Generally, the same principles that guide the teaching of young children apply also to adults. It is important to provide time for children's reading and equally important that the teacher finds some time to read. If children's discovery of several variants of Cinderella makes each one more memorable for being part of an integrated experience, the same will be true for teachers just getting acquainted with new themes or genres. Together, teachers and children can learn from each other and share the joy in books that heralds a lifetime of reading.

Summary

There are many compelling reasons for using children's literature in the classroom. It offers the personal satisfactions, insights, and aesthetic pleasure of the arts along with an imaginative power closely tied to children's narrative mode of thought. Research has shown that literature also has educational value, providing naturally for content learning and for the development of language, reading, and writing in ways that skill-oriented materials cannot duplicate. Though books may have value in themselves, their impact in school depends largely on the teacher. A point of view that honors children's response and an attitude that makes the teacher one of a community of readers and learners are both important contributions. All together, these interwoven ideas about literature and learning form a web of support for its use in the classroom. Had this been the work of another Charlotte (Charlotte A. Cavatica of E.B. White's *Charlotte's Web*), the words written large in the web would surely be "ENJOY" and "LEARN."

References

Allington, R.L. (1984). Oral reading. In P.D. Pearson (Ed.), *Handbook of reading research*. New York: Longman. 829–864.

Anderson, R., *et al.* (1985). *Becoming a nation of readers: The report of the Commission on Reading*. Washington, D.C.: National Institute of Education, U.S. Department of Education.

Applebee, A.N. (1978). *The child's concept of story, ages two to seventeen*. Chicago: University of Chicago Press.

Bissex, G. (1980). *GNYS AT WRK: A child learns to write and read*. Cambridge, MA: Harvard University Press.

Britton, J. (1968). Response to literature. In J. Squire (Ed.), *Response to literature*. Champaign, IL: National Council of Teachers of English. 3–10.

Bruner, J. (1986). *Actual minds, possible worlds*. Cambridge, MA: Harvard University Press.

Calkins, L. (1986). *The art of teaching writing*. Portsmouth, NH: Heinemann.

Carr, J. (1982). Writing the literature of fact. In J. Carr (Comp.), *Beyond fact: Nonfiction for children and young people*. Chicago: American Library Association. 3–11.

Cazden, C. (1966). *Some implications of research on language development for preschool education*. Paper prepared for Social Science Research Council conference, Chicago. (ERIC, Ed. 011329)

Chambers, A. (1985). *Booktalk: Occasional writing on literature and children*. New York: Harper & Row.

Chomsky, C. (1972). Stages in language development and reading exposure. *Harvard Educational Review, 42*, 1–33.

Cohen, D. (1968). The effect of literature on vocabulary and reading achievement. *Elementary English, 45,* 209–213, 217.

Cullinan, B.E., Jaggar, A., & Strickland, D. (1974). Language expansion for black children in the primary grades: A research report. *Young Children, 29,* 98–112.

DeFord, D.E. (1981). Literacy: Reading, writing, and other essentials. *Language Arts, 58,* 652–658.

Eckhoff, B. (1983). How reading affects children's writing. *Language Arts, 60,* 607–616.

Fielding, L.G., Wilson, P.T., & Anderson, R.C. (1986). A new focus on free reading: The role of trade books in reading instruction. In T.E. Raphael & R. Reynolds (Eds.), *Contexts of Literacy.* New York: Longman.

Hardy, B. (1978). Narrative as a primary act of mind. In M. Meek, A. Warlow, & G. Barton (Eds.), *The cool web: The pattern of children's reading.* New York: Atheneum. 12–23.

Hickman, J. (1986). Children's response to literature. *Language Arts, 63,* 122–125.

Huck, C.S. (1977). Literature as the content of reading. *Theory into Practice, 16,* 363–371.

Huck, C.S. (1980). *Making connections between research on child language and teacher education.* Speech given at IMPACT conference sponsored by the International Reading Association and National Council of Teachers of English, Cincinnati.

Huck, C.S. (1982), "I give you the end of a golden string." *Theory into Practice, 21,* 315–321.

Huck, C.S. (1986), To know the place for the first time. *The Bulletin, 12,* 12–15.

Huck, C.S., Hepler, S., & Hickman, J. (1987). *Children's literature in the elementary school* (4th ed.). New York: Holt, Rinehart and Winston.

Iser, W. (1974). *The implied reader.* Baltimore: Johns Hopkins University Press.

Nagy, W.E., Herman, P.A., & Anderson, R.C. (1985). Learning words from context. *Reading Research Quarterly, 20,* 233–253.

Ninio, A., & Bruner, J. (1978). The achievement and antecedents of labelling. *Journal of Child Language, 5,* 1–15.

Rosenblatt, L. (1938). *Literature as exploration.* New York: Noble and Noble.

Rosenblatt, L. (1978). *The reader, the text, the poem: The transactional theory of the literary work.* Carbondale, IL: Southern Illinois University Press.

Smith, F. (1982). *Writing and the writer.* New York: Holt, Rinehart and Winston.

Tierney, R.J., & Pearson, P.D. (1982). Toward a composing model of reading. *Language Arts, 60,* 568–580.

Wells, G. (1986). *The meaning makers: Children learning language and using language to learn.* Portsmouth, NH: Heinemann.

2

Selecting

Children's Books:

"The Rarest Kind

of Best"

Betty Marion Brett

The session had gone on for more than an hour. The discussion had been animated, the opinions diverse and dogmatic. Occasionally, a raised voice betrayed its owner's frustration. There were pauses as individuals reflected. The participants were graduate students who had been challenged to think about the nature of literature and the literary experience and the relationship between children's literature and literature generally. To focus their discussion the students had been given three statements to examine:

> Only the rarest kind of best in anything can be good enough for the young. (de la Mare, 1942, p. 9)

> Children are a part of mankind and children's books are part of literature, and any line which is drawn to confine children or their books to their own special corner is an artificial one. (Townsend, 1971, p. 9)

> A child's range of choice in his reading will always depend upon what is at hand, and this will largely depend upon his elders. (Smith, 1953, p. 12)

The students were of different backgrounds. Although some were English majors, none had done studies in children's literature. Some were parents; all were teachers. All could read; some were readers. Again and again they returned to the statements for interpretation and analysis. They were obviously wrestling with new ideas. I listened:

> "My children are primary, so I don't worry too much about literature or the literary experience as long as they are reading."

> "My children know best what they like. It would be presumptuous of me to tell them what to read."

> "How can the critics who are adults know what books are best for children?"

> "But there are so many books. How can children — or even adults — know which ones are best? I don't know myself!"

> "This book is garbage. And the critics say it's great!" (The book being held up is *A Swiftly Tilting Planet* by Madeleine L'Engle).

> "Just what is John Rowe Townsend talking about?"

I listen carefully. I console myself. It is still the first week in the term, and I have heard all of this before. It is passingly strange how frequently such viewpoints surface in undergraduate classes, in parent-teacher meetings, in teacher in-service sessions, as well as in graduate classes. In any group there is usually at least one person who, with pride in personal enlightenment and liberalism, insists that for adults to choose books for children is an infringement upon the rights of those children to make their own decisions. The same individuals are usually unwilling to allow children a similar freedom in food selection, however, reasoning that although children may know what they like, they cannot be expected to know enough about balanced diets to always make wise nutritional choices. The fact of the matter is that in their choices of consequence, children need and deserve the guidance of adults.

Children may know what they like, but their taste and preferences are very much a matter of time, place, and circumstance and are determined by what they know best. Children lack the experience in both life and literature to be able to make valid decisions about where excellence resides. Certainly they cannot be expected to develop preferences for experiences they have not shared. It is mere folly to pretend that all books are of equal literary merit, just as it is folly to believe that children who are surrounded by an equal number of excellent and inferior books will automatically choose the best ones.

It is often argued that it is better for children to read something than nothing. This is a legitimate point of view if the sole purpose of the reading exercise is the acquisition of reading skills, in which case any collection of words may serve as word recognition practice. Road signs, candy wrappers, cereal boxes, comic books, and poorly written trade books may all be equally useful. This approach, however, fails to take into account either the nature of literature or the nature of the literary experience. The literary experience provides vicarious experiences; it deepens insights, sharpens sensitivities, evokes both thought and emotion, and helps the reader to interpret the world. Some books do this better than others. So much depends upon the quality of the books that children have accessible to them. Adults in positions of influence who provide children no assistance in their choice of reading material are guilty of a betrayal of trust and an abrogation of responsibility.

Not all books are literature. This is as true of children's books as it is of books written for an adult audience. Literature for children is, nevertheless, a part of all literature, characterized by those qualities of excellence that are the hallmarks of good writing. Since it is literature for children, however, it must always take into account the nature of its audience. In subject matter, theme, language, and approach it must reflect the author's perception of what childhood is like. Books that are genuinely children's literature recapture something of childhood with its honesty, its excitement, and its anticipation.

Children's Literature — A Philosophical Perspective

The grade two classroom was alive with excitement and buzzing with activity. It was Education Week, and many special activities were going on. Katherine offered to show me around. First, she showed me all the displays, the writing, and the artwork, and then she headed for her favorite spot. Walking briskly past the table where the reading series books were arranged, she paused only long enough to say, "These are readers. You don't need to see them," and she hurried me to the book corner. Several pals of hers were also there. A number of them were gathered around David, who was ensconced in the sagging armchair holding a copy of Lee's *Jelly Belly*.

David read dramatically from the nonsense verse, or was he merely recalling what he had already heard and read so often? It did not matter. He had a captive audience. Occasionally they all joined in the recitation. Peals of laughter erupted as they commented on the preposterous situations and humorous illustrations. So engrossed in their own enjoyment were they that we slipped by unnoticed. "These are our *good* books," Katherine observed, by way of explanation, as if no more needed to be said. Certainly anyone who knew anything about reading would know the difference between a mere "reader" and a good book! "This is one of our newest ones," she remarked, as she handed me *In Coal Country*. "And this is my favorite part," she added, opening the book to the second page where the image of the little girl hurrying to meet her father as he comes home from his midnight shift at the mine is reflected in the lens of his miner's lamp. "Just read what it says," she ordered. I read:

> In the morning I listened for the whistle that signalled the end of the hoot-owl shift. Sometimes I walked up the run to meet Papa. He was always covered with grime and dirt, but I could see the white of his eyes smiling at me. (Hendershot, unpaged)

I stopped. Katherine took the book and looked intently at the picture. Smiling as if to herself, she said, "My daddy carries a lunch bucket, too, but he doesn't work in a mine. He builds things. My sister and I wait for him and Mommy to come home when they are away." She laid the book carefully on the table, but before she moved on she noticed some other books that were obviously favorites. "It was sad when her grandfather died," she said, pointing to Aliki's *The Two of Them*, "but she will never forget him, will she? He was very kind. My

grandfather is like that. My grandma is, too." I did not spe
destroy the magic of the moment. I need not have worried. He
tion had already jumped to the next book. "I have always lov ...us
book as long as I can remember," she confided. "My grandpa and
grandma read it every night when I was young." The book was
Margaret Wise Brown's *Goodnight, Moon.* She replaced it reluctantly.

Young Katherine and the other children, who were so preoccupied
with their own enjoyment of the "good" books, had obviously experienced the truth of Smith's statement that "all books written for
children are not necessarily literature" (1953, p. 14). Having learned
that there is something special about what she called "good books,"
Katherine dismissed the others as being unworthy of attention. There
will be time enough later for her to learn about literature as vicarious
experience, about credible characterization, well developed plots,
significant themes, appropriate settings, and effective style. There
will be time enough for her to learn of different artistic techniques
in text and illustration. For Katherine and the other children, the present is all important. She is enjoying books and reading; she is identifying with situations and characters; she is responding both emotionally and intellectually. She is experiencing what literature really
is, and for her it is both personal and pleasurable. Literature just now
is enlarging and enriching her vision of the world, although at the
moment she may be unable to verbalize the depth of the understanding. The books to which she returns with such obvious joy are those
that are providing for her a rich literary experience.

Just what the nature of the literary experience is for an individual
child we may guess at, but we cannot really know for certain because
the interaction between child and book is both individual and private.
Although some confidences may be shared with peers or with a
trusted adult, there are many genuine responses that will remain
inaccessible. We may never be aware of it, but there may be some
children who, like Harold Coleman in Byars' *After the Goatman,* will
date their earliest flashes of insight into the imponderables of life and
death from a particular book or from a particular literary moment of
illumination.

The best children's books, of course, will serve a number of quite
distinct functions. They will provide information. Quite effortlessly,
in the context of an enjoyable story, children may gather a great deal
of information about people, places, and things. No one would suggest, however, that the communication of information is the sole or

even a significant function of literature. Admittedly, the best books provide tremendous opportunity for the development of language and other associated skills. Nevertheless, no one would seriously suggest that the primary function of literature is to serve as a vehicle of instruction in the language arts. The best children's books will provide opportunities for children to explore both life and the human condition. In convincing and captivating style such books may lead to understanding oneself and others, probe prejudices, enlarge the reader's capacity for compassion, and develop an increased awareness of what it means to be truly human.

The best children's books are literature. Such books evoke emotions; they invite thought and reflection; they engender ideas. While they are not necessarily serious, they may have profound statements to make about what the Little Prince in Saint-Exupery's book termed "matters of consequence." They explore universal truths with honesty and integrity. Concerned with the whole of human experience, they provide a link with life. While they generally celebrate the sheer joy of living, they dare to deal in tears as well as laughter. Their total perspective of life is positive, for they affirm the wonder, the expectancy, and the optimism that are so much a part of childhood.

The best children's books, in the words of Smith (1953), give those who enjoy them "a steadying power like a sheet anchor in a high wind, something to hold to" (p. 15). They are, if one accepts the philosophy of C.S. Lewis (1980), as worth reading at the age of fifty as they are at the age of ten. The challenge to concerned adults is to ensure that children have the opportunity to experience them and respond to them. That this will happen by accident is unlikely, given the brevity of childhood and the number of books available. The collection of "good" books in Katherine's classroom had resulted from careful evaluation and selection. Involved in such a selection process must be an awareness of what is available and a discriminating judgment rooted solidly in an understanding of excellence in both the literary and graphic arts.

Children's Literature — A Critical Perspective

It is generally agreed that a vigorous and informed criticism is essential to the healthy growth and development of the arts. This is true of literature as it is true of the arts generally; it is true as well of that body of writing referred to as children's literature. All who carefully and conscientiously select and evaluate books for children are engaged in a search for excellence, a search that demands informed judgment and some sense of the prevailing critical climate.

Children's literature in the best moral and humanistic tradition was born in the middle of the nineteenth century. That it has achieved its present level of excellence is attributable, at least in part, to the lively and growing body of criticism that has come to be associated with it. Gone are the days when no self-respecting author would admit to writing for children. Today most authors would be proud to join the ranks of Betsy Byars, Monica Hughes, Katherine Paterson, Barbara Smucker, Ivan Southall, John Rowe Townsend or Jill Paton Walsh, all of whom write children's books. The works of these authors and of others too numerous to list have been recognized by the critics as works that bear the marks of artistic craftsmanship.

The criticism of children's literature, firmly established in such landmarks of the past as Hazard's *Books, Children and Men* (5th ed., 1983) and Smith's *The Unreluctant Years* (1953), has in the last two decades or so included an increasing emphasis on the developmental nature of children as well as the growing concern for the manner in which contemporary social issues are depicted. Hence, there have emerged three approaches to the criticism; or perhaps it is more accurate to say that the present approach to the critical evaluation of children's books is a three-pronged one: work centred, child centred, and issues centred. These three approaches are unified by critical concerns that, defying any such categorization, deal with the whole. They are unified, for example, by an emphasis on artistic excellence regardless of the subject matter. A brief examination of each approach may be helpful in an attempt to discover what implications there may be for those involved in selection policies and practices.

A work-centred criticism is primarily concerned with the relative importance in children's books of the generally accepted literary conventions of plot, setting, characterization, theme, style, and point of view, and the individual and collective contributions of those conventions to the development of a successful narrative. It is concerned with form and language; it is concerned with literary technique. It involves interpretation, analysis, and comparison. This work-centred criticism, as well, includes discussion of the distinctive features of particular genres and helps provide answers to very practical questions. What, for example, are the distinguishing characteristics of historical fiction? Can books like Smucker's *Underground to Canada,*

Greenwood's *A Question of Loyalty*, Lunn's *Shadow in Hawthorn Bay*, or Brandis' *The Tinder Box* be considered first-rate historical fiction when assessed by those timeless qualities that mark the writings of Esther Forbes, Hester Burton, Rosemary Sutcliff, or Leon Garfield? Or how do *Gretzky! Gretzky! Gretzky!* and other books in the Picture-Life Series in Canadian Biography compare with Fritz's *Can't You Make Them Behave King George?* Does *The Keeper of the Isis Light* by Hughes have anything significant to say about the folly of judging by appearance? What can the reader learn from Le Guin's *A Wizard of Earthsea* that may be helpful in dealing with personal arrogance and fears? How effectively are the ideas communicated? Does fantasy always illuminate reality?

Child centred criticism draws from both literature and psychology, establishing an interesting relationship between the two. Focusing on the uniqueness of the audience in children's literature, this criticism makes statements about the relationship between author and audience and between text and reader. It affirms that a knowledge of the nature and the limitations of the developing child is essential if authors and artists are to communicate with children. Such knowledge will determine both the subject matter and its treatment. In any critical evaluation of books for children the focus cannot be on the work alone. To ignore the child is to deny the existence of a distinctive literature for children. While consideration of the literary quality must always be paramount, a function of both the author and the critic is to see the child at the centre and the match between reader and text. This is not, however, to deny the truth of Lewis' statement that a child's story that is enjoyed only by a child is not a good children's story.

A child centred criticism demands that those who select books for children ask very important questions about some of the books being marketed as children's books, even some of those that have won awards for excellence. Moreover, it focuses attention on what may be a rather ironical development in children's literature, a development in which the continuing search for excellence without reference to the nature of childhood may result in so-called children's books of literary excellence that are really beyond the reach of all but the exceptional child. Without minimizing the importance of books of excellence and challenge for the few, it must be emphasized that there is a need for good books for all children. Those who write, those who illustrate, and those who select books for children must be aware of the child's capacity to comprehend and to respond intellectually and emotionally. One may ask, for example, what it is that makes *The Last Free Bird* by Stone or *Hiroshima No Pika* by Maruki a children's book? Or what is the appeal of Willard's *A Visit to William Blake's Inn* to most children? Or why is Paterson's *Jacob Have I Loved* marketed as a children's book?

A trend of the last two decades has been the broadening of the subject matter of children's books to include a variety of issues and social concerns. Alcoholism, drug abuse, family violence, divorce, homosexuality, child assault, abortion, and death are all dealt with in books for younger children. Any valid criticism of those books must be concerned with both the appropriateness of such topics and the honesty of the treatment afforded to them. An issues-centred criticism has concern for both the legitimacy of the subject matter and the artistry of the presentation. It offers guidelines, for example, by which the depiction of minority groups, the elderly, and the handicapped may be appraised. It establishes conditions under which violence may be effectively and justifiably included. It makes a clear distinction between what is literary and what is merely social commentary.

The measure of a book's literary excellence is not determined by the relative number of male or female characters or whether those individuals are black or white, old or young, strong and healthy or suffering from mental or physical impairment. Regardless of the social issues, it is the author's perspective, vision, and sensitivity in the treatment of the narrative that will change into a work of literature what might otherwise be no more than crass propaganda. Literature will use social issues as the raw material of an artistic creation, going beyond the issue to illuminate life and the human condition.

Issues centred criticism can provoke much thought on the part of those who select and evaluate books for children or who are involved in stimulating book-related discussions. Is the violence in *Grover* by the Cleavers really necessary, for example? Does the fact that the Black characters in Armstrong's *Sounder* remain nameless mean that the author is racist? Is it really so that only Black authors can write about Blacks? Did Fox's treatment of the slave trade in *The Slave Dancer* show that, regardless of the colour of the traders' skin, their despicable behaviour is unacceptable in a civilized society? Are the language and the sexual references in Major's *Holdfast* gratuitously included for sensational purposes, or are they essential to the integrity of the plot? Are contemporary picture books like Hazen's *Two Homes to Live In* or Stinson's *Mommy and Daddy Don't Live Together Anymore* much more than thinly disguised social tracts? Who is the audience for Munsch's *Love You Forever?* Is the violence in Lee's *Lizzy's Lion* appropriate? Does the fact that a book is popular justify its promotion in the classroom?

Issues centred criticism affirms that literature is more than the voice of pressure groups with causes to champion. Authors and illustrators should have neither their subject matter nor their language prescribed. As artists they must have the freedom to explore and create. This freedom, though, must never be taken as license to distort, falsify, or sensationalize. Nor should a writer's attempt to evoke themes or address subjects once considered taboo automatically be construed as bold and original artistic achievement. Social issues should not be introduced into children's books merely as token gestures, nor should they be treated superficially once they are introduced. The challenge to both authors and artists is to recognize the issues that shape the lives of characters and to use these issues constructively in the creation of a literary work. The challenge to those who select and evaluate such books is to distinguish between concerns that are genuinely artistic and those that are purely political or topical. This challenge must be boldly addressed or both children and their literature will be the poorer.

The responsibility of critically evaluating and selecting books for children is a formidable one. The search for excellence demands the best professional judgement. Truly professional judgement will be both informed and sensitive. It will be informed about the nature of the literary work and the nature of the developing child; it will be sensitive to all social issues that impinge upon the lives of children; it will be sensitive to the manner in which these issues may indeed become an integral part of their literary experience.

A Personal Response

I looked up in response to a soft tap. In my office doorway stood one of the graduate students. "I came by to confirm that we are going to work with realistic fiction next," she said. "I plan to catch up on some reading during the weekend." I suggested that she include in her reading LeGuin's *Very Far Away from Anywhere Else*, Little's *Mama's Going to Buy You a Mockingbird*, and Hughes' *Hunter in the*

Dark. She agreed to add these to her already bulging case. She hesitated, as if she wished to say something else, then began, "This will sound silly, but I wanted to tell you that I had a strange dream last night. I was told by my doctor that I was going to die. Now normally I'm terrified of death, I don't want to talk about it or even think about it. Certainly the possibility of my own death is not something I have ever been able to deal with philosophically." She paused. "Strangely enough," she continued, "I was able, in my dream, to accept that possibility without shock or fear." She went on to explain that the only reason she could offer for such a dramatic attitude change was the fact that she had just finished reading Babbitt's *Tuck Everlasting.* Then with her words literally chasing each other, this very able but very quiet student, who had scarcely spoken out in class in the eight weeks of term confided, "I can't believe that so much has happened to me in just a few weeks. I simply can't believe the excellence I am encountering, both literary and artistic. And the ideas! I wouldn't have believed it possible that I could learn so much about so many things simply by reading children's books. I can't help thinking what a pity it is that all our teachers don't realize how those books can influence a child's view of the world as well as support and enrich everything in the curriculum."

The student is right. It is, indeed, a pity that not all teachers are convinced of the rich potential of literature to enrich both the curriculum and the lives of the children. The blessing is, though, that so many teachers are aware and that there are so many classrooms alive with books and book-related activities. Many teachers have discovered the world of children's literature and its tremendous potential for personal enjoyment, for discussion, for interpretation through art, music or drama, and for integration into science, history, and other subjects. Such teachers know that the entire programme of studies may be literature based. The possibilities are limited only by the breadth of their vision and resourcefulness, the depth of their knowledge and commitment, and the imaginative heights that they and their children are prepared to explore together.

Summary

Although children readily learn that some books bring them more pleasure than others, they cannot be expected to discover for themselves the "rarest kind of best" that is available in literature.

They need and deserve guidance. Teachers and others who assist in this search for excellence need to exercise professional judgement informed by their understanding of three views of the critical evaluation of children's books: work centred, child centred, and issues centred. Teachers who are confident in their own knowledge of books and sensitive to their potential will enrich children's lives by offering them a chance to know the best in literature.

References

de la Mare, W. (1942). *Bells and grass.* New York: Viking.

Hazard, P. (1983). *Books, children and men* (M. Mitchell, Trans.). (5th ed.). Boston: Horn Book, Inc.

Hunter, M. (1976). *Talent is not enough.* New York: Harper & Row.

Lewis, C.S. (1980). On three ways of writing for children. In Sheila Egoff, G.T. Stubbs, and L.F. Ashley, (Eds.), *Only connect: Readings on children's literature* (2nd edition). Toronto: Oxford University Press 1980. 207–220.

Smith, L. (1953). *The unreluctant years.* New York: Viking.

Townsend, J.R. (1971). *A sense of story.* Boston: Horn Book, Inc.

3

Changing

Conceptions of Early

Literacy Learning

Moira McKenzie and Gay Su Pinnell

Our conceptions of early literacy learning have changed fundamentally in recent years. We now see it in much broader terms than simply teaching children to read and, eventually, write. It embodies an understanding of the whole context and values of literacy that children meet in their everyday lives in their homes and communities. We recognize that literacy is culturally diverse and culturally learned. We know that reading and writing, like oral language, are learned in use, as they function for purposes seen to be relevant to the learners.

We know more about stories and storying; how we represent events in our lives in stories, and how our own stories are nourished and extended through our experience with literature.

Recently, we visited a kindergarten class where these understandings were reflected. When we walked into the room we were immediately aware that the children were engaged in a variety of purposeful learning. Evidence of opportunities for learning abounded. On one table there were growing plants, each labelled with the grower's name and what he or she had planted. Corn and beans were growing more or less vigorously. There were caterpillars and pupae, accompanied by information books and stories — including Carle's *The Very Hungry Caterpillar,* of course. Children urged us to join them watching as a butterfly began to emerge from its chrysalis. They talked about its gradual emergence, the dampness of its wings, and speculated on the kind of butterfly, how long before it could fly, and so on. They eagerly recounted their experience of the whole process from caterpillar to butterfly.

Two children were observing and sketching the guinea pig. Marty wrote on her picture FHDBABBS (Friskie had babies). They were keen to tell us about the babies she had had recently and where they had gone to new homes. Another girl was delivering mail from the classroom mailbox. Each child had a personal mailbox made from half a milk carton and clearly labeled with the owner's name. Eva, the mail carrier, was looking closely at Jason's name on a letter and James' name on a mailbox. She asked, "Does this say Jason?" The teacher, Jean Sperling, helped her decide by looking at the likenesses and differences in the two names, and Eva delivered the letter to the right mailbox.

Some children were writing letters; others were painting and drawing. Arnold Adoff had just visited the school and the paintings and murals around conveyed the children's enjoyment and understanding of his visit and his books. The classroom had a well-displayed collection of children's literature, read to them frequently, and children were reading and sharing favorites. Two children together on the floor were reading an enlarged version of *The Very Hungry Caterpillar.* "I can't read this page," said the girl to the boy. "O.K. I'll read it," he said, and he did. "I can read the next one," said the girl, and she pointed and read, "'On Monday, he ate through one. . .'" etc. Other children were busy making books, recording their plant growth, making get-well cards to send to a friend with chicken pox, while others were building with blocks, playing with dinosaurs and checking them in the accompanying books.

The reading and writing going on was real, surely representing the children's interests and concerns as the examples show.

Figure 3–1.
"We planted seeds."

Literacy Is Learned in Use

We know from research (Halliday, 1975; Heath, 1983) that the context in which literacy is used plays a major part in shaping how literacy learning comes about. The driving force behind much current research is that literacy learning is not just a particular set of skills but the result of conditions that allow children to be part of a literate community, doing the things that literate people do. In so doing they begin to learn how the written language system works and gradually gain control over it.

We know a great deal about the beginnings of literacy from recent research (Clay, 1972, 1975; Harste, Burke, & Woodward, 1984; Holdaway, 1979). We have learned that children's early experiences of written language come from two main sources: the words and signs and symbols encountered in everyday life and the books and stories they share with parents and others. Children soon recognize the golden arches of McDonald's, the service station where parents buy fuel, and the signs in the supermarket that relate to the goods in the displays. They see written language used in TV advertisements and relate them to the cereal or sweets they have in their homes and find on the supermarket shelves. All homes seem to receive a vast amount of junk mail, as well as official documents related to income tax, insurance, or social security. Most families need to make shopping lists or send greeting cards, and children become involved in these activities, and are often invited to take part, even before they can write. The evidence is that most children read and write for real purposes from a very young age; they begin to know both the purpose and function of reading and writing in the life of their community and get to know something about how you do it. Much written language is available to young children, but it is *contextualized;* it takes its meaning from the situations where it occurs and the function it serves.

Books and stories offer children experience of a different kind of written language. The language of books is *decontextualized;* the words themselves constitute the story or rhyme, without referring directly to the children's own personal world. In stories, language is used to create symbolic worlds where meanings are made through the syntactic and lexical features of written language and the conventions of literature.

Responding to Books

Children who have frequent experiences with books may begin very early to exhibit literate behavior. Eight-month-old Hannah recognizes her own books and can turn pages to look at pictures. She can also make connections between one text and another; for example, in one of her waterproof books used frequently as a bath toy, the picture of the monkey squeaks when squeezed. In a new zoo book with heavy cardboard pages, she repeatedly tries to squeeze the picture of the monkey. One-year-old Emily, already knowing and enjoying a number of books and stories, surprised her father one day when he said, ''Zippety Zip,'' as he zipped up his jacket. Emily's eyes turned to her book *Zippety Zap!* by Harriet Ziefert. Her father thought it was a coincidence, but the next time he did it, Emily went off and got the book for him to read to her.

As with everything else in their environment, young children encounter written language in various forms and try to make sense of it and use it. Those who have had rich experiences with written language know a great deal about literacy. They have a good ''set for literacy'' (see Holdaway, *The Foundations of Literacy,* 1979), meaning that (1) they have high expectations of print for making sense and providing enjoyment; (2) they are familiar with the language of books and can use it in approximations of reading; (3) they have discovered how stories are structured and can predict using their knowledge; (4) they understand some of the basic conventions of printed language such as that the print carries the message and that reading involves moving left-to-right; (5) they have done their own experimenting with writing, experiencing the power of producing written messages; and (6) they have positive attitudes toward reading and writing because that has been their experience so far.

Children Learn from Sharing Books with Adults

It is widely accepted that enjoying bedtime stories enables children to build a repertoire of books and stories they know well, which influences their language development, making it possible for them to predict the language met in books and so get a good start in reading and, generally, to be successful early in their school lives (Durkin, 1956; Clark, 1976; Wells, 1981). Recent studies of young children in home situations have illustrated how children begin to take on the tasks of literacy (see Teale & Sulzby, 1986; Bissex, 1980). An analysis (Fox, 1983) of young children's tape recorded oral monologues indicated examples of language that were not only narrative but literary, thus illustrating that young "children can and do learn complex rules of narrative production before they can read and write, rules which we are sometimes more accustomed to find underlying the texts of mature adult writers" (p. 24). According to Fox these young children seemed to transform their literary experience and to use it for their own narrative purposes.

Dombey's (1983) investigation into early story reading provides insights into the way a mother helps her child make sense of stories. She describes the mother-child talk as "weaving the language of informal conversation with the language of a certain kind of narrative." In the following excerpt from her example, a mother is reading Southgate's story of *The Little Red Hen* to Anna, just three years but already an eager explorer of stories and picture books.

> Mother: (Reading). The Little Red Hen took the wheat to the mill and the miller ground it into flour.
>
> Anna: (Pointing to the picture.) Why you got a hole in there?
>
> Mother: Well, in a mill they're upstairs — and it's like going into an attic and you climb up. You know when you go in the attic and you climb up and up the ladder and go through a hole. It's like that in the mill. (Dombey, p. 28)

We see immediately how the parent acts as mediator as she answers Anna's questions by relating the hole in the mill loft to the attic in their home. In the way she answers Anna she is demonstrating the active role readers must take in constructing meanings that make sense in the light of their own knowledge and experience. Dombey puts it this way —

> She is learning to interrogate the text, learning that for a story to be created within her mind, the listener (or the reader) cannot rely on a passive receptivity, but must play an active part in the asking of questions, the drawing of inferences and the constructing and testing of hypotheses. (Dombey, p. 41)

In enjoyable reading experiences, and the conversations and explanations that accompany them, children develop attitudes and expectations basic to reading and to learning generally. They learn to bring meaning to reading text in order to get meaning from text. Knowing how to draw upon relevant knowledge from our life — or another book — experience in this way is *learned behavior.* Heath

(1983) explored how children in cultures where books are shared in this way begin learning such behaviors very early in their lives, with adults who mediate literacy experiences and guide them in learning to make sense of books. Wells (1986) found that children who were most successful in early schooling were those who had enjoyed particular kinds of experience with adults and books. This knowledge should have a powerful influence on what books we choose to share with children in school and how we choose to share them. Cochran-Smith's research (1984) was designed to study how adults in one setting, a nursery school, set out to "make readers." She describes how the nursery teacher put into practice some of the knowledge now available about literacy learning.

Literacy Learning is Culturally Diverse

Sharing books in the ways discussed above occurs in particular cultures. Heath's work provides us glimpses into how children, all native speakers of English, are initiated into literacy in three small communities in North Carolina. Over a ten-year period Heath studied ways in which children were socialized into language and literacy in two working-class communities she named Tracktown and Roadville. She related her findings to data collected from a third group, who were teachers in the same area, which she called Maintown. She found that the three communities placed different values on literacy and used reading in very different ways. In Roadville, reading was valued for itself and how it could contribute to children's school learning. Children were given books and taught to know facts such as colors and numbers, letter names, and sounds. Their attention was focused on literal interpretation of texts, and fiction was suspect, not to be trusted. In Tracktown, books played a very small part in community life, but there was great emphasis on story telling. The community valued verbal adroitness, play with words, or making analogies, competences undervalued in their schools. In Maintown the interactions between parents and children with books were similar to those described in the previous section, with great attention given to the dialogue that accompanied the book.

A Point of Entry for all Children

There is little doubt that teaching in most schools is slanted towards success for the Maintown type of preschool experience where much crucial literacy learning takes place. Problems arise for children when their equally valid learning experiences are not recognized and developed in school. Research shows that almost all children from literate communities develop a remarkable knowledge of contextualized written language. Most children share that common currency of childhood — television with its stock of stories, cartoons, and films. In school, children should be encouraged to tell their own stories, from their own lives and happenings as well as those heard or seen. Some of the cartoons derive from folk and fairy tales, which can be shared through story telling, in the books we make with the children, and in the picture books we share with them. They will meet Cinderella and Snow White in a different, literary form and enjoy meeting old friends in new ways just as book-wise children enjoy meeting again their favorite books.

Encouraging children to tell their own stories, related to their own lives and experiences, in and out of school, is a way for children and adults to share their present understanding of events or situations. In this way they begin to create a *shared context* for negotiating and developing meanings. Wells (1986) says that "making sense of an experience is to a very great extent being able to construct a plausible story about it" (p. 196). Stories read to children, such as Hoban's *Bedtime for Frances*, or Sendak's *Where the Wild Things Are*, reflect back to them events and feelings in their own childhood in a literary form, which in turn gives more power to their outer story telling and to their imaginative and dramatic play. Wells has this to say:

> In conversation, children discover the forms of oral language that correspond to their inner storying. But in listening to stories read aloud they not only extend the range of experience they are able to understand but also begin to assimilate the more powerful and more abstract mode of representing experience that is made available by written language. (p. 200)

It seems that children enjoying real experiences in social situations interpret them in the stories they tell about them. The stories and picture books read to them and talked about nourish their own stories and add to their ways of telling.

What then has happened to the notion of "reading readiness?"

Reading Readiness or Emergent Literacy?

We need to ask ourselves what we really mean by being "ready to read" when children seem to be engaging in literate behavior almost as soon as they are born. We need also to revise outdated notions of basic skills and of skill mastery. There are important early learnings about reading and writing, but these need to be seen as part of the child's building a holistic understanding of the purposes, processes, and conventions of the written language system. Early, high-quality experience with children's literature appears to be a powerful factor in literacy development (Strickland & Taylor, 1986). As they experience hearing written language read aloud and produce their own attempts, supported by others, children develop the kinds of competencies that will serve them well in the more formal school curriculum.

In good kindergartens, such as the one described at the beginning of this chapter, children have wide experiences with spoken and written language. They hear stories read aloud, not just once but many times each day, and this reading is accompanied by conversation with a supportive adult. Even before they can exactly match words and print, these young children behave as readers as they produce their own approximations of books like Hutchins' *Rosie's Walk* or Campbell's *Dear Zoo*. They also behave as writers as they get their thoughts on paper in the best way they can.

Creating Rich Learning Environments is Philosophically Sound

Whether or not they had studied education as a process, most people visiting this kindergarten classroom would have pronounced it ''good education.'' Children were obviously happy and engaged in worthwhile activities. They were reading, exploring, and reflecting on their experiences through art, writing, and dramatic play. They were relating new learning to their present knowledge and interests. Their activities were connected; that is, linked together in ways that helped them develop larger understandings. Children were working for real purposes rather than on isolated and seemingly meaningless tasks; at the same time, they were developing the important skills and knowledge they need for intellectual growth generally and for literacy and math development.

Good educators and parents have intuitively created and appreciated many such learning environments. A tradition in the United States, however, has prescribed quite a different curriculum for the young child's classroom. Most kindergarten and first grade children do not spend time on activities such as those described above. Instead, they work to match letters and sounds; they fill in the blanks on countless ditto sheets; they work their way through a "readiness" book that requires knowledge of sounds but no reading; they spend their time on drill. That, along with the continuing emphasis on skills tests for evaluation and on mastery of a rigidly sequenced set of skills, offers little entry to literacy for many children. It makes it important to think more deeply about what makes good practice good.

In the present day, the classroom described above might be called "literature based" (see Huck, Hepler & Hickman, 1987) or "whole language" (Goodman, 1986; Newman, 1985). But it also belongs to a tradition of thinking about good education for children. In 1845, Horace Mann, returning from an inspection of schools in Europe, criticized American schools of the nineteenth century for focusing on words and letters instead of language in a more holistic sense. He urged enrichment of the curriculum through music, hygiene, and drawing. Experimental schools, such as the Mann School at Columbia University and the Dewey Laboratory School in Chicago, provided examples of good practice (see Huck, Lewis & Young, 1953). Dewey (1916) talked about education as "the continuous reconstruction of experience" and advocated active learning and choice. William Kilpatrick (1923) described the "project curriculum" used in Ellsworth Collings' experimental school in McDonald County, Missouri:

> He did not teach "subjects" as these are commonly understood. The actual aims of his school were not the conventional knowledge or skills, but the bettering of the present child life of his pupils. His starting point accordingly was the actual present life of the boys and girls themselves, with all their interests and desires, good and bad. This first step forward was to help guide these children to choose the most interesting and fruitful parts of this life as the content of their school activity. (Kilpatrick, p. 6)

Collings, a school superintendent, believed that "actual learning is never single" and many concomitant learnings always exist. The curriculum is a series of guided experiences so related that what is learned in one serves to elevate and enrich the subsequent stream of experience.

Language Research Supports Good Practice

Language research of the last twenty years has helped to illuminate the traditional theories of good practice (see King, 1975). From research on early language acquisition we know that children actively construct their own structures and meanings at every stage of language learning. Building on Piaget's (1954) studies of cognitive development, explorations of how children engage in these processes indicated the importance of experience and social interactions with others (Bruner, 1975). Research centered on the social and interactive functions of language (see Halliday, 1973, 1975) suggested that language learning begins with meaning and that young children focus on what language is for as they are socialized in the family and community. All of this research on language reaffirmed the importance of children's using both spoken and written language meaningfully within a supportive context.

Good Teaching Prevails

Most recently, research on the beginnings of literacy has again confirmed the definition of good practice while contributing to teachers' understandings of the "whys" of what they do in such environments. When Jean Sperling talks about her classroom, she refers to research that demonstrates how children form their own models of written language and gradually learn how to use and understand them. Researchers (see Teale & Sulzby, 1986) have described becoming literate as an emerging process that begins very early as young children encounter print in the environment and as they participate in the reading of stories. Harste, Burke, and Woodward (1984) say that children naturally use written language and in the process take ownership of their own learning.

What, then, should classrooms be like? In many ways, good classrooms will have the opportunities for active learning and choice described in the early writings of Dewey (1916) and others. The curriculum will be productive in that it helps children develop understandings and at the same time leads to further activities that extend opportunities for learning. These generative learning activities were and are good practice. But now teachers are learning how children develop significant understandings of text that underpin the processes of learning to read and write. They know how to support language and literacy learning sensitively through the activities and materials they provide and through their own interactions with children. They do this by closely observing children, making hypotheses about their learning and development, and tailoring their own actions to be most helpful to them. Teachers like Jean Sperling have gone far beyond just stimulating a series of "activities;" they aim to engage children in worthwhile first-hand experiences and to follow them in constructing meaning and taking on new learning. These "noticing" teachers assess while they teach, always looking for evidence of learning and ways of making connections with other learning. The result is an activity-oriented classroom, rich with literature, that provides a broad range of avenues to literacy guided by a teacher whose work is strengthened by sound knowledge of how children learn language and become literate in a real sense.

Summary

Classrooms that support early literacy learning are the teaching product of active learning and active and informed teaching. These classrooms help children continue the learning they began before school, expanding their knowledge and their strategies for learning more. These are places where, as in Jean Sperling's classroom, children can enjoy a favorite tale like "The Three Bears," attending to book language and story structure. They can use their knowledge of written language and story to compose a new text that they can read. They can attend to visual details of print as they write, and become familiar with conventions as they construct and reread their stories. They may create a spoken text by taking dramatic roles and exploring the story's meaning through play. We recognize this as good practice, and through the efforts of researchers in language and literacy, we understand more about why that practice is good for children. Teachers, too, are entering the research world to develop their own theories and understandings. Their observations and their depth of knowledge inform their decisions, creating good practice while they teach.

References

Bissex, G. (1980). *GNYS AT WRK: A child learns to write and read.* Cambridge, MA: Harvard University Press.

Bruner, J.S. (1975). The ontogenesis of speech acts. *Journal of Child Language, 2,* 1–20.

Clark, M. (1976). *Young fluent readers: What can they teach us?* London: Heinemann.

Clay, M.M. (1972). *Reading: The patterning of complex behavior.* Auckland: Heinemann Educational Books.

Clay, M.M. (1975). *What did I write?* Auckland: Heinemann Educational Books.

Cochran-Smith, M. (1984). *The making of a reader.* Norwood, NJ: Ablex.

Dewey, J. (1916). *Democracy and education.* New York: Macmillan.

Dombey, H. (1983). Learning the language of books. In M. Meek, (Ed.), *Opening moves: Work in progress in the study of children's language development* (pp. 26–43). Bedford Way Papers 17, Institute of Education, University of London. Distributed by TINGA TINGA, a branch of Heinemann Educational Books.

Durkin, D. (1966). *Children who read early: Two longitudinal studies.* New York: Teachers College Press.

Fox, C. (1983). Talking like a book: Young children's oral monologues. In M. Meek, (Ed.), *Opening moves: Work in progress in the study of children's language development* (pp. 12–25). Bedford Way Papers 17, Institute of Education, University of London. Distributed by TINGA TINGA, a branch of Heinemann Educational Books.

Goodman, K. (1986). *What's whole in whole language?* Portsmouth, NH: Heinemann.

Halliday, M.A.K. (1973). *Explorations in the functions of language.* London: Edward Arnold.

Halliday, M.A.K. (1975). *Learning how to mean: Exploration in the development of language.* New York: Elsevier North–Holland, Inc.

Harste, J.C., Woodward, V.A., & Burke, C.L. (1984). *Language stories and literacy lessons.* Portsmouth, NH: Heinemann.

Heath, S.B. (1983). *Ways with words: Language, life, and work in communities and classrooms.* New York: Cambridge University Press.

Heathcote, D. (1980). *Drama as context.* Aberdeen: National Association for the Teaching of English.

Holdaway, D. (1979). *The foundations of literacy.* Sydney: Ashton Scholastic.

Huck, C.S., Hepler, S., & Hickman, J. (1987). *Children's literature in the elementary school* (4th ed.). New York: Holt, Rinehart and Winston.

Huck, C.S., Lewis, I., & Young, D.A. (1953). Appendix: Chronology of significant developments in American elementary education (1633–1953). In H.G. Shane, Ed., *The American elementary schools.* Thirteenth yearbook of the John Dewey Society. New York: Harper and Brothers.

Kilpatrick, W.H. (1923). Introduction. In E. Collings, *An experiment with a project curriculum.* New York: Macmillan.

King, M.L. (1975). Insights from studies of language acquisition. *Theory Into Practice, 14,* 293–298.

McKenzie, M.G. (1987). *Journeys into literacy.* Huddersfield, Eng: Schofield & Sims, Ltd.

Newman, J.M., (Ed.). (1985). *Whole language: Theory in use.* Portsmouth, NH: Heinemann.

O'Neill, C., & Lambert, A. (1982). *Drama structures.* London: Hutchinson.

Piaget, J. (1954). *The language and thought of the child* (3rd ed.). London: Routledge and Kegan Paul, Ltd.

Taylor, D., & Strickland, D.S. (1986). *Family storybook reading.* Portsmouth, NH: Heinemann.

Teale, W.H., & Sulzby, E., (Eds.). (1986). *Emergent literacy: Writing and reading.* Norwood, NJ: Ablex.

Vygotsky, L.S. (1978). *Mind in society.* Cambridge, MA: Harvard University Press.

Wells, G. (1986). *The meaning makers: Children learning language and using language to learn.* Portsmouth, NH: Heinemann.

4

"Please Don't Stop There!": The Power of Reading Aloud

Barbara Friedberg and Elizabeth Strong

A group of ten- and eleven-year-old children were asked what they liked about hearing stories read. Ten-year-old Becky remarks, "It's like standing back and looking at a painting all at once." Eleven-year-old David says it provides him the opportunities to "make a better image of what's going on in the story and in my mind." For eleven-year-old Sarah, it allows her time to "get lost in a character," often the main character because she does not "have to stumble over words." She can sit back, relax, and just "think." Satisfaction and enjoyment are what reading aloud provides five-year-old Jason and seven-year-old Dolores. When their first grade teacher finished reading *The Little Red Hen* by Galdone, where that overworked hen had just announced her intention to eat all of the cake herself, Jason immediately responded, "That's appropriate." Dolores added, "It served them right, they didn't help. I'll bet the next time they'll help 'cuz they'll want some cake." These statements reflect some of the pleasures that reading aloud offers children who hear stories at home and school.

Influence on Language and Literacy Development

The powerful influence of storytime and read aloud sessions on children's literacy development, as well as on their personal growth and understanding of their world, has long been acknowledged by many educators and researchers. From infancy on, hearing and responding to stories and poems have shown to be most beneficial in extending and enhancing children's language development (Cazden, 1965; Snow, 1977; Ninio & Bruner, 1978). Listening to clusters of words like "a sloth of bears" and "a nursery of raccoons" in *Wild Animals* by Brian Wildsmith, or hearing sensory language such as, "I could feel the cold, as if someone's icy hand was palm-down on my back" from *Owl Moon* by Jane Yolen, or responding to precise poetic language like Sylvia Cassedy's description of the "Parlor" in *Roomrimes* heightens children's linguistic knowledge and competency and broadens their understanding of the world.

Kindergartners Susan and Kevin show how they enlarge their language storehouse and construct the meaning of unfamiliar words in *The Lion and the Mouse* by Dole. As the story unfolds, Susan cross-checks her meaning of "lair" by telling herself in a low voice that "'Lair' is the lion's home," while shortly after Kevin hears the words "seized him," he immediately whispers, "'seized,' he caught him." It is apparent from these examples that when these children hear new words they quickly seek meanings from the context of the story and from their previous experiences so that they can make sense of what they hear. Sometimes, however, meanings come later, as Susan found out when she encountered "gratitude" and asked, "What's that?" Although she was not furnished an immediate definition nor did she grasp the meaning from the context of the story, she did find out what "gratitude" meant during the follow-up discussion. When she asked, "What's 'gra-gratitude'?" Tim replied in a knowing manner, "Oh, that's when you say, 'Thank you.'" Read aloud sessions and the talk that accompanies them provide children many opportunities to enhance their language facility, learn how to mean (Halliday, 1975) and how to make sense of their surroundings.

Children not only learn how to negotiate meanings of new words and discover additional meanings for familiar words in different contexts, they also learn the importance of relating life experiences to literature (Ninio & Bruner, 1978; Cochran-Smith, 1984). Reading to children often triggers associations between their experiences and the content of the stories and poems. This gives them greater insight and deeper understanding of the embedded meanings interwoven in the stories and their decontextualized print. As six-year-old Paul listened to Galdone's retelling of *The Little Red Hen,* he linked his experience of watching his mom bake cookies with the little red hen watching her cake bake. When the little red hen took the cake from the oven, "a delicious smell filled the cozy little house." Hearing these words, Paul tilted his head, lifted his nose in the air and sniffed as if he were surrounded with the "delicious" aroma, and commented, "M-m-m-m, it's good!" Links of this nature make the stories and poems more memorable, helping children to connect their real life experiences with stories, and, in turn, stories extend and enrich their lives outside of books.

Links and Connections

Storytime and read aloud sessions provide children opportunities to make connections with other stories and poems. This intertextual awareness helps the children to build a frame of reference for literature, which broadens and deepens their literary landscape (Yolen, 1981). It increases their understanding and appreciation of the literary structures that stories and poems are built upon. The delight and humor in *The Jolly Postman* by the Ahlbergs can best be enjoyed and understood if a child has had previous exposure to the fairytales and Mother Goose rhymes. Without some background knowledge of these literary references, the child would miss a great deal of the fun and meaning of this story. For example, if a child has not heard "Little Red Riding Hood," or has no idea who Meeny, Miny, and Mo are, interpreting the underlying message of the letter from Harold Meeny of Meeny, Miny, Mo and Co., Attorneys at Law, to B.B. Wolf Esq., could be difficult. Similarly, older children who have no knowledge of dryads or fauns, may find it difficult to accept them in C.S. Lewis' lands of Narnia, and those who know nothing of Merlin may not recognize the importance of wizards in Le Guin's *A Wizard of Earthsea*.

Through reading aloud to children of all ages, important literary connections and references become known, increasing their knowledge of how, in Yolen's (1981) phrase, "stories lean on stories." This literary knowledge reduces the uncertainties that may exist in children's minds as they hear stories and enhances their ability to predict what will happen next, an essential part of learning to read and in sustaining interest in the written word. If primary children, for example, recognize the underlying "rule of three" in folktales, they can predict that if the first little pig builds a house so will the second and third, though the material will differ. A seventh grade teacher helped her children understand the mythical background of selkies by sharing two picture books, *The Seal Mother* by Gerstein and *The Selkie Girl* by Cooper before reading the novel, *A Stranger Came Ashore* by Hunter. This linking provided her children with a broader understanding of the ways of the selkie, an important character in Hunter's book.

Another teacher gave her children a similar experience when she read the 1988 Caldecott winner, *Owl Moon* by Jane Yolen. She linked Byrd Baylor's *I'm in Charge of Celebrations* to the delightful time the young child and the dad had going owling. The students then created their own "Celebration Days."

As children hear more stories and poems from different literary genres, their critical eye and ear enable them to make their own links. Billy, a first grader, upon hearing the title of Galdone's *The Three Billy Goats Gruff*, asked, "Is this the one where the troll is under the bridge?" By the third page, he had gathered enough of the storyline to say, "I remember this one." From then on he began to chime in on the, "Trip, Trap. . ." and to predict what was going to occur next. Ben, from the same class, began to realize after hearing a number of versions of "The Three Bears" that some stories have the same storyline but some of the language differs. After listening to the opening sentence of *When Goldilocks Went to the House of the Bears* by Rendall, he quickly remarked, "Ours didn't start that way. Ours said, 'Once upon a time. . . .'"

A Sense of Story

When children begin to make links of this nature, they are beginning to learn how things work, how story is constructed. They are developing a sense of story that enables them to have certain expectations about how characters will act (Applebee, 1978) and how specific stories will unfold. For example, a story that starts, "Once upon a time. . ." is usually a fairy tale, and it most likely will end, "They lived happily ever after." Internalizing these elements of language, style and literary structures and developing a sense of story are especially important to the acquisition of literacy (Bruner, 1986; Snow & Ninio, 1986; Huck, Hepler & Hickman, 1987; Spencer, 1987).

Children who hear stories and poems regularly have the opportunity to learn reading-like behaviors without anyone specifically teaching them. In fact, Snow and Ninio (1986) claim that there are very few rules of literacy that are explicit or can be taught explicitly. "Reading and comprehending texts depend on many tacit 'contracts' and 'metacontracts' between literate persons concerning the use of books and the meaning of texts — contracts which have very little to do with the ability to decipher a written word" (p. 121). Because children become so involved with story, they give themselves "private lessons" (Spencer, 1987). They not only learn how books work and how story goes, they learn how and when to turn pages, how print conveys a message, and how illustrations can be most helpful in making sense of the text.

Developing Imaginative and Critical Power

Perhaps one of the most important reasons for reading aloud is to stretch children's imaginations. Northrop Frye (1964) maintains that the stories and poems children hear and enjoy are the primary means of developing an educated imagination. Such imagination is pertinent in the lives of all children, regardless of their future endeavors. Without an educated imagination, he claims individuals cannot visualize new relationships or stimulate new developments in any area of study. Stories of all genres sharpen our observations and perceptions of the world, develop our emotional sensitivity, and extend our acquaintance with life (p. 4).

Literature arouses young children's imaginations as they struggle to solve the mystery of who took the teeny-tiny bone in Galdone's *The Teeny-Tiny Woman.* As seven-year-old Marlon argued, "It couldn't be the dog, 'cause it didn't say anything about a dog [in the story]." Taking the book from the teacher, he scrutinized each illustration searching for an answer. Not finding a satisfactory one, he returned to the story the following day to continue his search but still did not locate anything. As he put the book back on the bookshelf, he sighed and said, "I guess it must have been a ghost," and walked away. Children in third and fourth grades are often left to wonder who the 'stranger' is in Van Allsburg's picture book, *The Stranger.* Nine-year-old Rachel thought that the stranger "might be a spirit of the summer. The way he acts is so strange because he doesn't sweat when he works all day. The Bailey family wonders just like a lot of people who listen and read. Nobody knows who it is. There are so many different answers for this strange, puzzling man the Baileys call a 'hermit'." Since the author never reveals the identity of *The Stranger,* children must speculate and wonder.

Hearing stories can lead children to ask "What if" questions. After children have heard Banks', *The Indian in the Cupboard,* a discussion could evolve from the question, "What might happen if I could bring one of my plastic or stuffed toys to life?" Following the reading of Walsh's *The Green Book,* children could consider the question, "What if our planet were to be destroyed and we had to immediately depart for an unknown destination taking only one item with us? What would I take? Why?" Stories can push children's thinking beyond the bounds of the written texts and help them develop their ability to stand back from life and see things differently (Donaldson, 1978).

Children who live in homes and attend schools where books are valued and heard every day become critics of stories and poems at an early age. Vandergrift (1980) states that "Long before the child can decode words on paper, he is making choices among various. . .stories read to him. From the time of his first, 'Tell me a story,' he is exercising a kind of personal judgment that is the first step toward criticism" (p. 12). Growth in literary criticism occurs over time as children hear and read books, as they listen attentively and respond appreciatively to literature, and as they become aware of the books that are most meaningful, valuable, and enjoyable to them.

A Focus for Children's Reading and Response

Snow and Ninio (1986) claim that one of the most valuable impacts of hearing stories and poems on the nurturing of literacy is their source of enchantment and wonder. This triggering of delight and enjoyment entices children to return to their pages, revisiting their content and participating in them with deeper meaning. One six-year-old was so enthralled with the rereading of different versions of *The Great Big Enormous Turnip* by Tolstoy that he revisited the story more than forty times in a two-week span, through independent and partner reading, drama, writing, and art. This child, who had been identified as at risk of failing first grade, was able to read the story without difficulty at the end of the two weeks and found great delight in reading it aloud to his class. Through revisiting this story, he had become familiar with the language patterns and storyline, heightening his risk-taking ability and building his confidence as a reader.

When children hear the same stories and poems, they become focal points for much collaborative talk (Wells, 1986) and writing. This body of shared literature becomes the cornerstone for the development of a community of readers and writers. Read Patricia MacLachlan's *Sarah, Plain and Tall* to eight and nine year olds or Sid Fleischman's *The Whipping Boy* or Katherine Paterson's *The Great Gilly Hopkins* to a group of ten and eleven year olds, then elicit their responses and observe the intensity of their concentration and involvement. Take note of their in-depth discussion; that is, how it evolves and extends, how the children negotiate meaning. Notice how they borrow and improvise the story language, literary form, and ideas in their writing. Janet, Amanda, and Brenda, a group of fourth graders, had an enjoyable time following the letter format of *The Jolly Postman* and wrote:

Dear Mary, Mary Quite Contrary,

How did your garden grow? We at Frank's Nursery and Crafts wanted to tell you that you are eligible to enter the $500 and up sweepstakes. You have a 1 in 500 chance to win a trip over the moon with the cow.

Sincerely,
Frank's Nursery

The power of reading to children is also reflected in their success in school. Research (Durkin, 1966; Cohen, 1968; Clark, 1976; Applebee, 1978; Heath, 1983; Teale, 1986; Wells, 1986) has shown that children who have listened to stories and poems from an early age experience the most success in school. This success is heightened when teachers continue to read daily to them. The importance of rereading stories and poems to children has also proven to be advantageous. Studies (Beaver, 1982; Martinez & Roser, 1985; Morrow, 1988; Yaden, 1988) have revealed that repeated stories generate more talk, more complex questions, and more in-depth responses, as well as stimulate greater interest in reading the story independently.

Choices for Teachers

Teachers who value reading aloud and acknowledge its importance to children's learning and personal growth read daily for specific purposes whole books, chapter excerpts, and poems. One middle grade teacher states that she always reads three kinds of literature to her children each day — a chapter book, a picture book, and a poem. Sometimes reading aloud is purposely planned, as when children are hearing a continuous story; other times it may be woven into a discussion of a particular learning activity because it serves to make a connection, enhance an idea, evoke a question, or help solve a conflict.

These teachers also recognize the important effect reading aloud has on their entire curriculum. As one sixth grade teacher asserts, "Each period of history and each culture becomes richer if books are read which help children to understand and appreciate that group of people and their values. In fact, any curriculum area can be richly enhanced with fine literature from all genres." In his recent study of medieval life such books as Aliki's *The Medieval Feast* and de Angeli's *The Door in the Wall* were shared. When the children studied the Civil War, Lester's *To Be a Slave* was read, while in their language arts class the teacher read *Across Five Aprils* by Hunt. When studying the American Revolution, the children heard *My Brother Sam Is Dead* by the Colliers and parts of *Johnny Tremain* by Esther Forbes. Barbara Cooney's authentic pictures for *Ox-Cart Man* by Hall were shared with nine and ten year olds when they were studying the colonial period, while Jean Fritz's well-researched books then lead into the longer novels of that period.

Summary

Daily reading aloud should occupy prime time in every classroom. Introducing children to good books provides many educational values. It helps children develop language, build a frame of reference for literature, and discover the structures that stories and poems are built upon. It makes available to all children the satisfactions and imaginative power of literature. Reading aloud also keeps children interested in books and helps foster their desire to read on their own. The title of Daniel Fader's book, *Hooked On Books*, becomes a never-ending goal and is a more difficult task to achieve in today's television oriented world. Reading aloud is one proven way to interest children in reading good books. Once children have heard a book read aloud effectively, they invariably want to read it themselves.

In our quest for solutions to today's problems, we frequently neglect to look at the mistakes we have made in the past and continue to repeat our errors (Tuchman, 1984). This applies to education as well as our history. We know that reading aloud to all children is valuable, beneficial, and worthy of time spent. We must, therefore, reassess our educational priorities and seek to give reading aloud a dominant place in our curriculum.

"Oh please don't stop there. You do that every time. You stop at the most exciting part. At least tell us what is going to happen next." These words are often chorused at the ending of a read aloud session when the teacher deliberately stops at a place where anticipation reigns high until the next day. These are the words we need to hear more often in every classroom to show how reading aloud is honored and valued.

References

Applebee, A. N. (1978). *The child's concept of story, ages two to seventeen.* Chicago: University of Chicago Press.

Beaver, J. (1982). Say it! Over and over. *Language Arts, 59,* 143–148.

Bruner, J. (1986). *Actual minds, possible worlds.* Cambridge, MA: Harvard University Press.

Cazden, C. (1965). *Environmental assistance to the child's acquisition of grammar.* Unpublished doctoral dissertation, Harvard University.

Clark, M. (1976). *Young fluent readers.* London, England: Heinemann.

Cochran-Smith, M. (1984). *The making of a reader.* Norwood, NJ: Ablex.

Cohen, D. (1968). The effect of literature on vocabulary and reading achievement. *Elementary English, 45,* 209–213, 217.

Donaldson, M. (1978). *Children's minds.* New York: Norton.

Durkin, D. (1966). *Children who read early.* New York: Teachers College Press.

Fader, D. (1976). *Hooked on books.* New York: Berkeley.

Frye, N. (1964). *The educated imagination.* Bloomington, IN: Indiana University Press.

Halliday, M.A.K. (1975). *Learning how to mean: Exploration in the development of language.* Wheeling, IL: Whitehall.

Heath, S.B. (1983). *Ways with words: Language, life, and work in communities and classrooms.* New York: Cambridge University Press.

Huck, C.S., Hepler, S., & Hickman, J. (1987). *Children's literature in the elementary school* (4th ed.). New York, Holt, Rinehart and Winston.

Martinez, M., & Roser, N. (1985). Read it again: The value of repeated readings during storytime. *The Reading Teacher, 38,* 782–786.

Morrow, L. (1988). Young children's responses to one-to-one story readings in school settings. *Reading Research Quarterly, 23,* 89–107.

Ninio, A., & Bruner, J. (1978). The achievement and antecedents of labelling. *Journal of Child Language, 5,* 1–15.

Snow, C. (1977). The development of conversation between mothers and babies. *Journal of Child Language, 4,* 1–22.

Snow, C., & Ninio, A. (1986). The contracts of literacy: What children learn from learning to read books. In W.H. Teale & E. Sulzby (Eds.), *Emergent literacy: Writing and reading.* Norwood, NJ: Ablex. 116–138.

Spencer, M. (1987). *How texts teach what readers learn.* Victoria, Canada: Abel.

Teale, W. (1986). Home background and young children's literacy development. In W.H. Teale & E. Sulzby (Eds.), *Emergent literacy: Writing and reading.* Norwood, NJ: Ablex. 173–206.

Tuchman, B. (1984). *The march of folly.* New York: Knopf.

Yaden, D. (1988). Understanding stories through repeated read-alouds: How many does it take? *The Reading Teacher, 41,* 556–560.

Yolen, J. (1981). *Touch magic: Fantasy, faerie and folklore in the literature of childhood.* New York: Philomel.

Vandergrift, K. (1980). *Child and story: The literary connection.* New York: Neal Schuman.

Wells, G. (1986). *The meaning makers: Children learning language and using language to learn.* Portsmouth, NH: Heinemann.

5

Literature:

A Foundation and Source

for Learning to Write

C. Ann Terry

Read me a story so that I can travel beyond my world. Read me a story so that I can imagine pictures of unseen things. Read me a story so that I can hear words — words to ponder, words to reside inside my head, words that I safely tuck away until I create my own story someday.

The Power of Story

Consider for a moment the importance of story in our lives. Without our having the ability to understand or tell stories, our lives would change drastically. How would you convey to the teacher next door a story about an event that occurred during the lunch period or a tale about a happening on the playground? All of us use narrative many times each day to structure our experiences and relate them to others. We also think in narrative as we relive events, plan for the future, or attempt to find solutions to problems. At times, we create imaginary stories that play around with the question "What if . . .?" These imagined stories, sometimes called daydreams, are common and significant to us all. For some, they become published literary works, plays, musicals, television shows, scientific theories, or lucrative inventions. For all of us, they are a part of daily life.

Sense of Story

How do we acquire our knowledge and sense of story? At one time, listening to tales was a favorite pastime among people, and storytelling was viewed as an art. Today, in most homes, I suspect very little formal storytelling occurs, whereas the reading aloud of stories happens more frequently. In any event, it is through hearing and listening to stories at an early age that we develop and begin to refine our sense of story. "Though very young children may not be able to tell us in any full sense what they expect to find in a story," says Applebee (1978), "these expectations are reflected more or less directly in their attempts to tell stories to us." Story conventions appear over and over again in children's stories, such as in beginnings often associated with folktales, "Once upon a time" or "Long, long ago," or as endings such as "Happily ever after" or "The end." "The extent to which these conventions are recognized and used by children can be taken, to a certain extent, as an indication of the degree to which stories have begun the long march from the child's initial recognition that a story is in some way different from other uses of language, to the final firmly established recognition of story as a mode of communication," says Applebee. Needless to say, as children grow older and are exposed to more stories, they add to their existing knowledge of stories. They recognize story structure and make predictions as they read based upon their knowledge of story structure. They become acquainted with various genres and therefore understand that stories may take place in the past, present, or future. Children often mimic the language of stories, repeating patterns or refrains, as in "Trip-trap, trip-trap, trip-trap. Who's that tripping over my bridge?" They realize the importance of characters in stories and recognize common characteristics among characters, such as witches portray evil traits while the prince or princess in stories represent only good qualities. When children possess this type of knowledge about stories, they have a firm literary foundation upon which to build and write their own stories.

Literature and Writing

The key to providing children with a firm literary foundation for writing their own stories is an obvious one: Provide children with a wealth of rich book experiences. As teachers we must ensure that children have such book experiences. We know that many children are in homes where books are not owned, not valued, seldom read, and seldom shared. Television may be their primary source for hearing and learning about stories. For example, while visiting a fifth grade class, I listened to a teacher and a student discussing story characteristics as they conferred about a piece of writing. They talked about the beginning being a "grabber" and savored the well chosen action verbs in the piece. Finally, the teacher said, "Next, you might consider actions that build and lead to a climax in your story." The boy looked a bit puzzled as the teacher began to explain what she meant. Suddenly, the boy's eyes lit up, and he shouted, "Oh, yeah! I understand now. It's like the car chase. Two cars chase one another in and out of dangerous places until the bad guys in the lead car are caught by the good guys, like the stories I see on television."

Both researchers and children's literature specialists agree that exposure to literature appears to make a difference in children's writing abilities (Rentel & King, 1981; Huck, Hepler, & Hickman, 1987; King & McKenzie, 1988). In a representative study, Mills (1974) reports the results of a four-year longitudinal study in which children in the treatment group read children's books and discussed the stories prior to writing. These children scored significantly higher in their free writing than children in the control group, who did not use children's literature in this manner. The children in the treatment group learned how to write from hearing and talking about literature.

In her often quoted study and book by the same title, GNYS AT WRK, Glenda Bissex (1980) reports on the evolution of her own child's writing. Her son Paul, the "genius" in her study, learned to read and write at the same time. Bissex used a sign Paul hung on his door — Do Nat Dstrb: Gnys at Wrk — for her title. According to Bissex, reading appeared to have a substantial influence on the content and form of Paul's writing. Books served essentially as models for Paul's growing knowledge of the conventions of written language.

Books often serve as models for children's stories, and content from familiar books appears frequently in their writing. "Whether consciously or unconsciously, children pick up words, phrases, parts of plots, even the intonation pattern of dialogue from books they know" (Huck, Hepler, & Hickman, 1987). Teachers who share and discuss books consistently with their students see first-hand the influence of literature on children's writing. One such teacher, Searcy Dunn, a fifth grade teacher in Houston ISD, has what I call a "literature-based writing program" in her class. She believes, as I do, that it is extremely important for a teacher to share quality literature with children, especially if the literature serves as a model for writing. The students in Searcy's class know and enjoy books written by many well known children's authors, among them, Chris Van Allsburg. After reading *The Polar Express*, one of Van Allsburg's Caldecott Award winning books, a student in her class, Stuart Buchanan, chose to write a response to the story. About midway through his written response, Stuart writes, "While I was reading the book I fell asleep and had a dream. In my dream I was in the book feeling exactly how the boy felt." This part of Stuart's text appears to reflect a portion of the plot from another Van Allsburg book, *Ben's Dream*. Stuart, in reality, did not fall asleep in class while he was reading *The Polar Express*. Instead, he most likely borrowed an idea from a book that he knew well and used it in his response to *The Polar Express*. He probably thought it made his response more interesting.

There is one book all ages can enjoy even if you are old it can make you feel the joy of Christmas. It makes you wonder if there is a Santa Claus at the North Pole, but Santa can always tell if you believe or not. I think you have to believe in order to have a special Christmas. The book I did this paper on was the Polar Express. While I was reading the book I fell asleep and had a dream. In my dream I was in the book feeling exactly how the boy felt. I knew everything about how he felt through problems and joyful moments. I also knew how Santa felt about himself when he gave all those kids a present. My heart made me remember lots of joyful moments. That means my heart has a lot of love.

Figure 5-1
Stuart Buchanan's Piece

Poetry and verse serve along with stories as models for children's writing. They pick up refrains or patterns and use them in their own work. In ''Alligator Stew,'' a verse composed by second-grader Jennifer O'Brien, we discover the influence of Dennis Lee's humorous verse ''Alligator Stew,'' and Maurice Sendak's familiar rhyme, *Chicken Soup with Rice*. The refrain, taken from *Chicken Soup with Rice*, is somewhat altered, but distinguishable in Jennifer's verse.

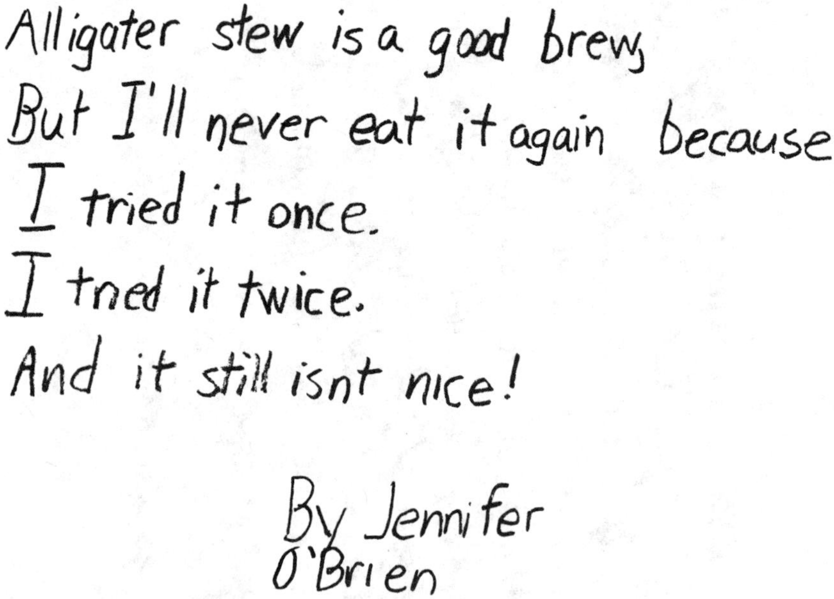

Alligater stew is a good brew,
But I'll never eat it again because
I tried it once.
I tried it twice.
And it still isnt nice!

By Jennifer
O'Brien

Figure 5-2
Jennifer O'Brien's Verse

The connection between literature and writing is significant. In the words of Frank Smith (1982), ''. . . the development of composition in writing cannot reside alone, but requires reading and being read to. Only from the written language of others can children observe and understand convention and idea together.''

A Pragmatic Approach

Young writers intuitively become aware of form, structure of events, patterns of language, and other conventions that are typically associated with literary discourse. I think as teachers, however, we have an obligation not only to expose children to many rich literary experiences and events in our classrooms in order to build a firm foundation for writing but also to capture and make the most of "teachable moments" that occur naturally during such literary experiences and events.

In an essay that appears in *Innocence & Experience* (1987), Joan Aiken describes both her father, Conrad Aiken, and her mother as teachers of writing.

> My mother was pragmatic in her approach to my writing. When giving me dictation, she nearly always chose poetry; I have reams from the *The Oxford Book of English Verse*, written down in careful copperplate, which got poetic language and verse forms very thoroughly in my head. And many of her casual remarks were pungent and memorable in themselves. "Look at the squirrel, how he suddenly stops and strikes an attitude," she would say, and I would write a poem about a squirrel. Or my mother, coming into a kitchen, would exclaim, "I dropped a pea in the larder—that sounds like the first line of a poem!" and I would scoot upstairs to the tiny writing-desk that I shared with my sister and write. . . . My mother was a direct teacher and believed in learning by imitation. "Write a poem like Wordworth, like Chaucer. . ." and I would produce accordingly.

Conrad Aiken made no such suggestions to his daughter, but he gave her *The Oxford Book of French Verse*, Keats' letters, Webster's plays, and volumes of poetry. He opened his extensive library to his children and made suggestions about what books to read.

Conrad Aiken provided his daughter with a literary foundation for writing, giving her numerous books to read, whereas her mother saw literature as a source for writing and studying the writing of others. Her mother capitalized upon teachable moments, planting ideas that grew into tangible works, and she suggested example works for thoughtful study and emulation. In order for students to grow as writers, we must do as Joan Aiken's parents did. We must use literature in our classroom in both ways: surround children with books and use them to teach the art and skill of writing. When we use literature in these ways, books become both a foundation and a source for learning to write. Within the context of reading and sharing books in our classrooms, we should become cognizant of teachable moments, just as Joan Aiken's mother did, and provide subtle instruction during such moments. As children grow older and are developing as writers, we should plan reading and writing experiences in which they can observe and study various conventions that typify particular kinds of writing. An ultimate goal is to have students understand how real writers work, how real writing gets done, and finally how to apply their understandings in their own writing.

What is the best way to learn how real writers work and how real writing occurs? We study writers and how they go about the act of writing, and, most importantly, we read, study and talk about their works. We want to select quality writers, such as Natalie Babbitt, and quality works for study, such as *Tuck Everlasting, The Eyes of the Amaryllis, The Search for Delicious,* and *Knee-Knock Rise.* We discuss the plot, or plan of action in stories, as it relates to Natalie Babbitt's stories. We may map out the action of one of our favorite stories by Natalie Babbitt. We study how the author has developed characters and made them believable in her stories. We discuss the significance of setting in Babbitt's books and compare themes in her books. We consider style and discuss how she uses metaphor and imagery to make her stories work.

The following web (pp. 58 & 59) presents a menu of literary experiences related to Natalie Babbitt's books. As we review the web, we envision how students gain a greater understanding of how literary elements work together in story-making. We also envision how teachers serve as guides through the various web experiences, using questions and discussion to help students make the connection between their own development of stories and the literary devices employed by authors such as Babbitt. When students explore quality stories in depth and engage in a variety of related book experiences such as the ones shown on the Natalie Babbitt web, they acquire knowledge that empowers them as writers. Once again, literature serves as a foundation and source for learning to write.

> Let me read stories so that I can discover how ''real'' writers write.
> Let me discuss stories so that I can learn the secrets of story-making.
> Let me write stories so that I can grow and develop as a writer. Let me share my stories so that I may enjoy the pleasure of authorship.

Summary

We develop our sense of story by listening to stories told or read aloud from an early age and, as we develop our knowledge of stories, we have a firm foundation upon which to build and write our own stories. It is clear that exposure to literature makes a difference in children's writing abilities. Books serve as models for children's stories; furthermore content from familiar books appears frequently in their writing. Young writers become intuitively aware of form, structure of events, patterns of language, and other conventions but teachers have an obligation to make the most of teachable moments to call attention to things authors do as we share literature with them. Teachers provide specific suggestions for using literature to help children learn about writing.

References

Aiken, J. (1987). On imagination. In B. Harrison & G. Maguire (Eds.) *Innocence and experience: Essays and conversations on children's literature.* New York: Lothrop, Lee & Shepard. 45–65.

Applebee, A.N. (1978). *The child's concept of story, ages two to seventeen.* Chicago: University of Chicago Press.

Bissex, G. (1980). *GNYS AT WRK: A child learns to write and read.* Cambridge, MA: Harvard University Press.

Huck, C.S., Hepler, S., & Hickman, J. (1987). *Children's literature in the elementary school* (4th ed.). New York: Holt, Rinehart and Winston.

King, M., & Rentel, V.M. (1981). *How children learn to write: A longitudinal study. Final report.* (NIE-G-79-0137). Columbus, OH: Research Foundation, Ohio State University. (ERIC Document Reproduction Service No. ED 182 465).

King, M.L., & McKenzie, M.G. (1988). Research currents: Literary discourse from a child's perspective. *Language Arts, 65,* 304–314.

Mills, E.B. (1974). Children's literature and teaching writing composition. *Elementary English, 51,* 971–973.

Slauson, E. (1987, Spring). Natalie Babbitt—A web of possibilities. *The Web.* (Available from The WEB, The Ohio State University, Room 200 Ramseyer Hall, 29 West Woodruff, Columbus, OH, 43210).

Smith, F. (1982). *Writing and the writer.* New York: Holt, Rinehart and Winston.

Getting to know Natalie Babbitt

— Read articles about the author
— Discuss how childhood hobbies and interests directly influenced the author's themes, settings, and illustrations of her books. "Natalie Babbitt" in Fourth Book Junior Authors, "Natalie Babbitt" by Jean Mercier

NATALIE BABBITT

Themes

— The cycle of life
    Compare Tuck Everlasting and A Gathering of Days
— Aging
    See similarities in The Eyes of the Amaryllis and Our Snowman Had Olive Eyes
— Pressures to Be Something You're Not
    How dealt with in Dick Foote and the Shark and Shadow of A Bull

Plot

— Map out the action of favorite Babbitt book
— Compare plot structures in several Babbitt books

Genre

— Determine the genre of each Babbitt book

Setting

— Consider the influence of the setting on plot and characters in The Eyes of the Amaryllis

Characterization

— Compare Gaylen to the boy King Arthur
— Decide if Mrs. Babbitt's comparisons between Hercules in Goody Hall and legendary Hercules were appropriate
— Discuss how the characters represent attitudes in Knee-Knock Rise
— Choose favorite character and list and changes in their personality
    The Book of King Arthur and His Noble Knights
    Hercules and Other Tales From Greek Myths
    The Search for Delicious

Illustrations

— Examine, compare, and contrast style of illustrations in:
    Phoebe's Revolt
    The Something
    The Devil's Storybook
— Draw pictures of main characters from her non-illustrated books
    Tuck Everlasting
    The Eyes of the Amaryllis

Figure 5-3
Natalie Babbitt and her Works

Style

— Examine the smooth incorporation
  of poetry into the plot and dialogue
  in her stories
— Find examples of imagery,
  metaphoric descriptions, and
  symbolism
— Discuss the appropriateness of
  the names of her characters
— Note clarity of style and the balance
  between narration and dialogue.
  Choose a representative sentence or
  paragraph
— Observe the consistency of Babbitt's
  style in writing and illustrating

Reading Aloud

— Share a story each day from
  The Devil's Storybook

Writing

— Write original Devil story
— Write and perform a mini-play
  from one of her short stories
— Create a poem that tells a story
— Write a letter to Mrs. Babbitt
  telling her your favorite book
  and why

Tuck Everlasting

— Discuss the necessary
  components of a good
  fantasy
— Compare the significance
  of the water in this book
  to what it represents in
  The Search for Delicious

Other Great Fantasies

Charlotte's Web
The Lion, The Witch, and The Wardrobe
The Hobbit
Tom's Midnight Garden

Adapted from ''Natalie Babbitt — A Web of Possibilities'' by Esther Slauson

Figure 5-3 (Continued)

Bibliography of Books for The Web on Natalie Babbitt

Babbitt, N. (1967). *Dick Foote and the shark*. New York: Farrar, Straus & Giroux.

Babbitt, N. (1968). *Phoebe's revolt*. New York: Farrar, Straus & Giroux.

Babbitt, N. (1969). *The search for delicious*. New York: Farrar, Straus & Giroux.

Babbitt, N. (1970, November 8). Happy ending? Of course, and also joy. *The New York Times Book Review*, 1, 53.

Babbitt, N. (1970). *Knee-knock rise*. New York: Farrar, Straus & Giroux.

Babbitt, N. (1970). *The something*. New York: Dell.

Babbitt, N. (1971). *Goody Hall*. New York: Farrar, Straus & Giroux.

Babbitt, N. (1974). *The devil's storybook*. New York: Farrar, Straus & Giroux.

Babbitt, N. (1974). The great American novel—and why not? *The Horn Book, L*, 176-185.

Babbitt, N. (1975). *Tuck everlasting*. New York: Farrar, Straus & Giroux.

Babbitt, N. (1977). *The eyes of the amaryllis*. New York: Farrar, Straus & Giroux.

Babbitt, N. (1977, December). Learning the language. *Language Arts*, 953-961.

Blos, J.W. (1979). *A gathering of days*. New York: Scribner's.

Commire, A. (1974). *Something about the author*. Detroit: Gale Research Book Tower.

Coolidge, O.E. (1964). *Hercules and other tales from Greek myths*. New York: Scholastic.

DeMontreville, D. (1978). *Fourth book of junior authors and illustrators*. New York: H.W. Wilson.

Hepler, S. (Ed.). (1982). *The best of the web, 1976-1982*. Columbus: Ohio State University.

Herman, C. (1977). *Our snowman has olive eyes*. New York: Dutton.

Kingman, L. (1978). *Illustrators of children's books: 1967-1976*. Boston: Horn Book, Inc.

Kirkpatrick, D.L. (1983). *Twentieth-century children's writers*. New York: St. Martin's Press.

Lewis, C.S. (1970). *The lion, the witch, and the wardrobe*. New York: Macmillan.

Malory, T. (1949). *The book of King Arthur and his noble knights*. Philadelphia: Lippincott.

Pearce, A.P. (1958). *Tom's midnight garden*. Philadelphia: Lippincott.

Sutherland, Z. (1981). *Children and books*. Glenview, IL: Scott, Foresman.

Tolkien, J.R.R. (1966). *The hobbit*. London: Unwin Paperbacks.

Tway, E. (Ed.). (1981). *Reading ladders for human relations*, 6th ed. Urbana, IL.: National Council of Teachers of English.

White, E.B. (1952). *Charlotte's web*. New York: Harper & Row.

White, M.L. (Ed.). (1981). *Adventuring with books: A booklist for pre-K–grade 6*. Urbana, IL.: National Council of Teachers of English.

Wojciechowska, M. (1964). *Shadow of a bull*. New York: Atheneum.

Worth, V. (1972). *Small poems*. New York: Farrar, Straus & Giroux.

6

Using Literature

Across the Curriculum

Barbara Chatton

A fifth grade teacher is packing her bag of essential teaching materials to take to science camp in the Rocky Mountains. She includes Jean Craighead George's *One Day in the Alpine Tundra,* Ron Hirschi's *Headgear,* and Sylvia Johnson's *Animals of the Mountains* as resource materials. She drops in Jim Arnosky's *Secrets of a Wildlife Watcher.* She adds Jane Yolen's *Ring of Earth* to provide poetic inspiration for some writings about the seasons. She puts in *I'm in Charge of Celebrations* by Byrd Baylor. She tucks in William Steig's *Abel's Island,* which she will read aloud to her students while they are at camp. On the very top she places Jamie Gilson's *4B Goes Wild,* about a group of fourth graders at science camp, to provide a little laughter at the end of each day.

This fifth grade teacher uses literature across the curriculum of her classroom and continues to provide that enriching experience for her students when she and her class go to science camp together. She realizes that to help her students become critical readers and thinkers she must include reading and good books as an integral part of every classroom day. In a time when students may have few reading experiences outside of school, this teacher wants to provide her students with daily experiences with good stories, poetry, and informational books. She wants her students not only to read but to read with pleasure, with increasing comprehension, and with a growing ability to use the knowledge they discover in the books they read.

Functions of Literature

Good literature, first and foremost, entertains. Books that make children laugh or feel pity or pose provocative questions set the stage for further study. A good story or poem piques a child's interest in subjects and ideas about which the child has had little previous knowledge. One second grader listened to Whitney's *Vasilisa the Beautiful* and wanted to know more about Russia and its tales. An older child became fascinated with Michelangelo after trying to solve the statue mystery in Konigsberg's *From the Mixed-up Files of Mrs. Basil E. Frankweiler.* Another wanted to learn more about Black American history after reading about Cassie's experiences in Taylor's *Roll of Thunder, Hear My Cry.* Teachers can take advantage of this natural curiosity and use literature to invite further study. A poem such as Hoberman's "Cricket" might start children speculating about insect bodies and their functions. The letters in Cleary's *Dear Mr. Henshaw* may help students understand that letter writing is a way of thinking about yourself and of communicating rather than simply a set of skills to be mastered.

Teachers can use books to provoke interest in a variety of ways. For example, read aloud from books that provide ties to the content of the sciences, social studies, and reading and language programs. Create displays of attractive books that highlight and explore ideas and questions raised in the classroom. Post poems that explore a topic that will be studied in the classroom so that children can consider the poem before, during, and after study. Feature books in learning centers as direct ties to the activities included in the centers.

Entertaining books may enhance children's interest in working in these areas; they also deepen their understanding of what they do there. *Note of warning! Take care not to stretch too far to tie a book to a skill or activity or to use the same strategy too frequently. Children may begin to think of books and poetry as teaching devices rather than as positive and entertaining growth experiences if every activity or lesson is introduced in the same way.*

Once children's interest in a subject has been aroused teachers can use literature to develop a climate for discovery in the classroom. Inquiry learning, which encourages students to pose questions to be explored and then to discover potential solutions through experimentation and study, is fostered in classrooms in which there is a literary environment.

Literature Raises Questions

In the literature-filled classroom questions are posed throughout the day as children react to what they read and hear. As one first grader said upon hearing Browne's *Gorilla,* ''It's like the book has questions that you have to answer in your head to try to figure it out.'' Good books, stories, and poems raise questions that pique interest and curiosity. Teachers encourage students to work toward ways of answering the questions literature raises. When two students found differing pieces of information about Mars in the science fiction books they were reading and got into an argument over which was right, the teacher asked them how they might settle the argument. They checked encyclopedias, nonfiction books on Mars, and an article the school library media specialist helped them to find in a magazine. As they synthesized what they had learned from these other sources they resolved their argument. The students also agreed to present to the class the information that they had found out about Mars as they went about answering their question.

Another student found a cat poem and declared that it didn't describe her cat at all. Her teacher showed her Livingston's collection, *Cat Poems* and Hopkins' *I Am the Cat,* and in these books she found poems that she did like. After seeing so many poets' descriptions of their cats she decided to write her own poem about her cat. When she had written and edited the poem her teacher helped her to mount it and several of her favorites from poetry collections for a special display in the classroom.

These students were able to seize upon an idea or question as they read and to pursue it through study and experience. In both cases the teacher capitalized on the learning experience and gave children a chance to share their knowledge with others. In order to foster this literary spirit of inquiry, classrooms and library media centers need to be equipped with strong collections of current informational books, poetry, and fiction so that children can explore written material and make connections. Ideally library media specialists are available to aid teachers and students in the discovery process. Use of collections should be flexible: teachers should be allowed to keep materials in their classrooms during the times when subjects are studied or give children freedom to use the library as they find questions and topics to explore.

Literature Avoids Fragmentation

Frequently in elementary schools the information presented to children is fragmented, with no clear ties made to the larger world of knowledge or to the child's own experiences. The study of animals in a basic science series, for example, may include learning the differences among mammals, birds, and fish, discussions of animal behavior, eating habits, and so on. The information presented in brief lessons focuses on only one of the topics. Literature can be used to enrich these basic lessons. Books illustrate animal communities and categories in ways that deepen children's understandings.

Children might work in small groups, focusing on the study of one animal, comparing informational materials, finding poetry and stories, and looking for folklore that shows their animals in special ways. They might enjoy listening to their teacher read aloud from books such as North's *Rascal,* which show humans and animals interacting. They might add their own chapters to Barrett's *Animals Should Definitely Not Wear Clothing* or *A Snake is Totally Tail* to show what they know about animal characteristics. All of these activities that focus on books, reading, and writing about animals will reinforce the lessons of the basic science texts so that students understand and remember the material they have covered.

Literature Makes Connections

One of the important functions of literature is that it provides the reader with insights into the human condition and asks the reader to rethink his or her own experiences in light of what has been read. Because it does provide these experiences, literature can be used across the curriculum to arouse curiosity, to enhance understanding, and to help children to see connections among ideas and topics they study in school.

A significant factor in helping children to put information into a larger context is the connections that students make between their own understandings and new information. Literature can play an important role in this bridging function as it helps students to feel a sense of empathy for people or animals they may be studying. Upper elementary children may study the American Revolutionary War in their social studies text by locating sites of significant events on maps, learning important dates, and studying the actions of important people. What they can miss from these experiences is a sense of connectedness to past events: a sense that these events have significance for their own lives. Literature such as Forbes' *Johnny Tremain* and the Colliers' *My Brother Sam Is Dead* opens doors to history by providing opportunities for readers to get to know young people who live in different times and places. Through their connection to the characters readers can better understand what it might have felt like to have lived through historic events and what their significance really is.

Art in picture books provides another type of "bridge" experience for children trying to make sense of a subject. Cooney's illustrations for Donald Hall's *Ox-Cart Man* clearly evoke the hard work and long journey to market in nineteenth century New England. Stephen Kellogg's pictures enhance and clarify the concept of large numbers in *How Much is a Million?* And Heller's brilliantly colored pictures for *Chickens Aren't the Only Ones* help children to clearly see all of the egg-laying species.

Literature Enhances Problem Solving

Use of literature across the curriculum enhances children's problem solving abilities. The characteristics of problem solving include the awareness of likenesses, differences, and analogies; the ability to identify crucial elements in a problem; the ability to visualize and the ability to generalize. Involved readers are problem solvers. A fifth grader reading Raskin's *The Westing Game* exhibited a number of problem solving characteristics as he read and responded to this mystery including making connections to his own experience of mystery stories. He continuously re-sorted and categorized the elements of the story to decide which were the significant clues and drew the floor plan of an apartment building to help him to visualize events.

Young readers often solve problems in the plots of books they read by focusing on analogies to their own lives and experiences. The most natural reaction when reading a book is to imagine what one would do in the character's place. A small child may call out why he would choose the grey and white cat in Gag's *Millions of Cats*. Another child will offer a solution to Lionni's *Swimmy* and his problem with the big fish. An older student might have ideas about what Cracker could do to help Alma in Byars' *Cracker Jackson*. Problem solving is required by literature; the reader who is involved and identifies with characters has an opportunity to live through a variety of situations, real and imagined, and to try his or her hand at solutions.

Much nonfiction for children is stylistically presented to encourage readers to use problem solving strategies. Seymour Simon's *Animal Fact/Animal Fable* offers alternative solutions for children to ponder and respond to. Tomie de Paola's *The Quicksand Book* comically presents the child with a problem and discusses methods for solving it. Millicent Selsam's *Where Do They Go? Insects in Winter* poses questions for children to think about as they read.

Literature Fosters Critical Thinking

Literature also fosters critical thinking. Teachers can encourage critical thinking by the kinds of questions they ask their students and by the kinds of activities they suggest. Thoughtful questions and activities encourage children to tie reading to their own experiences outside of school and in the classroom. They also ask children to analyze and synthesize works in terms of what they know. Further, good questions ask children to evaluate what they read in terms of criteria they develop. In sum, good questions encourage children to think critically about books even as they are being entertained and informed.

Literature aids reading and language arts by providing children with concrete and meaningful experiences in the act of reading, writing, and oral language use. As children read from various genres of fiction, poetry, and nonfiction, they begin to develop strategies for reading and writing for different purposes. The content and style of books can encourage children to read more critically and with increased comprehension. Books can encourage experimentation with styles of writing. For example, some students spontaneously emulate the style or form of writing from a book they enjoy as they respond to it. After reading Zolotow's *Someday*, one child presented his teacher with a paper that said, under a lovely drawing, "Someday there will be a rainbow without any rain." An older student mimicked the style of McNulty's *How to Dig a Hole to the Other Side of the World* when she wrote her report on a planet, calling it "How to take a trip to the other side of Mars." Students can also see that communicating effectively requires editing and revision as they watch Lois Lowry's Anastasia in the *Anastasia Krupnik* books and Rabble in *Rabble Starkey* struggle to revise their written works.

Literature Expands Horizons

Literature used in the social studies curriculum provides students with historical, social, and cultural insights beyond their own personal experiences. It can clarify the concept of time as do Goodall's *The Story of an English Village* and Pryor's *The House on Maple Street*, pictorial time lines that clearly show historical change. Or it may ask the reader to consider a situation or an idea in a new way. Literature often focuses on choices a character must make. Through reading about people of the past or in other cultures who have been faced with difficult choices, students learn about the decision making process and that many decisions require difficult choices with no guarantee of consequences. Insights provided by novels about history or culture also help children to understand their personal beliefs within a broader context. Literature can help children to participate in a common history and culture as well as to better understand diversity within it. In addition, books such as Beverly Naidoo's *Journey to Jo'Burg*, set in South Africa, and Mohr's *Going Home*, set in Puerto Rico, allow children to meet people outside of the borders of the United States and to experience the lives of children in very different settings.

Music and art education help children to understand and respond to expressive qualities in the arts and to know something of composers, artists, styles, and media. Brief biographies of musicians such as Lasker's *The Boy Who Loved Music* and Goffstein's *A Little Schubert* can provoke children's interest in hearing their music. Children might want to match their favorite stories, poems, and picture books with pieces of music that reflect their mood or tone or to create art works to express their responses to these writings. The art in fine picture books can be used across the grade levels to introduce children to artistic styles and media. Children might illustrate their own stories using what they have learned about art. They might choose to provide further illustrations or create a new cover for books they have read when lack of pictures or the type of pictures leaves them dissatisfied.

Literature can support both the content and processes of the sciences. Stimulating and pleasing books for children have been written about most areas of the sciences. Scientific processes can be explored through books that encourage children to closely observe the world in pictures or to keep careful records of observations as Brady does in *Wild Mouse*. Well-written science books encourage children to ponder, experiment, classify, and make inferences from what they are learning. Books help children to empathize with other creatures on the earth and to develop an understanding of their interrelationships as McNulty does through the dialogue in *Mouse and Tim*. Students can be encouraged to consider the social implications of scientific study as they read science fiction or poetry about science such as the poems included in Morrison's *Overheard in a Bubble Chamber*.

Literature can be used in the field of mathematics to help children visualize problems to be solved. Simple counting books typically present a series of pictures to illustrate the abstract concept of numbers. Mathematical game books such as *Anno's Counting House* ask children to engage in more sophisticated problem solving activities. Songs, games, and poetry that involve counting out such as Keats' *Over in the Meadow* and Lewin's *Cat Count* provide opportunities for children to play with numbers in a literary way.

Literature is helpful in the study of physical, health, and environmental education as it provides resources for understanding problems in these fields. Books such as MacLachlan's *Through Grandpa's Eyes* and Slepian's *The Alfred Summer* help children to understand aging and disabilities. Books such as Parnall's *The Mountain* and Peet's *The Wump World* can open children's eyes to environmental problems. Literature can also support studies of self-image, social behavior, and coping mechanisms.

Recent studies show that children are not spending time reading outside of the classroom (Anderson, 1985). Sadly, classroom time for reading is often devoted to worksheets and other activities that require little reading skill and provide little practice (Anderson, 1985). Test scores indicate that students are able to decode what they read but may not be able to understand it or to evaluate it effectively (Applebee, 1988). The greatest benefit of using literature across the curriculum is that meaningful reading is taking place all day long in a variety of settings and with a variety of texts. Reading integrated with the curriculum motivates and encourages further study. It provides an entertaining and enriching context for learning. It also stimulates children's thinking and reasoning skills and suggests alternative ways of looking at the world through another's point of view by recognizing the distinctive style of an author. Reading suggests various methods of study of the world including observation, analysis, and evaluation. It suggests methods of writing about our own experiences so that others can understand what we know. Literature used across the curriculum extends and enriches the life of the classroom and the attitudes, knowledge, and understandings of the students who work there.

Summary

Literature serves many functions in the elementary school curriculum. First and foremost, it entertains but it also extends meaning and helps children raise questions about their world. Literature across the curriculum avoids fragmentation; it enriches brief lessons on specific topics that seem to be isolated bits of information. Literature also makes connections; by using trade books we help children relate what they are learning to what they already know. Literature enhances problem solving, ability to recognize analogies, and capacity to visualize and generalize. Children learn to think critically, to evaluate books for their accuracy and develop criteria for making judgments about the quality of what they read. Finally, literature expands horizons and provides students with historical, social, and cultural insights. Literature used across the curriculum enriches the life of the classroom and enhances the vicarious experiences of students.

References

Anderson, R. *et al.* (1985). *Becoming a nation of readers: The report of the Commission on Reading.* Washington, D.C.: National Institute of Education, U.S. Department of Education.

Applebee, A.N., Langer, J.A., & Mullis, I.V.S. (1988). *Who reads best? Factors related to reading achievement in grades 3, 7, and 11.* National Assessment of Educational Progress. Princeton, NJ: Educational Testing Service.

Part II

Strands:
Celebrating Books and Authors in Four Genres

Introduction

What materials — specifically, what kind of books — are central to a child's literary education? Among Charlotte Huck's favorite genres are picture books, fantasy, historical fiction, and poetry. In the following chapters, different voices speak about each of these genres. For example, Barbara Kiefer gives a historical view of the development of picture books and describes some of her extensive research into children's responses to the art of illustrations. Marilyn Reed, an administrator, interviews five teachers to describe their varied approaches to the use of picture books in the classroom. Marcia Brown, an artist who has three times been awarded the Caldecott Medal, explains her goals as an illustrator and the careful research she undertakes in the development of an authentic interpretation of a story.

The many forms of fantasy play a significant role in the development of children's imagination. College teacher Dan Woolsey describes the various types of fantasy and shows how children relate its deeper truths to the realities of their lives. Middle school teacher Virginia Stelk shows how she captures some of the magic in fantasy to engage preadolescents in learning. She also traces the roots of fantasy in the real worlds in which much of it is set. Madeleine L'Engle, a fantasy writer and winner of the Newbery Medal for *A Wrinkle in Time*, captures the elusive qualities of fantasy as she tries to define it and probe its dimensions from the inside. Her statements underscore the distinctions between truth and facts.

Historical fiction is central to a school curriculum. First, Linda Levstik, who teaches at the university level, shows how it can give children a gift of time that stretches back as far as their imaginations can take them and yet allows them to see themselves as part of the people whose lives make up our past, present, and future. In a subsequent chapter, Lillian Webb, a gifted teacher, takes us inside her classroom to see how she uses historical fiction with students. She not only teaches history from the content of literature, in the process she teaches children a great deal about the literature itself. Finally, Mollie Hunter, a writer of historical fiction who has won the British Carnegie Medal for her book *The Stronghold*, explains what it is like to live surrounded by the history of her Scottish ancestors. She tells how the silent mystery of the ruins of a wall or an arrangement of stones draws her into their past. Through her writing she probes what life must have been like for the people who created the ancient constructions and established the facts of history recorded in books.

Poetry is at the heart of a child's literary education; it educates the heart as well as the mind. In this section, Rebecca Thomas reviews the research on children's preferences in poetry but shows how she moves students beyond their stated preference to embrace a wider range. Centering on the work of winners of the National Council of Teachers of English Award for Excellence in Poetry for Children, Thomas makes a case for a long and loving experience with poetry. Next, university professor Amy McClure works with classroom teachers Peggy Harrison and Peg Reed to show how poetry invites participation *in* an experience rather than just telling about it. These authors summarize traditional approaches to poetry and then provide an alternative method for fostering poetic response, one that Peg Reed and Peggy Harrison implement in their classrooms. They demonstrate that children are much more responsive to poetry when they are in a supportive literary context. Eve Merriam, one of the recipients of the NCTE Award for Excellence in Poetry, expresses her beliefs about poetry and her regard for Charlotte Huck in poetic form. She has selected a bouquet of her own poems for Charlotte that speak eloquently and lovingly about their subject.

7

Picture Books

for All the Ages

Barbara Kiefer

A small booklet titled "How Can I Prepare My Child for Reading?" (Grinnell, 1984) lay on the desk in my home office. My then nine-year-old son glanced down at it in passing and remarked, "Oh, there's that book you used to read to me." I was about to refute this statement when I picked up the booklet and looked more closely at the small black and white photograph on the cover. A mother is holding her toddler, who is pointing to a picture book that is resting in his lap. The book is only about two inches across and is set at right angles to the viewer, but on closer examination I recognized it as Robert Kraus' *Whose Mouse Are You?* Jon had been correct. This was a favorite book I had read to him many times when he was two years old. How was it that many years later a quick glance at a tiny black and white photo that bore little resemblance to the original still brought instant recognition?

Picture books have been considered such common accoutrements of early childhood, at least in literacy-rich homes, that we sometimes take them for granted assuming that, like tricycles and building blocks, they will be discarded and replaced with more sophisticated entertainments as the child grows older. For Jon, however, and presumably other children like him, picture book experiences are not put aside but remain so vividly etched in the mind that a brief encounter can trigger a flood of memory. Perhaps this is because, unlike tricycles and blocks, the picture book is not a toy; it is an art object, one that provides a unique aesthetic experience that may profoundly affect not only a single child like Jon but our entire civilization. For Jon is one of thousands, young and old, who have been involved in memorable and long-lasting experiences with a picture book.

Although during the twentieth century the picture book has remained the province of young children like Jon, many of today's picture books are visually and intellectually demanding and deserve to be enjoyed by a wider audience, which includes older children, adolescents, and adults. It seems that now more than ever artists and writers have discovered the picture book as a challenging medium for their talents, just as new developments in printing techniques have made it possible for the picture book to continue to develop as an art form, as it has over the centuries.

In spite of current debate as to the picture book's appropriate audience (Kimmel, 1982; Nodelman, 1982) or difficulties in agreeing on a clear definition of a picture book (Bader, 1976; Marantz, 1977; Shulevitz, 1988; Silvey, 1986), the picture book is a vital and important art object because, like language and culture — indeed like the human race — it has changed over time. A product of society, of technology, and of culture, the picture book represents a combination of image and idea that is basic to our human nature. As philosopher Suzanne Langer writes, ''Image making is the mode of our untutored thinking and stories its earliest products'' (1942, p. 145).

An Historical View

Cave Paintings

If this is so, perhaps the first picture books may well have been the Paleolithic cave paintings like those found at Lascaux, France, or Altamira, Spain, and which date from 15,000 B.C. Using the products of technology available (there were, of course, no paper, no written alphabet, printing presses or binderies) those artists of long ago created products that were, in their cultural roots and their social and individual responses, similar to the picture book of today. The paintings were first a result of a cultural need, the need to represent basic aspects of survival of the individual and the race through image and myth, and an artist's need to convey some meaning through visual symbols.

In ensuing years technological advances have been responsible for the changing form in which the artist has chosen to convey and record pictorial images and ideas. At the same time the changing needs of society, as reflected in the culture of a particular age, have determined content and designated the audience.

Scrolls

The invention of papyrus scrolls saw a form more closely resembling today's picture book emerge in Egypt around 2,700 B.C. In these papyruses, especially those referred to as the *Book of the Dead,* the combination of pictorial image and verbal story was both a portable and a permanent object that was accessible to those who had knowledge of the writing system and that was immune from individual interpretation and change inherent in the oral storytelling tradition.

The purpose of these scrolls was still very similar to the cave paintings; that is, to record rituals and magic that would speed the soul through the underworld. Yet the appearance is remarkably similar to the layout of today's picture books. Pictures and words were fully integrated on these rolls, with pictures occupying the majority of the space. Often what seems to be a decorative border was added along the top or bottom of the scroll.

Clay Tablets to Parchment

A major advance in picture book history came in the fourth century A.D. with the invention of the Codex by the Romans. Based on multileaved clay tablets used in Greece and Rome at the time, this technique allowed bookmakers to cut pieces of vellum or parchment (made from animal skins) into sheets that were folded and sewn together in the fold and then bound with thin pieces of wood covered with leather. The Codex was much easier to use than scrolls and allowed both sides of the page to be used. Moreover, the Codex seemed to have encouraged a more disciplined sense of layout and design in picture books. While earlier artists had experimented with placement of pictures and words, the full-page framed illustration, sometimes alone, sometimes facing the written text, much as we would find in many of today's illustrated books, was the result of the Codex. This approach to layout seemed to result in greater delineation between pictorial text and written text. Each illustration told its own story, and while all the paintings in a book may have been connected by a common theme, they did not always represent a connected flow of image or story which unfolded and continued with the turning of the page (as is common in today's picture book).

Book Art as Fine Art

As the Roman Empire drew to a close, the church had become primarily responsible for the continuation of the picture book in Western culture, not only to present and glorify the message of Christianity but as a center for the crafts of bookmaking. In addition, church scribes continued to preserve and illustrate secular works although it was mainly religious texts that were thought worthy of illumination. Perhaps the best-known example of church art during this period is the magnificent Book of Kells, created by Irish monks in about the sixth century. During this period the picture book retained some of the mystical qualities of its earliest ancestors, for, among a largely illiterate population, the illustrations must have retained great power to effect a profound religious experience for the individual participating in rituals surrounding stories of the Old and New Testaments.

From the thirteenth century, however, the picture book began to be the province of the secular world with the social and cultural needs of a changing world determining its content just as technology would continue to affect its form. Universities and a more widely literate populace increased the demand for books. This trend gave way to the illustration of many more secular texts — histories, epic poems, fairy tales, fables, romances, and works of Dante and Chaucer.

Paper and Print Techniques

Several major technical advances took place during the early Middle Ages that affected book production, availability, and audience. The development of paper, an inexpensive book material, and the invention of inks suitable for wood block printing occurred in the early fifteenth century. The great revolution in printing, however, came with the invention of movable type during the 1450's. This invention signalled the end of the hand-illuminated book and the beginning of picture bookmaking as a commercial rather than a purely aesthetic process.

At first the audience for these printed picture books remained an adult one. The idea of producing a book for an audience of children was unheard of mainly because the concept of children as a separate social group was unthinkable, at least until the twelfth century, and it was not until the seventeenth century that Comenius' *Orbis Pictus* was published to "entice witty children." Its real purpose, however, was not to entertain but to instruct; this "educational" factor would remain a major focus of picture books for children well into the nineteenth century.

Following the invention of the first printing presses, further technological advances allowed the picture book to reach a larger audience at the same time this technology affected the processes and product of illustration. For many years, for example, illustrations were printed in black from wood blocks or metal plates. While color may have been added by hand, it was not until the 1800's, most notably through the efforts of British printer Edmund Evans, that color separations from an artist's original drawings were perfected. Evans was also responsible for producing the first quality picture books whose aim was to entertain an audience of children, attracting such notable artists as Walter Crane, Randolph Caldecott, and Kate Greenaway to the field of book illustration.

The Contemporary Scene

By the early 1900's, photographic techniques had replaced hand engravings as the method of translating original art to the printed page. Even these streamlined printing processes still required many tedious hours of color separation on the part of the artist. This method of book production often required that picture book illustrators be craftspeople, knowledgeable about printmaking techniques such as lithography and engraving as well as technical matters of commercial publishing.

Audience

From that time commercial publishing of picture books began to be aimed almost exclusively at *young* audiences, a reflection of changing attitudes of society. This fact may have been responsible for the *re*emergence (note Egyptian and early Roman and Greek scrolls) of a picture book format in which pictorial text often carried the weight of the book's meaning-expressive potential, with verbal text kept brief or eliminated altogether. It also encouraged a wide range of subject matter. Today we find nursery rhymes, poetry, songs, folk tales, fantasy, realistic stories, informational books, alphabet books, counting books, and concept books, as well as pop-up books among the many genres embraced by current picture book artists.

The Artist's Role

Moreover, with new techniques of laser printing developed in recent years, the efficient and faithful reproduction of original art to printed form has revolutionized the field of book production and attracted a wide range of artists to the field. For even as over the centuries society and culture have shaped the picture book's content, the picture book has always been a vehicle in which artists expressed visual meaning. Just as authors create character, settings, events, and themes through elements of language, words, sentences, and paragraphs, artists convey meaning through the elements of design — line, shape, color, value, and texture — and through principles of composition like rhythm, repetition, balance, and eye movement.

Unlike painters, who can take a more self-centered approach to art, devoting their careers to the exploration of these elements or experimenting with various media, picture book artists seek to express some specific meaning or narrative, sometimes in the company of verbal text, sometimes not. They are still storytellers in the most basic sense. They choose the elements and principles of design for their meaning-expressive qualities and seek to unify these not only on a single page or picture plane but also over the succession of images held within the boundaries of cover and endpages. They also consider technical choices inherent in book production such as original media, typeface, layout, paper stock, cover and endpages, spatial orientation or viewpoint, and pictorial content. The picture book artist thus has the potential to create an art object that is more than the sum of its parts (images and ideas) and can profoundly affect the reader's understanding as well as deepen the aesthetic experience surrounding the picture book.

Today the picture book artist's efforts to communicate meaning and the reader's response to that meaning provide a continuous link to other artists and audiences down through the centuries. Although the form and purpose of the picture book may have changed over the years, today's picture book artist has the same power to evoke a variety of responses — sensory, affective, cognitive, and aesthetic — as did those earliest storytellers who created the extraordinary images on cave walls. How similar also to experiences surrounding the cave paintings is the picture book experience for today's audience of children. For children, like that earliest audience, the ritual of picture book reading is also highly social in nature either in the one-to-one lap readings during the youngest years or within the context of picture book reading and response found in school settings. In addition, children have the opportunity for individual responses, which are also likely to change and deepen over time as they return to favorite books or broaden their experience with a variety of styles and genres.

Response to Picture Books

Over many years of observation of children responding to picture books (Kiefer, 1983, 1986, 1988), I have come to believe that picture books of many types and in many styles, created by sensitive artists (and authors) for audiences of many ages, can become the focal points for a variety of reactions and responses. In return, children (and adults) who have frequent opportunities to respond to picture books may not only be given lasting memories but may also develop deeper cognitive and affective understandings and a more critical aesthetic awareness.

I have found that children (in kindergarten through fifth grade) choose a variety of ways to respond to books. Often they react physically (especially young children) or want to act out the story. I found first and second graders asking to create plays in response to *Old Mother Hubbard* and *The Grey Lady and the Strawberry Snatcher* or to respond to picture books with art work of their own. Following the teacher's reading of *Song of the Horse,* for example, many children wanted to create pictures. As one fourth grader explained, "The illustrations just catch your eye and then you don't want to let go. You just want to get hold of it and keep it till you've done all the illustrations." Older children also respond to picture books through writing. In her book response journal a fifth grader noted:

> The illustrations of *Moss Gown* were different than other books. It made you feel funny. The illustrations were just great. In the front part of the book the colors were winter, in the middle part the colors were summer colors. . .

Children's verbal responses in written work during group read-alouds, in discussions, and in interviews showed their diligent attempts to make sense of the picture book, both its message and its medium.

Children used their own unique terms in discussing the picture books — "squiggly lines" to describe William Steig's style, "lushy" for Maurice Sendak's *Outside Over There*, or "color concussion" to explain the technique of wood block printing. At the same time children were incorporating artistic or book terms like media, acrylic, watercolor, or endpages into their vocabulary.

Functions of Language in Response

As students talked or wrote about books, I found their purpose was often an informative one, telling what was happening in the pictures or pointing out the details. They were also likely to compare objects found in one book to similar objects in another book. A second grader noticed the small board game lying under the tree in the opening pages of *Jumanji* by Chris Van Allsburg. "Oh, that's like the cover of his other books," she reported. Upon close examination this tiny one-inch box does indeed bear hazy images of a topiary garden that figures prominently on the cover of Van Allsburg's first book, *The Garden of Abdul Gasazi*. This child's remarkable attention to detail was not uncommon among the children I observed. It seems that they may scan or view pictures in a different way than adults do, moving from part to part rather than looking at the whole and thus finding the small details that so many illustrators seem to include in their picture books. Research in the psychology of perception (Coles, Sigman, & Chessel, 1977) supports this notion.

Children also use a heuristic or problem-solving function of language as they look at picture books. They wonder about the cause

Figure 7-1.
From *Jumanji* by Chris Van Allsburg. Children respond appreciatively to his detailed illustrations.

Figure 7-2.
From *Outside Over There* by Maurice Sendak. Children can return to Sendak's work again and again and make new discoveries about his illustrations.

of events or the media used in the original illustrations. They also make inferences about characters, events, and themes. "It's a dream," said a second grader looking at a sleeping shepherd in *Outside Over There*, "cause when you count sheep you dream."

Some children enter the world of the book for imaginative purposes in their oral and written language. They choose the character they want to be or actually speak as one of the characters. Looking at the woodcutter confronting the wolf in Hyman's *Little Red Riding Hood*, a third grader said in a gruff woodcutter voice, "So here you are, you old sinner. I've been looking for you all these years and this is where I find you."

The imaginative function also appears in the metaphors and similes children create as they look at picture books. They use words such as "pumpy" or "like mashed potatoes" to describe Tomie De Paola's distinctive clouds; and a first grader described the ripples behind the boat in *Dawn* as "like whipped cream that men put on to shave." Occasionally, imaginative language extends to the descriptions of entirely new mental images. This happens most often with black and white illustrations that children would describe as colorful. A first grader reported that the game board in *Jumanji* "looks like it's all different colors." Her friend agreed, "Like when you turn it you can see white and you can see a little bit red."

Many children make personal connections to books. Illustrations remind them of their lives outside the book — their home, their friends and possessions or important experiences. They also express their emotions with comments such as "that picture makes me feel like I'm on my Mommy's lap" (of *We Be Warm Til Springtime Come*) or "those colors make me feel sad." At other times children express personal opinions about picture books. "It's a good book because I like it," stated a first grader, while a fifth grader wrote:

> *Our King Has Horns* is not a Caldecott Book. A Caldecott book is a book of pictures, not text. Look at *Polar Express, Mufaro's Beautiful Daughters, Hey Al*, and *Jumanji*. They've all been to the top and they color in their picture [background?]. On those books you can feel the color of the sky and ground. In *Our King Has Horns* it's more of what air? What ground? If that's not enough to convince you, what is?

Awareness of Artistic Elements

As I have observed children responding to picture books and examined their verbal response, I have found that they are able to become "meaning makers" (Wells, 1986) in the deepest sense that their age and experience would allow.

While young children are more intensely focused on their own reaction to the book ("These are better because I like them") and often seem uninterested in who created the book or why an artist would choose a particular style, they *do* pay attention to elements and principles of design. They mention colors, lines, and shapes and refer to value and texture with words such as "bright," "light" or "bumpy." They notice borders or small vignettes that are part of double-page compositions. They are also aware of technical choices involved in book design, pictorial content, typefaces, endpapers, and original media.

Many older children, however, begin to be aware of the expressive potential of the artistic elements and to think of the artist as a maker of meaning. They talk about the emotive power of the elements of design. "The pictures look sad. They don't have a certain shape to them," said a third grader of *Hiroshima No Pika*. A classmate looked at Zwerger's *Hansel and Gretel*. "Some of the colors make it sort of sad — the browns," she explained. A fourth grader compared *The Crane Maiden* with *The Crane Wife*, two versions of a Japanese tale. "*The Crane Maiden* is too block-like, like it's all straight, made up of squares. *The Crane Wife* is made up of circles. It fits the story better because it's a smooth story and a ball rolls and a square won't."

Their understanding of the expressive qualities of the artist's choices also extend to more technical aspects of the book. Looking at the burnt sienna endpapers in Zwerger's *Hansel and Gretel*, a fourth grader reported, "They look reddish brown like somebody's put something there and just forgot about it and never got it up again. They put it in the forest and left it there forever."

Many children are able to go beyond their personal preferences for style, media, or color in illustrations to think about the picture book's artistic merit. When asked whether they would have preferred that Van Allsburg had used color for *Jumanji*, a second grader replied, "Just because they're not colored doesn't mean they're not good." One of his classmates explained:

> It's harder when it's in black and white. It takes more time and you can't just whip through the book. The monkeys in the closet would have been easier to see if they were in color. You *like* to take time.

I found that many children like to take time with picture books and that picture books that are artistically demanding or puzzling, like *The Grey Lady and the Strawberry Snatcher, Outside Over There,* or *Song of the Horse* are books that engender the most long-lasting and deepest responses on the part of children. It would seem that when artists are intensely involved in the creation of meaning through the medium of the picture book, they have the potential to destroy complacency, to uncover needs, to pique curiosity, to evoke enthusiasm, and to arouse passion.

These are possibilities that exist in classrooms where teachers give children many opportunities to look at and respond to a variety of good picture books, where teachers take time to read and discuss good picture books with children, where teachers give children time and encouragement to respond to books in a variety of ways, and where teachers return to picture books so that response can change and deepen over time.

In contexts like these, children of all ages may have the opportunity to build lasting memories, to extend artistic and literary understandings, and to deepen aesthetic awareness. Such contexts ensure that the picture book will remain the vital art object that it has been for centuries; a product of society, technology, and culture, yet also a process of communication between artist and audience.

Summary

Picture books, unlike tricycles and building blocks, are not discarded as a child grows older; instead they become a part of the vividly etched images we carry in memory most of our lives. This is because picture books are not toys but are art objects that provide a unique aesthetic experience that has a lasting effect. Picture books have become intellectually demanding and are used as an art form by an increasing number of talented artists. The development of painting and illustration historically reflects the social and cultural changes of our world. From Paleolithic cave paintings, through Egyptian scrolls, vellum illuminations, to the invention of printing with paper and inks, the works of art represent technological advances. On the contemporary scene, picture books have become the province of a young audience reflecting society's changing attitudes. Picture books have the same power to evoke a variety of responses as did the early cave paintings and scrolls. Children and adults responding to picture books create lasting memories and develop cognitive and affective understandings and a critical awareness.

References

Bader, B. (1976). *American picture books: From Noah's ark to the beast within.* New York: Macmillan.

Bland, D. (1958). *A history of book illustration.* Cleveland, OH: The World Publishing Co.

Coles, P., Sigman, M., & Chessel, K. (1977). Scanning strategies of children and adults. In G. Butterworth (Ed.), *The child's representation of the world.* New York: Plenum Press.

Grinnell, P. (1984). "How can I prepare my young child for reading?" An IRA Micromonograph. Newark, DE: International Reading Association.

Harthan, J. (1981). *The history of the illustrated book.* New York: Thames & Hudson.

Kiefer, B.Z. (1983). The responses of children in a combination first/second grade classroom to picture books in a variety of artistic styles. *Journal of Research and Development in Education, 16* (3), 14–20.

Kiefer, B.Z. (1986). The child and the picture book: Creating live circuits. *Children's Literature Association Quarterly,* 11 (2), 63–68.

Kiefer, B. (1988). Picture books as contexts for literary, aesthetic, and real world understanding. *Language Arts,* 65 (3), 260–271.

Kimmel, E. (1982). Children's literature without children. *Children's Literature in Education,* 13 (1), 38–43.

Langer, S. (1942). *Philosophy in a new key.* Cambridge, MA: Harvard University Press.

Marantz, K. (1977). The picture book as art object: A call for balanced reviewing. *Wilson Library Bulletin:* 148–151.

Nodelman, P. (1982). Letters to the editor. *Children's Literature in Education,* 13 (4), 195–197.

Silvey, A. (1986). Could Randolph Caldecott win the Caldecott medal? *The Horn Book Magazine,* LXII (4), 405.

Shulevitz, U. (1988). What is a picture book? *The Five Owls,* 11 (4), 49–51.

8

Teachers Using

Picture Books

Marilyn Reed

Picture books are used by teachers in a multitude of ways. How they are used depends greatly upon teachers':

- experience as children with picture books and other literature
- exposure to children's literature in teacher education courses
- level of administrative support for using books in the classroom
- curiosity in seeking a deeper understanding of literature and how it enhances children's learning
- attempts to keep abreast of new publications and ways to use them effectively.

Respect for the integrity of children's literature and the necessity of integrating it in all learning will guide the discussion in this chapter.

Who can better answer how teachers use picture books than the teachers themselves? I asked five teachers to share their thoughts. They teach different age levels of children, are of different age and sex, and have had different kinds of training and experience. All have been part of an alternative educational program within a public school system and were all hired by the same administrator. Their responses provide insight for other teachers seeking an understanding of a literature-based program.

I asked the five teachers some broad, open-ended questions: (1) How do you use picture books in your classroom; and what are some of those books? (2) Where did you learn about picture books and how to use them? The responses they gave were personal and individual.

How Do Teachers Use Picture Books?

Sue Bauchmoyer, Kindergarten/First Grade

Sue uses picture books most often in theme related units. She reads through stacks of books and sorts them according to genre or theme. For example, in preparing for her next unit on fairy tales, she groups variants of a particular tale. The Cinderella stories include an English version, *Tattercoats*, a Perrault version illustrated by Marcia Brown, and a Grimm version illustrated by Nonny Hogrogian. She then figures out what extensions she might have the children do, first for short-term projects and then how those might extend into long-term projects.

Sue also uses picture books to help children learn about art. During discussions following read aloud by the teacher, she discusses the different illustrators and the background, detail, and media used in the illustrations. She encourages children to try the different media used, attend to the format of the books they hear and read, and then relate that to the books they write, illustrate, and publish themselves. For example, during a study of ABC books, they discussed books by Burningham, Wildsmith, and C.B. Falls and the use of thick paint, white on color, color on white, and wood prints. They experimented with these concepts as they created their own ABC books.

Using picture books helps Sue's children learn language. They compare words they did not know, become aware of patterns and rhythm, and join in spontaneously as they listen to and predict the use of language patterns. Sue sees evidence in their own work when children use expressions such as "there was no doubt about it" or "as a matter of fact."

Sue uses picture books to help build a sense of story, especially predicting that something is going to happen. Children become familiar with the beginning, middle, and ending of stories, which carries over into their own writing. Picture books of poetry are also used for their predictability and surprise.

Children in Sue's classroom use picture books for DEAR time (drop everything and read) and for other reading. Good picture books with patterns and repetition appeal to children's interests as they learn to read. Despite earlier evidence that shows that boys lag behind girls in reading achievement, Sue's master's degree study showed that boys read as well as girls at this age level when they can choose what they read. In Sue's study, the boys' comprehension improved as well.

Discussion always follows the silent reading time for children to share what they have read, to listen to new language in books, and to discuss what others have read. The children mimic the teacher's questions and comments and, in time, internalize those same questions as they continue their individual reading journeys. Choosing to read a book their friends have shared paves the way for understanding the importance of rereading good books to acquire the many layers of meaning they offer.

Reading with a partner is routine in Sue's class: children read to each other from the books they are presently reading. Discussion follows where each child questions and responds to questions similar to the model experienced in total group discussions although the dialogue is cast in children's natural language. Most of the time the children choose their partners, but sometimes Sue makes the choice, although it is rarely done by ability level.

Terry Trubiano, First/Second Grade

Terry also chooses picture books by theme. She creates a web of possibilities, an open-ended type of plan for an integrated curriculum study, and then jots down books that come to mind. She asks librarians at the school and public libraries to pull books related to the theme. Terry carries her planning web with her and seeks the help of other teachers who can offer suggestions as to books that should be included in the study and responses and extensions that she could include. When she has about one hundred books, she sorts them into categories within the theme and makes an index card for each book that includes something about the book and ideas for extensions. For example, Yagawa's *The Crane Wife* would be good to use with Matsutani's *The Crane Maiden*, Bangs' *Dawn*, and Yamaguchi's *The Golden Crane* for a comparison chart. Both the teacher and students use the cards that are filled with ideas.

Terry makes a plan for the approximate period of time for the unit. If she feels a theme will sustain interest for five weeks, she divides it into five topics. At the beginning of the unit, she works with her group as a whole to introduce ideas for study and extensions. For example, the whole group makes a comparison chart together so the children are familiar with this process. She might introduce making a collage or a felt board story, and as she discusses and questions, the children get the idea. She then asks for four volunteers to work on a felt board presentation of a story she has just read, and a small group goes to work. This gets them back into the book to search for whatever part of the story they are working on and to look for parts of the books they hear other groups discussing. She models the process for the group that they will use later on when they will do more extensions on their own.

The process of making a comparison chart is unfamiliar to some teachers, and I asked Terry to share how she does that. She said that in a study of Japan, she used the above mentioned books about the crane maidens. She read them aloud to her class in a two-day period, during which they discussed similarities and differences. Then she put up a chart with the titles in a column on the left. Across the top they wrote in some possibilities for comparison. They could compare: who found the crane?; was there a magic clock?; did the crane change into something else? She then would ask who would like to work on the magic clock; and who would like to work on how the crane changes; and who would work on how the stories ended. Again, these extensions lead students back into the book rather than away from it.

The art of picture books is a fascinating area for children to learn; Terry introduces the same media to her students that illustrators use in picture books. She models the sketching, shading, hatch marks, black and white drawings, collage, full color, whatever is involved. The children experience this wide range of media as they discuss what the illustrator had in mind in illustrating the text.

Sample Comparison Chart on Versions of
The Crane Wife

	Who found the crane?	Was there a magic clock?	Did the crane change into something else?
The Crane Wife			
The Crane Maiden			
Dawn			
The Golden Crane			

After the first couple of weeks as the children use these ideas, their range of choice becomes greater as they explore the theme. Discussion is constant. For example, one day she shared that she had just read Karla Kuskin's *A Space Story*. The children got so caught up in the story during the reading that they hardly got through the story. The book asked questions, the children asked questions, and the teacher asked questions. ''What do you know about Mars that the author did not include?'' ''Which planet comes next?'' were some of the questions. A natural follow-up of a recent study the class had done on space, these questions naturally led into book extensions for morning work and to DEAR time later in the day. By living in this environment of inquiry, Terry feels the children more often raise questions on their own than she does.

Terry's next unit will be on favorite books in the classroom. As she scans the many books on the shelves in her classroom, she sees many that have not yet been shared because they have not fit into a particular theme, and she knows they are too good to miss. Thus she develops another unit of study around favorite, as yet undiscovered, picture books.

I was curious about how Terry happened to choose the study of Japan for first and second graders. She was so excited about how this had happened. She started the year with a unit based on *The Jolly Postman*. During this study she began each morning with a Super Writing Workshop when the children wrote poems, letters, and stories. They began to understand that writing is communication by writing on topics of their own and having that writing valued. They developed a respect for books by publishing their own. In the books that they wrote, her students included endpapers, copyrights, and a message about the author as well as other parts of picture book formats.

Through contacts made by another teacher who originally lived in England, they wrote to English schoolchildren. When the comptuer teacher learned of this, he asked if Terry's students would like to have pen pals through the computer, which resulted in pen pals in Japan.

The children learned that it was more fun to write letters to Japanese children if they knew more about Japan. So began the study of Japan. They explored the folklore, the crane as a symbol, geography, volcanos, origami, and the bullet train. From this they could ask questions in letters they wrote such as ''Have you ever climbed Mt. Fuji?'' or ''Have you ever ridden the bullet train?'' They studied picture books for information, for traditional tales of the culture, and for stories about Japan today.

Terry never believed children would write a whole page about book illustrations or discuss favorite authors and illustrators in their everyday conversations. She is continually excited about how this evolves and how the understanding of good books has become the very heart of her children's learning.

Fred Burton, Third/Fourth Grade

Fred's response to how he uses picture books in the classroom was: (1) we write from picture books; (2) we write about picture books; and (3) we learn through picture books.

Children write from picture books by using them as a springboard for writing. For example, he uses Horwitz's *When the Sky is Like Lace* to discuss alliteration and rich language, then the children try those components on their own. O'Neill's *Hailstones and Halibut Bones* exemplifies the relationship between illustration and poetry, and Lobel's *Fables* helps the students learn how to write fables.

Children write about picture books as aesthetic objects. They discuss how art enriches pictures as well as words to create a feeling or to make explicit a particular part of the story. They put this information into their own words through their writing.

Children learn through picture books in several ways. For example, they learn content through such books as de Paola's *The Popcorn Book* and Holling's rich geographical description in *Paddle-to-the-Sea*. They learn about format by examining the parts of a picture book and considering ways the parts might be reorganized. Simon's *Animal Fact/Animal Fable* introduces an alternating format that states a fable and then a fact about animals. The children extended this idea in their own publication, *Eye Fact/Eye Fable*. Reading picture books enables children to learn about different styles of writing, which they in turn can either borrow or improvise. For instance, *Inside: Seeing Beneath the Surface* by Jan Adkins helped children pick up on a flippant style of writing.

Quality language and stimulating dialogue, learned through using picture books, shows up in children's writing. Some picture books are used for fun or, as Fred said, ''Just for the heck of it!'' Children love unusual books, such as Chris Van Allsburg's *The Stranger, The Mysteries of Harris Burdick,* and *The Polar Express,* or Mitsumasa Anno's visual puzzles. *Anno's U.S.A.* takes two weeks to read as students examine and discuss a page each day to find all they can in the illustrations.

By reading many picture books, students learn to create their own picture books. They write for an audience younger than themselves and extend that writing into longer stories for their own classroom. The books they write become part of their classroom library of student publications that others check out to read.

Sherry Goubeaux, Fifth Grade

Sherry uses picture books at the fifth grade level primarily for information since there are many nonfiction books that are both interesting and informative. For example, books on disability such as Kuklin's *Thinking Big,* Wolf's *Don't Feel Sorry for Paul,* and Powers' *Our Teacher's in a Wheelchair* invite repeated reading for their positive view of the disabled.

Sherry also uses picture books to share poetry first thing every morning when both the teacher and children read poetry aloud. They draw from single editions such as Ernest Thayer's *Casey at the Bat,* James Whitcomb Riley's *Little Orphant Annie,* and Prelutsky's *The Headless Horseman Rides Tonight,* as well as anthologies such as Sandburg's *Rainbows are Made* and Kuskin's *Near the Window Tree* explaining the origin of each poem.

Some picture books contain complex stories meant for older readers. Sherry uses Van Allsburg's *The Wreck of the Zephyr, The Stranger, Jumanji,* and *The Polar Express* for their many levels of meaning. She also presents folktales and other traditional literature through picture books, such as Hodges' *Saint George and the Dragon,* Yagawa's *The Crane Wife,* and Grimm's *Snow White.*

The fifth graders in Sherry's class study the art of picture books on a continual basis; they explore the media, techniques, and styles of different illustrators. When the illustrative techniques are not explained at the end of a book, students try to determine how they were done and experiment with them in their own work. They also discuss whether the illustrations extend the text or whether another medium might be more appropriate. For example, they probe Sendak's *Outside Over There* for its symbolic art, the Anno books for the story told through the illustrations, and Conover's *The Wizard's Daughter* for its story within the illustrations.

These students also learn about the layout and design techniques of bookmaking through picture books, then they apply their knowledge by writing, illustrating, and publishing their own books. Not only are the student-made books widely used in the classroom, but some are shared with their younger friends in kindergarten.

Sherry believes that picture books give children who do not have solid reading abilities a way into books. During Sustained Silent Reading, where students' reading choices are honored, picture books draw some children through the text and eventually on to more difficult reading.

For read aloud time Sherry often relates a picture book to a longer book she is reading. The transformations in Yagawa's *The Crane Wife* and deGerez's *Louhi, Witch of North Farm* enhance an understanding of the many changes that take place in *Amy's Eyes* by Richard Kennedy.

Lois Monaghan, Sixth Grade

Lois teaches English in the middle school and, therefore, has her students for one period per day. She uses picture books that are appropriate for the time she has and looks for ones that provide examples of literary value and use of language. She believes that picture books help students see the world in a new way.

Lois uses picture books as a way of play — play with story, play with idea, and play with a piece of literature. The books help students recognize the message, the theme, and to reach beyond the obvious — similar to drawing the meaning from poetry. They provide a way to help sixth graders experience myths such as Tomaino's *Persephone* and to give imagery to poetry as in Susan Jeffers's version of Frost's *Stopping by Woods on a Snowy Evening*.

The language in many picture books is worthy of sixth graders' respect. Steig's *Amos and Boris* continues to hold their attention. In working with picture books, Lois emphasizes reading the book, enjoying the book, studying the book, and appreciating the book.

Lois likes to have her students write picture books as a way to teach the elements of a story. The brief format requires them to maintain a tight focus and reach a satisfactory conclusion with an economy of words. It also helps her explain the visual images of a story as they work toward writing a short story.

During an outdoor education session on site in the woods, Lois sits in a cave with her students and shares Baylor's *Everybody Needs a Rock*. They talk about the meaning of the prose poem and develop ten rules for finding their own special rock. By relating literature to life and creating their own meaning, Lois believes that sixth graders gain confidence in reading and interpreting meaning from texts.

Where Did These Teachers Learn How to Use Picture Books?

All five teachers had courses in children's literature as undergraduates, and they all took several literature courses in graduate school at The Ohio State University. Three of them had undergraduate training in an alternative program with a major thrust in language arts and literature as the basis of an integrated curriculum. Their university teachers read aloud to them and had them experience the way books should be used in the classroom. Two of the teachers had a rather traditional undergraduate program, but their graduate studies spurred them on to greater use of picture books and other literature in their classrooms.

These teachers feel that one of the best ways to learn to use picture books is simply by using them frequently. By building a store of knowledge about authors and illustrators they can create meaningful experiences for children. Sharing these experiences with colleagues enhances that growth.

Summary

The five teachers profiled here use picture books to help students learn: (1) new information related to an integrated theme of study; (2) the content, concepts, and skills of literacy, language, and literature; (3) the art of picture books; and (4) how to enjoy books. Each of these components is refined and studied in more depth as students progress through elementary school. The responses of these teachers indicate that picture books can be used throughout the elementary school years for numerous educational and aesthetic purposes.

9

My Goals

as an Illustrator

Marcia Brown

Marcia Brown first wrote these words more than 20 years ago and yet they seem as fresh as newly baked bread. She remarks that 20 years before that date she was asked to write on the same subject and upon rereading her original paper found that her views had not changed in the intervening years. We are struck by the stability of an artist's view about her goals as an illustrator; they stand today much as Marcia Brown shaped them early in her career. Although today Marcia Brown would perhaps use more recent examples to illustrate her points, her basic message remains constant. It also shows that no matter how things change, important things remain the same.

—Editors' Note

"Each artist has his own way of working. After a while, he works in possibly the only way he can, given his own temperament."

When recently I was invited to speak on my goals as an illustrator, I was reminded that twenty years ago I was asked to give a talk and write a paper on this same subject. As I reread that paper, I saw that most of my ideas have not changed very much but have only become more pronounced. Just as when one watches landscape the distant things stay put while those nearby are changing constantly, so one's goals in illustration do not change often enough to provide good ammunition for the speeches illustrators are asked to make about their work.

Often reactions to performance in one of the arts will reveal something about another. A few evenings ago a friend and I heard and saw a performance of *Oedipus Rex* by Stravinsky, a modern musical score based on the classical theme and nourished in its composing by many heroic examples for voice and instruments from other periods. The "visual presentation" had been entrusted to a painter of considerable reputation who saw fit to vie with the composer for honors in creating a parallel composition of the costumes and décor. He used a prizefight, with Oedipus the popular hero, in the usual satin bathrobe and prize-fighter's shoes, in an effort to bring the ancient conflict of Oedipus into a modern arena, where it might appear to be more meaningful than in its own period. What was forgotten was the idea that the story so transcends its period, and evidently any treatment of it, that the attempt to pin it to the present seemed ludicrous. The thing did not come off. One wondered why there had been such a lack of faith in the work itself, which needed no help from anyone, and lack of faith in the audience.

I often think of illustrators as I think of performers of music. Those one can listen to longest are often those most selfless, those who are content to be a medium for the music. They put their own individualities at the service of the music to probe its depths and reveal its spirit, rather than to display the idiosyncracies of their own personalities. Techniques that hammer can dull the eyes as well as the ears.

Even though I may be the composer, I have come to think of the illustrator more and more as the performer of the spirit of a book. If one lives with a book from its beginning, one may be closer to that spirit. Some spirits speak so loudly their voices are unmistakable. Others are more delicate. No one way can be called the best way to interpret them to a child.

Feelings appropriate to the fine arts, especially painting, are often called forward in speaking about illustration for children. Little children readily look at all kinds and styles of art. They are probably the freest and most imaginative audience in the world. But illustration is illustration and not painting. It is communication of the idea of a book.

This all sounds obvious and has been said many times before. But every book I illustrate has to be considered in these terms.

By now most of us realize that ours is an age in transition, an age in which many old values are being turned upside down and many old solutions are no longer valid. We love dramatic descriptions of phenomena, but the word *explosion* is not too violent a one to describe the swift changes we are undergoing.

Twenty years ago we were pleading for more receptivity to the new. Now we can ask ourselves to take a long look at the guests we have so blithely invited in.

As foreign-born artists have been more and more absorbed into the American scene, national contributions to American illustration from other countries have diminished. Many publishers reprint translations of foreign picture books, just as other countries reprint some of ours in order to enrich their own lists. Commercial techniques are now exchanged so widely internationally that it is a bit hard to identify the individual contributions of a particular country. Many artists have come to the field of illustration from that of painting or printmaking and have brought great richness of technical experience as well as personal freedom to their work.

Today a sculptor can fashion clean rectangular boxes, or give an order to a cabinetmaker to fashion them, and announce that his work is signing the death warrant of all previous art. And the announcement is listened to and taken seriously. Critics write enthusiastically about shows of optical experiments that used to be part of a design student's art-school training. The latest fads from a fashionable art market are put forth for a child's consumption a few months after a brief foray in the advertising field. Many books seem to be put out for oversized children in adult skins. The huge and overwhelming single image on a page, when the object described is only an incidental detail in the story; the indiscriminate use of close and hot color harmonies derived from the fashion world; overblown illustrations in overblown color in which the thread of a story or fable is lost in the extravagant garment given it — these are in the books that are not content to persuade but scream for attention and all too clearly proclaim their origin in a highly competitive market.

Speaking of a complex contemporary musical score of more visual than audible interest, Harold Schonberg, music critic of *The New York Times*, wrote of "Decibel Power versus Expressive Power." They are not the same. We could describe such books of decibel power as books for the eye (often of enormous visual interest as objects) instead of books for the eye and mind and heart, in which the whole book and each of its parts functions to express in just proportion the idea within. Many people have confounded the aims and methods of illustration with those of fine art, which has its origin in an entirely different level of the unconscious. They forget that a book starts with an idea, whether or not it has a text, and illustration is at its service. Successful illustration extends, embellishes, illuminates, but never obliterates the idea.

In spite of the dashing compositions, the blowups, the typographical shocks, many of our books today are conventional. Each age sets up its own conventions. One has only to look at publishers' catalogues to see some of ours: The children who seem to call to the reader, "Look, Ma, I'm acting!" instead of going about their own business; the stereotypes of harebrained but charming elderly friends of children; the mechanical abstractions of trees and animals; the orange-pink color schemes, no matter what the subject; the huge blown-up image from contemporary poster technique, with the main interest in design; neo-Victorianism in fine pen-line techniques derived from nineteenth-century engravings and drawings; delicate and poetic ideas awash in a sea of textures and colors that all but drown them, that stultify and limit a child's response; use of collage and mixed media — such as crayon and woodcut — together, occasionally at the price of the graphic unity of the page; visual elements from other works that had a deeper origin in reaction to life — tag ends of art techniques filtered down from painting, through commercial illustration, finally to become manner and formula in the child's book; morbidity of technique — tattered rags and incrustations of decay that come from painting techniques. What do they have to say to a child, unless the decay is purposeful, a part of the story being told?

If my mentioning these trends, which can so often result in visual clichés (but which need *not* if the idea of the book remains uppermost in importance), seems negative, perhaps it is because we become so accustomed to virtues in what is close to us that we hardly notice them and are roused only by apparent faults.

Never before have illustrators been so sure of a welcome for their most extravagant and bizarre experiments. Never has such lavish production been put at the disposal of the little child's picture book. The barker's voice in the marketplace must be loud to be heard and his wares must glitter.

When experimentation and breaking down the visual means into their simplest elements occur at the total service of the idea, we can get something as imaginative as Leo Lionni's *Little Blue and Little Yellow*. Collage can be used to tell the story richly, with the textures employed adding a dimension of visual metaphor to the story, as in the same artist's *Inch by Inch*.

Artists are constantly enlarging their fund of means to tell a story. We can ask that the means remain means, that experimentation and techniques remain tools, not ends. The search for novelty can be our goal; it can also be our curse.

Some artists, like Maurice Sendak in much of his work, are harking back with wit and re-creation of atmosphere to some of the best of the nineteenth-century line illustrators — Cruikshank, Tenniel, and Richard Doyle — and are performing a most valuable service in revitalizing a tradition that is probably much more vigorous than many of our seductive eye-catchers that remain on the decorative level and hardly attempt to illustrate a story in depth.

There seems to be very great interest in the composing process, in the *how* of making a book. It might be a good idea if we were occasionally to ask *why*, and we might end up with "Why on earth?" There is a great interest in the contribution of the individual artist, but perhaps we are asking him to talk too much about how he works and are not looking hard enough at what he does.

Some time ago I was one of probably a great many people who received a questionnaire from the National Council of Teachers of English on the "composing process" — as good a name as any for it — to try to track down what is elusive in the process of making books. The questions were intelligently thought out, as such things go. But I suspect that what is elusive will remain so, since it is a subtle combination of personality, inner drive, and imagination in the author or illustrator himself.

Illustration and writing are often a lonely business, and artists when they get together often compare notes on ways of working. I am often asked why each of my books is apt to look different from the others. Each artist has his own way of working. After a while he works in possibly the only way he can, given his own temperament. I feel about each book very differently. My interest is in the book as a whole, not just in the illustrations. Every detail of a book should, as far as possible, reflect the intention the artist and designer had toward the idea of the book. These intentions need not even be expressible in words, but they should be felt. That quality of the individual book that is strongest — the simple vigor, the delicacy, the mood, the setting — should determine the color, not an arbitrary application of brilliance to whatever the subject.

The atmosphere of a book is extremely important; in older boys' and girls' books it is perhaps more important than depiction of events. A story that is very traditional in feeling can often suffer from illustrations that are stylistically too different in period. When one adapts a modern technique to illustrations for a historical period, one must think of the young child looking, with little knowledge of period. Do the costumes give the feeling of the period if they do not reproduce the details?

Freshness lies in the intensity of expression, not in the novelty of the technique.

In order not to drag the ideas or techniques that I have developed during work on one book into another, I try to take a good piece of time between books, painting or just taking in impressions by travel, in order to clear the way for the next.

Some books are of course related by period, and the same research holds for both; this is true of *Cinderella* and *Puss in Boots.* But the spirit of the two is completely different. The quality in a story itself and in the way it is told determines style. Puss is extravagant, swaggering. The king, a *bon viveur,* enjoys the outrageousness of the cat. *Cinderella,* with the tenderness of the godmother, the dream of the girl, the preposterousness of the sisters, is in a completely different mood.

People speak of some artists who use different techniques as if they had fifty up their sleeves ready to appear, fullblown, when needed. But the life of an artist is one of constant preparation. He almost never feels that he has realized his aim. When a book is finished, he is usually just beginning to feel how it might have been. Stacks of trial drawings and rejects attest to many efforts to find the right way to say what one has to say. One develops the technique necessary to express one's feeling about the particular book in hand. Sometimes this takes several months of drawing into a subject until one is ready to begin the actual illustrations.

People often ask how much time it takes to make a book. Five days, five months, three years — as long as is necessary to get down one's ideas and feelings about the book.

It might be useful for me to tell you of my work on three different books, each of which presented a different problem in illustration and bookmaking. They happen to be mine, and I use them because I know them best.

One is a picture book, one a picture-story book, and one an illustrated book for older children. All three are of folk origin: one is a fable, one of the oldest types of folktales; one is a synthesis of several European folktales through a poet's mind; one is a hero legend with chants from a people with an oral culture.

Myths and legends tell a child who he is in the family of man. In a book with ancient, mythic origins, some of the poetic depth of the story should be implied in the illustrations. The child, looking and reading, will understand and recall tomorrow more than he can tell you today.

Once a Mouse. . . is a picture book in which the pictures complete a very brief text and, I hope, add some comment of their own. Since the book is for very young children, the details are only those needed. The woodcut is a favorite medium of mine, one that relates to traditional graphic media and that can be very successfully combined with type on a page.

Though the words of the fable are few, the theme is big. It takes a certain amount of force to cut a wooden plank, and a definite decision. Wood that lived can say something about life in a forest. An artist can make his own color proofs in printers' inks, can mix his colors and give an approximate formula to a printer. Even though the transparent colors on an offset press are different from the thicker ones used at home, this proving can be of enormous help in seeing what one will get.

Each artist has his personal feelings about his way of working, and the finished book is what is to be judged as successful or not, but in my own books I like every color to be cut on a separate block in order to maintain the optical unity of the medium. A book is like a very small stage. Just as a violent drama on television is sometimes hard to take in one's living room, what is effective in a large print can often break up a comparatively small book page.

The story of *Once a Mouse.* . .moves in an arc from quietness to quietness; from meditation, to concern, to involvement, to anger and action, back to meditation. The colors I chose were the yellow-green of sun through leaves, of earth, the dark green of shadows, and the red that says India to me. Red is used as a force to cut into the other colors when its violence is needed. Excitements are fairly easy to make in illustrations — a chase, a fight, an explosion — and offer immediate release. The quiet power of inner life is much harder to achieve and must be felt more deeply.

Just before I went to Hawaii in 1962 I had reread *The Wild Swans* of Andersen. There are vast images in that story, vast implications and sonorities that can ring in a child's mind far into adult life. It is a story with strong contrasts: dark toads and bright poppies; the forest pool in its shadow and the shimmer of light through the leaves; the darkest part of the forest — no bird was seen, no sunbeam pierced the bloom — "yes, indeed, there was solitude here, the like of which she had never known." And then the free, vast spaces of the sea, the dark waves rearing up to show their white sides.

Between the black cypresses that would be there in an Italian graveyard shines the moon. Over the tumbrel bearing Elisa to her death the eleven swans descend, and the story ends with the miracle of the white flower in a dazzle of light and happiness.

To try to show these contrasts I used a broad lettering pen dragged over rough watercolor paper and sumi for the gray washes. I needed the simplest means of achieving dark and light. The rose color for the swans' beaks, for the dawn, for the poppies and the roses I got from rubbing sanguine powder into the plastic contact plate. I was afraid to trust delicate washes either to dropout halftone or hand-clearing. The drawings were frequently vignetted around the type to tie the two more intimately together and to give variety to the movement of the book.

When I was in Hawaii I was so enchanted with the natural beauty of the islands and the charm of the people, I did not even think of looking for material for a book. The Hawaiian folklore I knew was long, involved, and difficult for a Western child. And the wild swans had ensnared me for most of the winter and spring following that first visit.

But just before I left the islands, an elderly lady gave me a historic collection of legends gathered by her husband's uncle, who had grown up on the island of Kaua'i. One story interested me particularly, "The Story of Paka'a and His Son Ku." After the swans were in flight, I decided to return to Hawaii to see if I could get inside the atmosphere enough to do a book for children based on that legend, full of racial memories of the people, also full of courage, of a boy's struggle to find himself, to discover his own place, to leap, at least in thought, beyond the mores of his own culture. The leap beyond the usual, the accepted, is so often what defines the folk hero. His audacity embodies the longings of a people for something beyond — beyond the next promontory, beyond the blue-black water where the sharks dwell, beyond the next island, beyond a restrictive social structure controlled by taboos. The material thrilled me, and I went into it more deeply, reading in Polynesian and Hawaiian myths and anthropological studies, talking to proud people who retained after 150 years of foreign influence some of the old thought patterns and ideas of their fathers.

While I was writing the story of Paka'a, which swings back and forth from the delineation of character to the natural phenomena that form character and provide images of magnificence to describe it, I was naturally thinking of the illustrations. Full color would not only have been out of the question in cost for a long book for older children but would have intruded too insistently on a story that is one of internal struggle and growth as well as external action.

Except for enigmatical pictographs, of great interest to anthropologists but very primitive graphically, and wood and stone images of gods, there was almost no Hawaiian art that seemed effective to me as inspiration for illustrations for a legend for young people with probably a vague picture of a tourist's paradise. I had thought of a carved medium, woodcut or linoleum, one that might hark back to the elegantly simple carvings and also one that could depict the atmosphere in which such legends arose. I finally settled on linoleum, and two points of view evolved in the illustrations that are also in my telling of the story. One is the background of vast natural forces — the winds that were thought to bear the tales; the basalt cliffs that gave an ideal to men's character; the vast spaces of the sea, source of life and food, testing ground of prowess, image of both beauty and poignant and unfulfilled longing. The other is a simple delineation of character, pared down to its essence in the most direct of emotional confrontations. Linoleum, which can be cut or engraved, seemed to be the answer.

The color I chose for the printing was close to that I recall most strongly when I think of Hawaii — the deep green of the clefts in the great palis, where all softness has worn away in wind and rain but where living plants have clad the cliffs in velvet. I chose a deep, warm, almost olive green to harmonize with the warm-toned paper.

Margaret Evans, who designed the typography, chose Palatino, a type that has the strength and individuality in its cut to halt the eye on the individual word. I had tried to tell the story with strong, simple words, most of them Anglo-Saxon, words of action, with metaphors taken from Hawaiian life. The pictures would have to reflect the feelings of those words. Big things had to remain big. Action should have meaning, but thought and inner feeling are also action in illustration. I found this illustration for older children a challenge, with a more rigid type page than that of the picture book, with a very different mental approach from the reader.

In *The Little Prince*, Saint-Exupéry makes a statement in the context of one human relationship that perhaps we could apply to another: "One is forever responsible for whom one has tamed." Children walk, arms open, to embrace what we give them. To hand on to them the breakdown in communication that is all around us is a very serious thing. Those who work with children should be encouraged to hand on to them their personal involvement with the world. A child needs the stimulus of books that are focused on individuality in personality and character if he is to find his own. A child is individual; a book is individual. Each should be served according to its needs.

This chapter originally appeared in *Lotus Seeds: Children, Pictures, and Books* by Marcia Brown, published by Charles Scribner's Sons, New York.

10

Dreams and Wishes:

Fantasy Literature

for Children

Dan Woolsey

Invitation

If you are a dreamer, come in,
If you are a dreamer, a wisher, a liar,
A hope-er, a pray-er, a magic bean buyer. . .
If you're a pretender, come sit by my fire
For we have some flax-golden tales to spin.
Come in!
Come in!
(Silverstein, 1974, p.9)

Every genre of children's literature holds an allure for modern readers, but the stories that most insistently invite readers into a world of dreams and wishes are fantasies — those stories in which the incredible and the impossible are made convincingly real, where the new and the strange sit comfortably within a world that is believable, immediate and authentic.

What is Fantasy?

Though we all can recognize a fantasy story when we see one, it is not so easy to define the genre. J.R.R. Tolkien, the well-known author of *The Hobbit* and other benchmarks of modern fantasy, recognized this difficulty when he wrote that "Faerie cannot be caught in a net of words; for it is one of its qualities to be indescribable, though not imperceptible" (Tolkien, 1965, p. 10). In that same essay, however, Tolkien argues that an essential ingredient in such stories is an element of "arresting strangeness," that sense that we are entering another world or that we are looking at our own world with new eyes. Similarly, Elizabeth Cook writes that the quality unique to fantastic literature is "a sense of the strange, the numinous, the totally other, of what lies quite beyond human personality and cannot be found in any human relationship" (Cook, 1969, p. 5).

For our purposes here, a fantasy is a narrative that involves some violation of what are commonly accepted as the laws of reality. These stories may involve magical creatures, from talkative spiders who can spell out messages in their webs to fierce flying dragons who can communicate only in the old tongues; from tiny Borrowers who live beneath our floorboards to shapeshifting wizards who live in the farthest reaches of a land called Earthsea. The fantasy may revolve around magical objects: ancient swords, powerful rings, or wardrobes that lead to magical kingdoms. Or the magic may manifest itself in events that violate what is accepted as possible. Thus, small carved wooden soldiers may take on life and the quest to return to their rightful home as they do in Pauline Clarke's *The Return of the Twelves*. And in Penelope Lively's *The Ghost of Thomas Kempe*, a young boy struggles with a curmudgeonly old poltergeist who is wreaking havoc on his home and village, finally managing to return him to his final resting place.

The fantasist writes of these impossibilities without apology, asking the reader to step inside this new world and to accept these creatures and these incidents as truth. Readers who are willing to suspend disbelief, to "pay something extra" (Forster, 1949, p. 101), will gladly move into this new reality.

Still, for all of the "imaginative virtuosity" (Cameron, 1969) of these fantasies, the boundaries of this secondary world must be clearly marked. The skillful fantasist does not simply allow his or her imagination to run wild; this secondary world must be a disciplined creation, a world with definite and consistent laws and limits. A successful fantasy will have impeccable logic and internal consistency. Lloyd Alexander, the creator of such memorable and convincing secondary worlds as Prydain and Westmark, elaborates upon the importance of internal consistency:

> Once committed to his imaginary kingdom, the writer is not a monarch but a subject. Characters must appear plausible in their own setting, and the writer must go along with the inner logic. Happenings should have logical implications. Details should be tested for consistency. . .Writers of fantasy must be, within their own frame of work, hardheaded realists. What appears gossamer is, underneath, solid as prestressed concrete. What seems so free in fantasy is often inventiveness of detail rather than complicated substructure. Elaboration — not improvisation. (1973, pp. 242, 243)

Writers of fantasy must create settings, characters, and incidents that will make the fantasy believable. This may be accomplished through an accumulation of corroborating detail that firmly anchors the story in reality. In *Sweetwater,* by Lawrence Yep, Tyree is a sensitive early adolescent living with his close-knit human family in the hostile environment of a remote colonial settlement on the planet Harmony. Tyree's desire to become a musician leads him to seek a private place to practice his flute. He chooses Sheol, once an elegant part of the city but now abandoned due to flooding. Yep's description of Sheol is filled with descriptive detail and an ominous sense of other-worldliness:

> At night Sheol didn't look like it belonged to man anymore. The half submerged elegant houses looked like ancient monsters surfacing. Their great stone faces were covered with delicate beards of green seaweed or soft mustachios of barnacles. The seaworn doors opened like the mouths of Seadragons through which the water twisted and untwisted, and the windows were like eyes, hollow and black and waiting — with ripples fanning outward as though from some creature sleeping inside. (p.17)

While he is rowing through this fearsome landscape, Tyree hears a sad and beautiful song wafting across the water. He hurries to the source of the music and meets Amadeus, a member of the race of Argans, an intelligent race indigenous to the planet. Here, Tyree describes this strange creature:

> It was an Argan, an old one, sitting there calmly. The bristly fur on his back and arm-legs was all wrinkled, and he stooped slightly from old age. He looked very much like a four-foot-high Earth spider, though you would never suggest that to an Argan . . . He put down his reed pipes when he saw me and with six of his arm-legs slowly pushed himself off the portico. He walked delicately on two arm-legs like a ballet dancer imitating an old man, with his six other arm-legs stretched out to balance his overpuffed body. (pp. 18, 19)

We can accept Tyree and Amadeus and their strange world because they are carefully and vividly described, but also because beneath those alien surfaces we can see ourselves and our world. "True fantasy," writes Mollie Hunter (1975, p. 59), "is always firmly rooted in fact or in some instantly recognizable circumstance acceptable to the reader." In simple terms, then, effective fantasy is a marriage of the strange and the familiar, the magical and the commonplace. It may be unreal, but it is not untrue.

Types of Fantasy

Children's fantasy is a richly varied genre, and a comprehensive accounting of the field would require an entire book. However, we can roughly trace the boundaries of this imaginative literature. At one end of the territory we would find low fantasy, simple stories with an element of magic that are entirely set in the primary world. At the other edge of this diverse terrain are profound and complex sagas set in intricately constructed imaginary lands or "secondary worlds." Between those two borders, however, there are other fantasies in which the primary and the secondary worlds are side by side or where one is nested within the other. In these stories, characters may tumble through space and time, moving back and forth between here and there, between the past, the present, and the future.

Low fantasies are often based on eccentric characters who find themselves in preposterous situations. Thus, an unpretentious sign painter with an interest in Arctic exploration finds himself herding twelve rowdy penguins through a stage show in the Atwaters' *Mr.*

Popper's Penguins; a young country boy from New Hampshire cares for a baby Triceratops that hatches from Butterworth's *The Enormous Egg;* and a strange and lonely boy named James makes a fabulous transatlantic flight in a hollow peach with the help of 502 friendly seagulls in Dahl's *James and the Giant Peach.*

Also set in the primary world are the animal fantasies or "beast fables" (Tolkien, 1965). Many classic characters in children's literature are talking animals who take on human characteristics while remaining true to their species. The Victorian era brought us great animal heroes such as Peter Rabbit, Toad of Toad Hall, and Winnie the Pooh. No discussion of children's fantasy would be complete without mention of other talking beasts such as Wilbur and Charlotte, Frances the badger, Chester, *The Cricket in Times Square* by Selden and Hazel and Fiver, the courageous and visionary rabbit bucks of *Watership Down* by Adams. A recent addition to this group of articulate animals is Mathias, the young mouse warrior who leads the mice of *Redwall* by Jacques to victory over the villainous rat, Cluny the Scourge. These small creatures remind us of ourselves and the follies of our society. Their world is one that we easily recognize as our own. In them we recognize our own strengths and frailties, for we must acknowledge that we, too, are sometimes intelligent and loyal like Charlotte, sometimes naive like Wilbur, and at other times greedy and self-seeking like Templeton.

Low fantasies are often humorous and accessible, providing excellent stepping stones to the more complex fantasies at the other end of the spectrum, those that are located entirely in an imagined secondary world with a unique topography, flora and fauna, and laws of nature. Such stories are often called high fantasy, and they tend to be as serious as the above stories are humorous. They are complex narratives, drawing upon ancient roots — myth, legend, and the oldest dreams of our ancestors. These are stories of high adventure and enchantment, of quests for magical objects, self-discovery, and the battle between good and evil. These dramatic scenes are played out upon wide but well-defined landscapes and the consequences are universal in their impact. Be it called Middle Earth, Narnia, Earthsea or Prydain, this secondary world is a fully realized other-world.

Finally, there are those stories in which the borders dividing the secondary from the primary world are not easily drawn. In these stories characters are transported headlong across space and time; in these worlds, the past may intrude upon the present day, or the present moment may suddenly fade into the past. Thus, the displaced English child Tolly befriends three seventeenth century children who share his grandmother's ancient house in *The Children of Green Knowe* by Lucy Boston; a self-absorbed youngster joins the childhood play and dreams of his elderly neighbor in Pearce's *Tom's Midnight Garden;* and Sandy and Dennys Murry inadvertently stumble into one of their father's experiments and find themselves struggling to survive with Noah and his family in the harsh desert climate of a young Earth before the coming of *Many Waters* by L'Engle. These fantasies share many of the universal themes explored in high fantasy: the coming of age, the quest for wholeness and home and the fact that "today holds yesterday and tomorrow within it" (Curry, 1980).

Themes in Modern Fantasy

One of the key functions of fantasy literature is to interpret human experience with memorable and penetrating symbols or images, to shed light on the oft hidden realities of the workings of the human heart and mind. Ursula Le Guin reminds us of the illuminatory power of these tales:

> The great fantasies, myths and tales are indeed like dreams: they speak from the unconscious to the unconscious, in the language of the unconscious — symbol and archetype. Though they use words, they work the way music does: they short-circuit verbal reasoning, and go straight to the thoughts that lie too deep to utter. . .They are profoundly meaningful and usable — practical — in terms of ethics; of insight; of growth. (1979, p. 62)

Fantasy has this power because it deals with potent themes related to universal desires, conflicts, and values. It raises hard questions about who we are, how we should live in our world, and how we should live with each other. It sheds light on the constant struggle of good and evil within our world and within each of us, provides hints at the place of each of us within the broader sphere of space and time, and explores the meaning of life and death.

The best fantasies engage our minds and our hearts at the same time by presenting profound ideas and complex issues in a concrete form. Perhaps more than realistic fiction, well-written fantasy can clarify philosophical and moral dilemmas by embodying them in story lines that may not be directly applicable to our complex and muddied lives but which can delight, instruct, and inspire because of their open and evident design.

For example, the natural cycles and rhythms that give structure to life are indicated in clear and simple terms in *Charlotte's Web:*

> Life in the barn was very good — night and day, winter and summer, spring and fall, dull days and bright days. It was the best place to be thought Wilbur, the warm delicious cellar, with the garrulous geese, the changing seasons, the heat of the sun, the passage of swallows, the nearness of rats, the sameness of sheep, the love of spiders, the smell of manure and the glory of everything. (White, 1952, p. 183)

With humor and pathos, White celebrates the beauty and wonder of the natural world. He eloquently reminds us of the the importance of love, friendship, and sacrifice, the cycle of life and death, and the web of living creatures that gives order to the universe. Significantly, man is not at the center of this web.

That man must accept his place in the cosmos is also emphasized in Lloyd Alexander's *The Book of Three*, in which Taran learns the importance of accepting the mercy and kindness of others and about the interdependence of all living things. Young Tolly learns much the same lesson in Lucy Boston's *The Children of Green Knowe*. He arrives at Green Knowe an insecure displaced child, his emotional isolation symbolized by the flood that cuts the old house off from the outside world. With the gentle encouragement of Granny Oldknow, Tolly slowly becomes aware of the animals and people, both past and present, who share his world. Finally he discovers that the world is indeed a good place and that he has an important place in it. The world opens up to him, and he begins to move out of himself and into its glorious possibilities.

This movement away from self is an important element in many of the best fantasies. Like Tolly, Max in *The Return of the Twelves* by Pauline Clarke becomes aware of others for whom he is responsible. As he oversees the reawakening of the twelve toy soldiers and their dangerous journey to the museum, he comes to see that he is not just an individual but also part of a vast universe. In the same way, nine-year-old Omri in Lynne Banks' *The Indian in the Cupboard* learns that he is responsible for the well-being of the small plastic Indian who comes to life in his magical cupboard. As the protagonists in these stories come of age, they learn that what they choose to do or not to do is important because of its impact on those around them and those that will come after them.

In most fantasies the protagonist is a rather common and ordinary person at the beginning of the story. However, these characters grow and develop as they encounter difficulty and challenges. These heroes embody the universal struggle to come of age, to reach maturity, and to find a niche in the world.

Indeed, all of us often feel small and powerless. Hobbits are smaller than dwarves, yet Bilbo Baggins succeeds in achieving a quest that redeems his entire world in *The Hobbit.* Equally important to Bilbo is the fact that in the process of meeting the challenges that responsibility brings, he is transformed from a tame stay-at-home into a self-reliant individual who finds beauty and excitement in a world that he would never have discovered if he had remained at home in his safe hobbit hole. So, too, we can easily relate to Taran in *The Book of Three* when we first meet him as a lowly assistant pigkeeper given to passionate daydreaming, boasting, and rash impulsive acts. Yet, we make the spiritual journey with Taran as he gradually accepts the quest that is given to him. We see him mature as he copes with the difficulties that confront him and with the forces of evil and chaos that surround him. Ultimately, we see him fulfill his destiny as the High King who makes the ultimate sacrifice, giving up promised immortality in order to rule the Kingdom of Prydain.

Well-written fantasy is the natural vehicle, not only to recount the spiritual journey of the individual but also to depict the never-ending struggle of the forces of good and evil. Each of the heroes discussed above has to come to terms with the darker side of life. Nowhere is this more evident than in Ursula LeGuin's *Earthsea* Trilogy. As an adolescent mage in training, Ged abuses his powers and releases a fierce and relentless shadow into the world. He learns through bitter and painful experience that he alone is responsible for the evil that has been unleashed, and he can control this evil only when he faces it directly. Similar themes can be found in other great fantasies, such as Susan Cooper's *The Dark is Rising,* Alan Garner's *The Owl Service,* and various volumes of C.S. Lewis' Chronicles of Narnia, but most notably *The Lion, the Witch and the Wardrobe* and *The Voyage of the Dawn Treader.*

Why Read Fantasy?

These, then, are some of the thematic patterns that provide the warp and woof of this richly embroidered literature. This brief discussion has hinted at the importance of reading this literature and sharing it enthusiastically and sensitively with young people.

Fundamentally, well-written fantasy offers what any good piece of literature provides: the aesthetic experience of reading an engrossing story, replete with engaging characters, vivid settings, and compelling incidents that propel the reader through the story. Good fantasies go beyond the well-told story, however, inviting the reader to plunge wholeheartedly into a strange world of magic and wonder, to engage in free play of the heart and mind. Fantasies can encourage the development of imaginative thinking; these stories help us to entertain new ideas, to dream new dreams, and to see the world in new ways.

However, the deeper value of fantasy literature lies in the fact that at their best such stories can serve as a revelation to the reader. Interestingly, our word "fantasy" is derived from a Greek word that is literally translated: "a making visible." These stories provide profound insights into the realities of our existence. They provide glimpses at the complex answers to our deepest questions: Who am I? Where did I come from? What is my purpose in life? How, then, shall I live today? Thus, readers will be a bit different after entering the imaginative vision of the fantasist. As we read fantasy we are extended and stretched toward an understanding of ourselves, our place in the world and the paths that we might take in the future. As such, the reading of fantasy literature provides a forum for the rehearsal of "human life as it is lived, as it might be lived and as it ought to be lived" (LeGuin, 1977, p. 169). So, let us invite young people, "If you are a dreamer, come in, come in."

Summary

Difficult to define, fantasy here is considered a narrative that involves some violation of the commonly accepted laws of reality. Fantasy writers ask their readers to step inside the imaginary worlds they create and willingly suspend disbelief. Readers do this readily because the fantasy writer creates a secondary world governed by consistent laws and impeccable logic. Types of fantasy range from low fantasy, simple stories set in the real world but with an element of magic, to profound and complex sagas set in intricately constructed imaginary lands. Between these borders lie animal fantasy, time slip fantasy, and other variations that intrigue readers with their intricate plots and strong characters who face inner and outer struggles. Fantasy deals with potent themes related to universal desires, conflicts, and values. It raises questions about identity, relationships, and deals with the eternal struggle between good and evil. Fantasy engages our hearts at the same time it engages our minds by presenting profound ideas and complex issues in concrete form; we are forced to clarify philosophical and moral dilemmas as we walk with a hero through earth shattering experiences. Like many of the characters in outstanding fantasies, we realize that our world opens up to us and begin to move out of ourselves into its glorious possibilities.

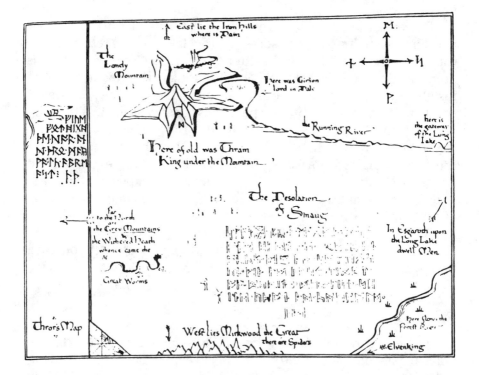

Figure 10–1.
Thror's Map from *The Hobbit*. Tolkien's Middle Earth is an extensively documented fantasy world, to the delight of readers everywhere.

References

Alexander, L. (1973). The flat-heeled muse. In V. Haviland (Ed.), *Children and literature: Views and reviews.* Glenview, IL: Scott Foresman.

Cameron, E. (1969). *The green and burning tree.* Boston: Little, Brown & Co.

Cook, E. (1969). *The ordinary and the fabulous: An introduction to myths, legends, and fairy tales.* London: Cambridge University Press.

Curry, J. (1980). On the elvish craft. In A. Chambers (Ed.), *The signal approach to children's books.* Hammondsworth, England: Kestrel.

Forster, E.M. (1949). *Aspects of the novel.* New York: Harcourt.

Hunter, M. (1975). *Talent is not enough.* New York: Harper & Row.

LeGuin, U. (1979). The child and shadow. In S. Wood (Ed.), *The language of the night: Essays on fantasy and science fiction.* New York: Putnam, 59–71.

LeGuin, U. (1977). In defense of fantasy. In P. Heins (Ed.), *Crosscurrents of criticism: Horn Book essays, 1968–1977.* Boston: Horn Book, Inc., 169.

Silverstein, S. (1974). *Where the sidewalk ends.* New York: Harper & Row.

Tolkien, J.R.R. (1965). On faerie stories. In *Tree and leaf.* Boston: Houghton-Mifflin.

11

Fantasy

in the Classroom

Virginia Stelk

"Look, Jordan, there's a dinosaur hanging over Mrs. Stelk's desk!"

"What are you talking about, Kevin? That's a dragon!"

"Dino? Dino is not a dragon's name!"

"What is — Puff?"

The conversation continues and spreads as the students file in and notice the big, inflatable "dragonosaur" over my desk. Eventually, they also notice the unicorns, hobbits, gnomes, ogres, gurgies, and other characters from my favorite fantasy books strategically placed around the room. Today is the beginning of a high fantasy unit with developmental readers in the seventh grade at Mount Vernon (Ohio) Middle School. The students, grouped homogeneously into sections

by reading ability, come into my room for their scheduled reading period. Despite the different ability groups, each group sounded like a theme with variations.

Using High Fantasy with Preadolescents

Why have a unit on fantasy with twelve and thirteen year olds? The primary reason is that this is the best age for it; it is a unit I have looked forward to every year for the past ten years. The preadolescent is full of questions about what's really right, what's "cool," and what is basically wrong.

They are all on a quest to find out who they are, and where they fit into society, yet they still feel the strong pull of family or at least want to feel it. In life, they want freedom to explore within limits. If we accept the premise that we should begin exploring by using the knowledge the students bring to class, almost every student of this age has at least some knowledge of the fantastic elements of fantasy; for example, the dragon over my desk. They know dragons from songs, movies, advertisements, and, hopefully, stories. The source of much fantasy derives from folklore: fairytales, myths, and legends. Like its predecessor, it integrates the imagined world with the real world.

Every student brings a variety of background experiences and needs to school, each one so very different from the other. For this reason fantasy works especially well with the preadolescent. Fantasy is not bound by time or space; it paints conflicts in primary colors or in black and white. It can, therefore, clarify conflict by putting it in its most basic terms.

By seeing life in fantasy cast in sharp relief, students can observe from a distance as conflicts are resolved. They can have opinions and thoughts about the conflicts without feeling guilty or thinking a teacher has a hidden motive in getting them to read the book. A teacher, therefore, must not think that there is one right meaning in a fantasy novel; students create their own meaning. Just as there are many valid interpretations of a fairy or folk tale, so, too, are there in fantasy. Some students may want to discuss a fantasy novel; others may choose to ponder silently its meaning for them.

Another reason I particularly enjoy a fantasy unit with preadolescents is its appeal to boys of that age. At ages twelve and thirteen, many boys are feeling a strong pull to sports, computers, and acceptable "manly" things. Reading books may be low on their list of things they like to do, even on a rainy day.

Many boys at this age are, however, interested in World War II, in the Middle Ages with its castles and the brave deeds of the knights, or in outer space travel as they see it in space adventure films. They may also like sports biographies or statistical information. These interests are reasonable for this age because young men are seeking their self-identity sexually and emotionally. They are leaning more toward their fathers than their mothers as they shape their own identity. Fantasy, however, appeals to these boys.

High fantasy, full of adventure and often battles, has a strong relationship to the Middle Ages in many of its settings. The far-away places of space adventure transfer easily to the imaginary setting of some fantasy and science fiction. The male characters in both high fantasy and science fiction are usually strong in spirit and determination, like sports heroes. This is not always the case in other genres.

I have always felt a strong commitment to motivate the preadolescent to become a lifelong reader. The seventh grade seems like one of the last chances to do this. High school and college curriculums have so much required reading that unless students truly enjoy reading a novel, they will not find time to start at that stage in school. Many twelve and thirteen year olds come to middle school with broad reading backgrounds, but others have never read a book on their own.

Fantasy covers a broad range of reading interests, from talking animals to high fantasy. I can always find a fantasy novel that someone has not read or one that can motivate a reluctant reader. Because high fantasy is based on lore that has been passed down from generation to generation — the beliefs and customs, the superstitions and prejudices — it is a good unit for preadolescents who are making their own quest for identity. Hopefully, they will enjoy reading a good book in the process.

Mythical Beasts

To introduce a fantasy unit, I frequently begin with a short unit on mythical beasts. The students read about the origins of dragons, unicorns, gnomes, trolls, fauns, mermaids, any mythical beast they choose. They write an informational paragraph on the beast, a poem about the beast (their own or one by another poet), and a short story that includes the mythical beast as a character. While they are working, I share two sample assignments with them.

For the information on dragons, I read from *Monsters* by Perle Epstein. The "Toaster" by William Jay Smith, "Steam Shovel" by Charles Malam, and "The Gold-Tinted Dragon" by Karla Kuskin are favorite dragon poems to share. For examples of dragons as characters in stories, I read about Eustace's encounter with the dragon in *The Voyage of the Dawn Treader* by C.S. Lewis and *Everyone Knows What a Dragon Looks Like* by Jay Williams.

I also like to share illustrative material about unicorns. Bulfinch's *Mythology* is a handy reference for basic information. The poems that I usually share are "The Unicorn" by Ella Young and "Unicorn" by Shel Silverstein. For variety, I rent a film, *The Unicorn in the Garden* by James Thurber. This beginning of a unit on fantasy is fun for all levels of readers and writers. Some of the illustrations the students do for their units are truly beautiful. The unit includes research, creative writing, and art, all webbed together. The following is an example of the way one seventh grader, Brooke Hitchcock, used her research to write a very creative poem.

Research:

Mermaids

The Mermaid is the name given to a mythical being. She is said to be half fish and half woman who lives in the sea. Her singing attracts mortal men and then she places a magical cap upon his head, so he can survive with her.

She spends her time combing her long golden hair. She eats sea plants, but will not eat any fish.

The only time that she ever leaves her underwater home is to sit on rocks and search for ships.

Some other sources say that mermaids cannot talk, but whimper and hum. If this is so, she cannot possibly attract men with her singing.

There are also mermen, who capture female's souls.

Poem:

The Mermaid

She sits ready, waiting, hoping
Watching the waves' repeated blows to the rocks on which she rests
Her long-awaited ship concealed behind low-lying clouds
Slowly, it emerges in the motionless sky,
the salt-cracked oars straining to move its monstrous bulk
Carefully, she begins her hypnotic song
Her voice calling, waiting, urging the man for whom she waits.

He stands in the crows nest attentive, listening, drawn to the song
    meant only for him
Then he's running, swimming, arriving to where she waits
She's hesitating, thinking, placing the magical cap upon his head
Then he's holding, loving, following her into the water
Wanting, needing
The mermaid

Quest Themes

Following the unit on mythical beasts, I use the first four books
of *The Prydain Chronicles* by Lloyd Alexander or *The Hobbit* by J.R.R.
Tolkien. The more able readers read the Prydain series independently.
I only ask them to read one of the first four books in the series, but
many read all five (six with *The Foundling*). I show the filmstrip of
The High King as a concluding activity. Those who have read *The High
King* independently note that parts of the book have been omitted
from the filmstrip. This creates an interesting discussion about mak-
ing films from books and often motivates others to read the book.
While students are reading independently, I share *The Foundling* for
background information on many of the characters and also because
I like to read in class every day.

I read *The Hobbit* by J.R.R. Tolkien with my less able readers. The
characters' names are not a stumbling block, and many have seen the
film on television, which gives them some background experience
with the plot. I read it with them, but not always word for word. Some
days, I read a chapter, and they read the next one. Other days (following a lot of motivation), they read independently. When they read
independently, it is for half the class period, followed by discussion
and a language experience activity. We also keep a daily journal of
what we read so that at the end of the book they have a summary of
what they have read. This summary is helpful with their extensions.

I allow my most able readers to choose a fantasy novel on their
own from a list of the fantasy books available in our school library.
I give brief book talks on each book and then let each one select a book.
Since I am so fond of *The Dark is Rising* series by Susan Cooper, I
usually read either *The Grey King* or *The Dark is Rising* aloud to the
class during the unit. Even the ablest readers enjoy hearing a book
read aloud; they are also excellent at sharing books with one another
through discussions and a variety of extensions.

Tracing the Roots of Fantasy

A fantasy unit also can bring wonderful experiences to the teacher. During trips to Wales, my husband and I have located many of the places referred to in Susan Cooper's *The Dark is Rising* series. We shared the books in our family and then visited Tywyn, Bearded Lake, Panorama Walk, Carn March Arthur, the estuary of the River Dyfi. We think we found the "Lost City," and we even climbed Cader Idris. After several trips to Wales, I corresponded with Susan Cooper, and she was kind enough to share the location of Will's House, Huntercombe Lane, and the Chiltern Hills of Buckinghamshire. We also visited those places as a family. It was exactly as described, even to the rooks on the roof of the parish church. We also took color photographs, which I matched with poetry to go with various chapters of the books. When I share the slides and poetry, it is a very special time for both the class and me.

As an outgrowth of visiting the real sites of *The Dark is Rising* series, we proceeded to find Caer Dathyl as described by Lloyd Alexander in *The High King*. We also read this series as a family. In Janet Hickman's "Roots of Fantasy" class, I read *The Island of the Mighty* by Evangeline Walton. A footnote at the beginning of the first chapter located Caer Dathyl in Pen y Gair in Caernarvonshire in modern Wales. Modern Caernarvonshire is Gwynedd on the old Welsh maps. My husband and I researched and found the place. When we arrived in Pen y Gair, we asked the location of Caer Dathyl from the people in the general store. None of them knew it, but they sent us to the lady next door whom they were certain could help us. At first, she directed us to a hillsite further south, but as we were leaving, she said, "The only thing around here is the Iron Age fort on that hill." Our mouths dropped open as she pointed to a hill across the river. We asked how to get to the top, and she gave us directions. After driving about halfway to the top, the dirt road ended, and we then climbed over stiles and among sheep to the top. It was obviously Caer Dathyl! We could clearly see outlines of rooms and stairways among the stones. It had indeed been a castle. We could see the river below and the route of the Cauldron Born. And, it had been burned to the ground! When I mentioned this discovery to Lloyd Alexander at the Ohio State Children's Literature Conference, he was not aware of the place. But we know it is the place! Isn't fantasy marvelous!

Matching poetry with books, small group discussions, art work, and other extensions and webbing it all together are truly representative of Charlotte Huck's teachings. In a middle school, each subject is taught independently and for a limited period of time each day. I have been fortunate to have a team teacher, Lois Hanson, who teaches language arts and social studies. Lois and I have found ways to correlate fantasy that students in my classes read with the content areas and vice versa. It is important that middle schoolers see that life is not separated into little compartments but is all part of a whole — their lives. I hope Taran and Eilonwy, Will, Bran, Jane, Simon and Barney, Bilbo and Frodo are also entwined in their lives, as well as a love of reading.

Summary

Fantasy is a magical ingredient in the curriculum for twelve and thirteen year old students because, at that age, they are full of questions about right and wrong and are on a quest to find out who they are and where they fit into society. They engage with the themes of fantasy partially because the themes do not deal with a specific problem in a specific time; instead they deal with universal questions set just apart from the real world. Preadolescents enjoy observing life outside themselves all the while imagining themselves in the thick of the moral or physical battle. The safety of the screen of fantasy allows them to test their mettle without fear of combat. Fantasy appeals especially to preadolescent boys who are interested in the adventures and battles often reminiscent of the Middle Ages. Male characters, strong in spirit and determination, serve as models for the young readers. A fantasy unit on mythical beasts involves research on the origins of dragons, unicorns, gnomes, and trolls before exploring poetry, short stories, and novels involving these creatures. A unit on quest themes leads students into the more complex novels by Tolkien, Alexander, and Cooper which stretch their imagination and satisfy their hunger for serious reading. Through trips to Wales, we located the very sites of many scenes in the fantasy novels we read.

12

Fantasy Is

What Fantasy Does

Madeleine L'Engle

There are as many definitions of fantasy as there are of myth, or of religion, or of what it means to be a human being. There are also an equal number of misapprehensions. One definition I like — though perhaps it is *too* broad to be adequate — is those things that were true, are true, and will be true. Another, interesting, but less satisfactory is: those things that never were, but always are. The dictionary's definition leaves me cold: nonrealistic story, play, and so forth; train of thought or of mental images indulged in to gratify one's wishes; fancy, whim, illusion, hallucination...

Fantasy is indeed a multifaceted word. Fantasy in literature, however, is not unreal. It is not something that is pleasant for little children but should be discarded for reality as soon as we come of age. It is not escapism. It is, rather, a search for a deeper reality, for the truth that will make us more free.

Stories of fantasy almost always start in the familiar world of the five senses, with what the reader can recognize; with kitchens, liverwurst sandwiches, stormy nights. Fantasy is rooted in and springs from the real. It is the real taken to that deeper reality that is beyond ordinary human perception.

We human creatures can be likened to a small radio. Most of the time we are tuned to a limited band, one that is adequate for the everyday world of getting up in the morning, doing our jobs, eating our meals, bathing, going to bed. We are also capable of being a much finer receiver than we ordinarily need to be. Fantasy tuning is incredibly fine tuning.

As I write this I am listening to a radio station that plays classical music. I turn on this small machine, which sits between books on one of the shelves, and out of it comes the precise strains of a Scarlatti Toccata. That seems miraculous to me.

Yes, but there are people who do understand how to put together a radio and how sound waves work. Yes, and there are also people who can plunge their hands into a fire of roses and who know where the back of the north wind is. That fire of roses may be fantasy, but it is also real for what fantasy does is to widen reality for us, breaking down the restricting limits of literalism we have allowed to be built around us.

I am working on a new fantasy now, one that is involving me in a lot of research about the Celts and the language they spoke more than two thousand years ago, about the nature of time as astrophysicists understand it today, and about the strange pursuit of being human. This book is an adventure story; it is also, for me, a way to work through grief at the loss of a husband after forty years; a way of renewing my belief that the human venture is magnificent and well worth all the struggle and the pain. If this work does not expand my own horizons it will not turn into a finished book. But as I write I can feel the air quivering, time changing, skies lifting and widening. I am moving into a reality that is greater than the ordinary daily world in which I get out of bed in the morning and move through the routine of the day, until the day's work is done and I can stretch out in a hot bath and get into bed and relax with a book. The world of which I am writing makes all these daily duties that might become mundane through repetitiveness become new every day.

When Dante wanted to write about human love and about divine love, he turned to fantasy, for his *Divine Comedy* is great fantasy. How often have writers turned to animals (Mole, Rat, and Toad, in Kenneth Grahame's *The Wind in the Willows;* a family of rabbits in Beatrix Potter's *Peter Rabbit*; barnyard creatures in Walter Wangerin's *The Book of the Dun Cow*) in order to find out more about human nature? These fantasies are far more real than slice-of-life stories.

A few years ago I moderated a panel of six twelve year olds from New York City schools, who were to bring in two of their favorite books for the audience of children's book writers and to discuss the kind of book they most liked to read. To the amazement of many of the writers, the books the young people brought with them were science fiction and fantasy. They were asked about some of the highly acclaimed books by slice-of-life writers. One boy said, "We live all that. Why would we want to read about it?" One girl said, "Oh, I read all those books when I was eight."

We far too often underestimate the capacity of children to understand fantasy, with all the demands it puts on the reader, as I discovered to my rue when editor after editor rejected *A Wrinkle in Time* as being far too difficult for children. The writer does not write fantasy for either children or adults, however; we write fantasy for the sake of the fantasy and for our own selves. And what great precedents there are! Fantasy is that wider language into which Shakespeare himself moved in writing *The Tempest,* his last play; and surely *King Lear, A Winter's Tale,* and *Twelfth Night* have many elements of fantasy. Fantasy is the language in which the writer tries to speak of those things for which there are no ordinary words. It can be very simple, perhaps deceptively so, as the story of Henny Penny is simple; or it can be complex indeed, as in (Scripture) *Daniel,* or John's *Revelation.*

Erich Fromm in his book *The Forgotten Language* says that the only language that transcends time, culture, place, and race, is the language of fantasy, fairy tale, and dream. Perhaps that is why, when we write fantasy, it stretches us, opens doors to new ideas, will not let us be content with easy answers. It is not possible for me to write two books of fantasy in a row because this genre is so incredibly demanding, not only in the research involved but also in the very creative process of the writer. The copy editor at my publishers, Farrar, Straus & Giroux, has had many difficult books to copy edit, by such writers as Solzhenitsyn, Malamud, T.S. Eliot, and yet she said that the most difficult book she ever had to edit was my fantasy,

A Swiftly Tilting Planet. It was a difficult book for me, too, especially cutting it down to the size considered publishable for a novel that is going to be marketed as a juvenile. Nowadays few people read the uncut *Gulliver's Travels* (which was certainly not written as children's fantasy — it is a very raunchy book) or even the uncut *Water Babies*. I read such books uncut, as a child, and as I leaf through them now, it is obvious to me that I must have read them selectively, cutting and skipping as I read, for certainly Kingsley is full of sermonizing, and so, even, is George Macdonald. But as I remember the books, all I remember is the story and the people.

In a fantasy I am, of course, interested in ideas, but these ideas must be set forth as story. Usually I, like the Victorians, sermonize, but I do not live in that more leisurely age so I try to cut the sermons out and toss them in the round file, leaving only the structure of the story to speak for itself — and the voice of the story is enough.

The story. When I was a child and lost in the confusions of the adult world around me, a world preparing for another terrible war, a world where my father was coughing his lungs out as a result of the first one, a world where I could see only through a glass very darkly, I found my way in story. Reading the story of others helped me live my own story more bravely and more fully, and the stories that sustained me were not those that were limited to the daily, ordinary world, but those that moved on to the extraordinary — Emily of New Moon seeing beyond the veil to the true fate of the doctor's lost young wife; Hans with a splinter of ice lodged in his heart; Cornelli discovering that she really did not have horns growing out of her forehead.

So, in my adult life, I seek to make sense and perhaps even beauty out of a world still lost in the horrors of war, where accidents strike at random and terrorism abounds, where love dies unexpectedly. Pattern and purpose emerge as I work at story, where people do more than they think they can do, where friendship is shown to be life saving, and love worth working for, and courage is bright against the face of evil's cloud.

Since my fantasies all happen to be based on post-Newtonian physics, quantum mechanics, cellular biology, astrophysics, there is always a great deal of research to do, but these new sciences that came with the discovery of the nature and structure of the atom are dealing with *being* itself, what life in the universe is all about. Much of what I study is over my head. I do not have the mathematical background to help me understand the various formulae filled with

Greek letters and numbers. My imagination is nevertheless stimulated by the ideas, and I understand just enough to send me hurrying on to the next book. In my current study of the nature of time I am full of questioning: why, if our planet is on a twenty-four-hour night/day rhythm, are our bodies, by and large, on a twenty-five-hour rhythm so that we have to reset our biological clocks every day? On weekends when we do not have to set the alarm clock and can sleep late, our body clocks get completely out of rhythm, and when the alarm clock goes off on Monday morning our timers are so out of sync that it feels like three or four in the morning to us, rather than six or seven. This fascinating piece of information is not likely to appear in the book I am writing now, or is it? At this point I do not know. But why is the human body clock out of sync with the planet? Thus far I have not come across an answer. Maybe the answer will be found in story.

I know that I am happy to be back at work on a fantasy again, after a book of nonfiction. Any writing is challenging, but there is something special about fantasy.

I am asked if my books are fantasy or science fiction. They are both. Fantasy is a wide word, embracing a wide world. Science fiction can be limited to the technicalities of space travel, but it need not be, and the science that undergirds my stories springs from the extraordinary world of subatomic particles — nobody could imagine anything more bizarre and colorful! What an extraordinary planet we live on! The nature of the universe is total interdependence, everything affecting and interrelating with everything else, and on our planet we are constantly warring, separating, turning our backs on each other. Story, like the universe, is integrating. Lear, becoming mad from all the tragedies he has brought upon himself, becomes purged and purified in his madness; the White Queen in *Alice Through the Looking Glass*, practices believing six impossible things every morning before breakfast; Eeyore finds pleasure in putting a burst balloon in and out of an empty honey jar. I learn from the small as well as the great, from a spider named Charlotte to Dante daring to enter the dark wood.

Perhaps that is the key. We must go into the dark wood, either in reading or writing fantasy, for the sunlight is only on the other side.

13

A Gift of Time:

Children's Historical

Fiction

Linda Levstik

*Mainly [my textbook] just says that the Americans were right but it doesn't tell you exactly why they were right, or why the British fought. . . Tim [in **My Brother Sam Is Dead**] was confused because what he saw wasn't too great for either side, and it wasn't very nice. . . How could they do such stupid things and all the social studies books leave out anything bad that the Americans did, and its always the British. . .?*

Fifth-Grade Girl

In the pages of a historical novel a young girl encounters the complexities of historical events, where facts from the past become living, breathing drama, significant beyond their own time. Issues that divided colonist from crown and neighbor from neighbor confront the reader with choices that have shaped the world and call for judgments about the historical content and literary credibility of the story. This fifth grader's response recognizes the difference between history as it is reported in her textbook and history as it is experienced by a fictional character, as well as in her own imagination. Historical fiction has given her a gift of time: time that stretches as far back as imagination and literature can take her, and time that allows her to see herself as one of the vast company of folk whose lives are our past, present, and future.

A Living Past

Historical fiction can create a sense of history so powerful that children enter imaginatively into the past and explore the "conflicts, sufferings, joys and despair of those who lived before us" (Huck, 1977, p. 469). Part of that exploration includes an opportunity to study and evaluate human behavior in a developmentally appropriate context. Narrative and story might be conceived of as the key to the secret garden of the past in which child and book together cultivate a sense of history.

Several writers (Egan, 1983; Levstik, 1981; Meek, *et al.*, 1978) have suggested that stories are an appropriate medium for introducing history to children. Story appears to be more easily understood than expository writing — perhaps because children have more experience with story — but historical fiction also satisfies on other levels.

Historical Subjectivity

Textbooks strive for objectivity and in their striving often lose the life of the past (Trease, 1977, p. 22). Historical fiction, on the other hand, thrives on subjectivity. It is an interpretation, acted out in a most subjective way, by individuals confronting historical realities. This subjectivity gives meaning to events by embedding them in a social system and making them subject to that social system's morality (White, 1980, p. 14–18). It also is one of the appeals of historical fiction to children (Meek, *et al.*, 1978). Consider, for instance, the child visiting an old battlefield. Historical markers describe patterns of troop advance and retreat, and tally the dead in each encounter. Turning points and consequences are detailed. Yet the child stands before a stone marker and asks, "Which side did Grandpa's family fight on? Are they buried here?"

Significance is counted in smaller, more personal terms than historical markers note. What was it like to be a person here? What was the nature of good and evil in that time and place, and with whom shall my sympathies lie? Hayden White (1980) argues that it is "possible to conclude that every historical narrative has as its latent or manifest purpose the desire to *moralize* the events of which it treats" (p. 18). Historical fiction, even more than nonfictional historical narrative, certainly invites the reader to enter into a historical discussion that involves making judgments about issues of morality. As White goes on to say, "unless at least two versions of the same set of events can be imagined, there is no reason for the historian to take upon himself the authority of giving the true account of what really happened" (p. 23). Nor for the storyteller to enlist the reader's sympathies in the subjective enterprise of historical fiction.

There are, of course, different forms of subjectivity. Some writers assume that children can (should?) deal with only one point of view or interpretation of a historical event. Their stories are painted in black and white with few touches of grey. In some cases, such as *Johnny Tremain* (Forbes, 1987), the story is well written but does not give the reader an opportunity to enter the heart or mind of, say, a sympathetic loyalist or to wrestle with the moral dilemma of loyalty during a revolutionary period. As Joel Taxel (1978) points out, such books reinforce simplistic images of historical events and eras and leave out significant portions of society — especially the poor, working classes, and minorities (p. 8).

Much has changed since *Johnny Tremain* was written, with more recent historical fiction more likely to challenge readers to make hard choices along with literary characters. In *My Brother Sam Is Dead* (Collier & Collier, 1974), both rebel and loyalist causes are flawed, and the agony of choices that destroyed families and the insanities of war are seen through the eyes of a character whose loyalties are torn between a loyalist father and rebel brother. *When the World's On Fire* (Edwards, 1973) deals with the incongruities of a war for freedom that nonetheless maintained slavery.

War is not the only place where the subjectivity of historical fiction is significant, however. In Pam Conrad's *Prairie Songs*, (1985), a young girl's love for the vastness of the prairie is contrasted with the loneliness and fear of a city bride newly come to a tiny soddy. The harsh realities of infant mortality, brutal weather, and isolation are juxtaposed against the beauty of an endless sky, the joys of trips to town and summer picnics, of family humor and warmth. In the same way, *Goodnight Mr. Tom* (Magorian, 1981) contrasts the horrors of an abusive parent and the ravages of war with the warmth and love of a foster home and the peace of a small English village. Both stories build on the complexity of human need and motivation, and on the diverse ways in which people respond to time, place, and circumstance. As a result, the subjectivity of well-written historical fiction can lead to a richer, fuller, and more empathetic understanding of history. Through historical fiction, children learn that people in all times have faced change and crisis, that people in all times have basic needs in common, and that these needs remain in our time. Children can discover some of the myriad ways in which humans depend on each other, and of the consequences of success and failure in relationships, both personal and historical.

Interpreting Human Experience

Historical fiction also provides a safe context for the exploration of the human experience that seems to be an important concern of older elementary-age children. In a study of sixth graders involved in a literature-based introduction to history, Levstik (1986) found that students reported being moved, inspired, and sometimes angered by what they read, and frequently added that they had learned something they labeled "the truth" about history. The frequency with which these children described their "need to know" about various topics in history was remarkable. Reading and discussing historical fiction appeared to help them explore the "unwished-for worst" (Hardy, 1978) as well as the "heroic best" possibilities for human behavior, and to test themselves and their own potential for good or evil. A clear example of this behavior can be seen in children's comments on *Gentlehands* (Kerr, 1978), *When Hitler Stole Pink Rabbit* (Kerr, 1972), and other Holocaust literature:

"I would have run away! Why didn't they run away?"

"I would have been terrified!"

"I've been fascinated by Hitler. . . . He got so powerful. And why did he kill those people? He was prejudiced . . . . He had a messed up mind. He was very confused." (Levstik, 1986)

These readers were not looking for historical information in the traditional sense. Rather, they sought emotional truth and the possibilities that other human experience might hold for their lives. They willingly read challenging books and actively participated in discussions. They constantly compared literary characters to themselves and to choices they might have made under similar circumstances. They empathized with characters in books, whether those characters were near or distant in time and space. Emotional distance and the need to understand human behavior determined whether a book was read or a historical era stirred interest. As one child explained: "I loved this book because it sees through the eyes of this person. I never knew how hard people had it. This book is so real. I find this period especially interesting for some reason that I don't know about" (Levstik, 1986). This grounding in story, with its emphasis on individual, human response to historical events has also been described as the beginning of historical understanding and the precursor to critical analysis of history (Egan, 1979; Britton, 1978).

Entering the Past

The structure of historical fiction has much to do with its impact on the reader, with the specific ways in which fiction helps the reader to understand history, and with the reluctance of some readers to enter the past at all. One of the difficulties of historical fiction is absorbing the reader into the historical era rapidly enough to maintain interest in the story. The reader must share the intimacies of the period — to be close enough to the characters "to feel their body-warmth, and to see the expression in their eyes" (Hunter, 1976) — for historical fiction to have full impact. This is not an easy task, for characters who are part of the past rarely comment on the common-places of their lives any more than a present-day character might think to provide extensive explanations of indoor plumbing or automobiles. Long introductory paragraphs can be cumbersome and delay entry into the story. Too many "tell-tale gaps" (Chambers, 1987) — places where the author depends on the reader's background knowledge — may decrease comprehension for less mature readers.

One technique used by some authors is a fantasy frame. The story begins and ends in the present, but the heart of the story takes a modern character into the past. This character serves as a reader's companion, noting those things a native to the time and place might miss and asking questions the reader might want to ask. Thus Kate, the modern character in *Halfway Down Paddy Lane* (Marzollo, 1981), comments on chamber pots, undergarments, the smell of boiled cabbage eaten amidst flies, and the treatment of millworkers during the early stages of the Industrial Revolution. Hurmence (1982) uses a similar technique in *A Girl Called Boy* when a modern girl walks into the antebellum South to be mistaken for a runaway slave. Survival depends on her ability to fit into the plantation system and forces her to note the details of everyday life.

A fantasy frame also makes explicit the connections between past and present. Characters are generally brought into the past by problems in the present. Rose, in *The Root Cellar* (Lunn, 1981), is orphaned and miserable, unable to adjust to her new family or rural life. Escape into the past puts her own problems into perspective and, finally, helps her to live in the present. Similarly, Abigail in *Playing Beatie Bow* (Park, 1982) comes to terms with her parents' divorce and imminent remarriage after living in the past and seeing the complexity of human relationships and of her own behavior. Modern problems that appeared overwhelming become manageable compared to crises that tested one's courage and ability to survive in times past. This sense of historical perspective — of asking what an action or choice will mean in the long run — is explicit in fantasy-framed fiction. Telltale gaps are few, and the story is generally more accessible to reluctant historical fiction readers.

The links between past and present are implicit in all good historical fiction. They are recognized in children's expressed ''need to know'' and in their willingness to wonder ''what would I have done?'' Speare's *The Sign of the Beaver* (1984) does not need a modern character to absorb the reader in a tale of survival and cross-cultural friendship. Instead, Speare begins with Matt, left alone in the Maine wilderness while his father returns to Massachusetts to gather the rest of the family. A series of mishaps lead to a relationship with Attean, a Native American whose friendship causes Matt to reexamine his most basic assumptions about his place in the world. Each chapter draws the reader on so that when Matt must decide whether to face winter alone and hope his parents might still return, or go with

Attean and his people away from the encroaching white settlement, the choice is truly agonizing and its outcome uncertain. Good historical fiction places the reader at those turning points where choices are not easy. Such choices occur throughout time and eventually test each of us on some level. Part of our response is based on our repertoire of possible human experiences, personal and historical. Literature extends that repertoire and lets us see ourselves as history makers and participants in the on-going life of the world.

The structure of historical fiction also links history to notions of causations and motivation. A narrative flows on a stream of cause and effect. In one sense, then, historical fiction forces history to conform to narrative norms — for causation to operate and for there to be a beginning point and a place where matters are resolved. Sometimes chance is part of the cause, as when Sam in *My Brother Sam Is Dead* (Collier & Collier, 1974) is arrested for a crime he did not commit and executed as an example to the unruly rebel troops. In other instances, religious bigotry motivates action, as when Nana Sashie's family in *Night Journey* (Lasky, 1982) fled anti-Jewish pogroms in Russia. Political uncertainty allows fanatacism and hatred to go unchecked in many historical novels, including O'Dells' *Sarah Bishop* (1980), Hilgartner's *A Murder for Her Majesty* (1986), and Sutcliff's *Bonnie Dundee* (1984). Injustice figures in such novels as Sebestyen's story of homelessness and labor unrest, *On Fire* (1985), Lord's *A Spirit to Ride the Whirlwind,* set in the Lowell textile mills, and Uchida's novels chronicling the tragedy of Japanese internment during World War II, *Journey to Topaz* (1985) and *Journey Home* (1985). In each case, the flow of narrative links action with reaction in a powerful emotional context, so that the reader feels, as well as knows, history. Readers can begin to understand the legacy of slavery in *A Girl Called Boy* and *Nettie's Trip South* (Turner, 1987), the mob psychosis that led to accusations of witchcraft in *The Witch of Blackbird Pond* (1958), or the struggle to build a life in a new country in *The Long Way to a New Land* (Sandin, 1981) or *In The Year of the Boar and Jackie Robinson,* (Lord, 1984).

Historical fiction also involves motivation. Why did characters behave in a particular way? What motivated their choices? When Meribah Simons, in *Beyond the Divide* (Lasky, 1983), is abandoned in rugged mountains with her wagon disabled, readers know the character of each member of the deserting party — know their weaknesses and fears and the events that have stripped them of the

Figure 13-1.
Good historical fiction lets readers *feel* history.

veneer of civilization. They also know Meribah's strength and the will to survive that has led her to this place. There is more in this scene of abandonment about what happened to people who journeyed west than could ever be found in a textbook. It is a study in human psychology and motivation and tells fundamental truths about the human condition. It is what children need to know about the past and about themselves.

Interpreting the Past

Henry Ford said history was bunk. An anonymous wit described it as "lies agreed upon." Children in a study by Levstik and Pappas (1987) defined history as "things everybody knows of in the past" (sixth grader), "real good stuff, like brutality of war" (fourth grader), and "what people did famous" (second grader). History is all this and more. It is more than the accumulation of discrete facts about the past and more than a chronological ordering of those facts. History is a process of selecting, organizing, and interpreting facts. Without interpretation there is little point in knowing about the past. Knowing the date for the Battle of Hastings, for instance, is irrelevant if there is no interpretive framework for that fact. Even school history, that creature of facts and chronology, is interpretation and, sometimes, lies. Every time children learn that Columbus "discovered" America, they learn an interpretation of history. How might Columbus' voyage to the Americas be interpreted by a Native American historian, for instance? Or how might Roger Williams or the Salem "witches" interpret the history of religious freedom in New England? One fifth grader, comparing her textbook with the historical fiction she had read, declared that she would never have lived in Massachusetts during the colonial era: "They didn't have religious freedom! They were stupid and killed people for their beliefs. I'd go maybe to Pennsylvania. It was more free there, I think."

This child is involved in making history. She is using facts and feelings to order the past in some meaningful way. She challenged her textbook descriptions of history on the basis of her reading in historical fiction. She disagreed with the textbook description of the Puritans' search for religious "freedom," and was appalled by the Puritans' discrimination against Quakers and by their willingness to believe in witches and to execute people on the basis of those beliefs, as described in Speare's *The Witch of Blackbird Pond* (1958). Literature fed her need to understand the past.

Whether one agrees or disagrees with her judgment, the fifth grader recognized the interpretive nature of history. She read extensively in historical fiction and had plenty of opportunity to discuss her readings with interested adults. It was literature, however, that first invited her to consider the consequences of historical facts. This is a major strength of historical fiction, that it can lead readers to consider the past from multiple perspectives and to recognize that history remains open to interpretation. Real historical understanding can grow from such roots, especially when nurtured at home or at school.

The power of a literary historical interpretation, however, places a burden on the novelist. Authors of historical fiction have a dual responsibility for literary quality and historical accuracy. Their audience is not as likely to challenge the accuracy of facts embedded in fiction (Levstik, 1986). E.L. Doctorow may be able to rearrange history for particular effect in his adult novels, but in historical fiction for children, events should not be moved around for the convenience of a story line. Nor should facts be altered, as Peck does in *A Day No Pigs Would Die* (1972), in which Shakers marry and live most un-Shakerly lives. Instead, accuracy of detail and legitimacy of interpretation are paramount. Novels such as Irene Hunt's classic *Across Five Aprils* (1964) succeed so admirably because they maintain historical accuracy, provide plausible, in-depth interpretation, and tell a fascinating story. Such books can be a springboard for discussion and further inquiry into complex historical issues. Each is also fine literature, well-written and challenging to the imagination. This is as it should be, for first and foremost, historical fiction is literature and should be judged on its literary merit. Fine reporting of history does not compensate for a weak story. On the other hand, a good story should not be an excuse for shoddy reporting of history.

When both story and history are linked by a well-crafted narrative, historical fiction can draw us all into the fabric of time, to discover that ordinary and extraordinary individuals built our world on a foundation of conscious and unconscious choices. We must also make choices for we, too, are part of the pattern of history.

Summary

Historical fiction creates a powerful sense of history in which students explore the joy, conflicts and sufferings of those who lived before us; it is the secret garden of the past. Textbooks may skim over individuals and events but historical fiction thrives on subjectivity, develops a story and places people and events in context. Historical fiction provides a safe arena in which students can explore the areas of human experience that interest them.

The narrative structure of historical fiction links history to notions of causation and motivation. Events of history are shaped into the norms of stories with the causes of events made explicit and the motivations of people made clear. Authors of historical fiction have a dual responsibility for producing books of literary quality as well as providing historical accuracy. Such books give students the gift of time so that time past melds with time present and helps them shape their future.

References

Chambers, A. (1985). *Booktalk: Occasional writing on literature and children.* New York: Harper & Row.

Egan, K. (1983). Accumulating history. *History and theory: Studies in the philosophy of history.* Wesleyan University Press, 66–80.

Fritz, J. (1980). Speech given at Bluffton College, Bluffton, Ohio.

Huck, C.S. (1977). *Children's literature in the elementary school.* (3rd ed.) New York: Holt, Rinehart and Winston.

Hunter, M. (1976). *Talent is not enough.* New York: Harper & Row.

Levstik, L. (1986). The relationship between historical response and narrative in a sixth-grade class. *Theory and Research in Social Education, 14,* (1), 1–15.

Levstik, L. (1981). A child's approach to history. *The Social Studies, 74,* 232–236.

Levstik, L., & Pappas, C. (1987). Exploring the development of historical understanding. *Journal of Research and Development in Education, 21,* (1), 1–15.

Meek, M., Warlow, A., & Barton, G. (Eds.). (1978). *The cool web: The pattern of children's reading.* New York: Atheneum.

Taxel, J. (1978). The American revolution in children's books: Issues of racism and classism, *Bulletin of the Council on Interracial Books for Children, 12,* 7–8.

Trease, G. (1977). The historical story: Is it relevant to today? *The Horn Book Magazine, 53,* 21–28.

White, H. (1980). The value of narrativity in the representation of reality. *Critical Inquiry, 7,* (1), 5–27.

14

Teachers Using

Historical Fiction

Lillian Webb

Children who read historical fiction with the help and encouragement of a knowledgeable teacher have opportunities for rich experiences with fine literature as well as for focused investigations of particular time periods. Historical fiction contains an abundance of stories in which the main characters exhibit strength in times of adversity; often characters mature during the course of a story.

Reading about such character development provides subtle role models for our students. For example, Tim Meeker in James Lincoln and Christopher Collier's *My Brother Sam Is Dead* is an admiring younger brother at the outset of the Revolutionary War. By the time his father is captured by the British and his brother Sam is arrested by his own troops, Tim is running the family's tavern, taking care of his mother, and formulating a plan for rescuing his brother from the stockade.

Students can identify with main characters of high-interest historical stories as they see the characters take charge of situations in which they find themselves. In another story, *The Sign of the Beaver* by Elizabeth George Speare, Matt is left in charge of his family's newly constructed cabin in Maine just before the Revolutionary War while his father returns to Massachusetts to fetch Matt's mother and the new baby. While he is alone during that long winter, Matt learns survival techniques from local Indians and struggles to build a relationship of friendship and trust with Attean, the Indian chief's grandson.

During class discussions about the behaviors shown by characters in these stories, students exercise their own judgment and decision-making skills. With guidance from the teacher, students hypothesize about how they would have dealt with the problems faced by story characters. Third graders who read *Bread and Butter Indian*, by Ann Colver, often discuss Barbara's decision not to share the existence of "her" Indian with her family. Why did she choose this course of action? What would you have done if you were in her place?

Reading and discussing stories of historical fiction allow students to see that problems faced by story characters are not unlike situations in which they might find themselves. In the story told by Tim Meeker, the plot of *My Brother Sam Is Dead* turns upon the basic disagreement between Tim's brother Sam and his father, Life Meeker. The father feels that a few pennies of tax are not worth a life; whereas, his brother Sam believes he is right in fighting for America's freedom against the tyranny of Great Britain. Like many sons as they approach manhood, Tim and Sam feel the need to distance themselves from their father's control. This is not a problem isolated within an historical period but a human problem that can be discussed in today's terms.

Using historical fiction in the classroom provides unique opportunities for students and teachers to incorporate the humanities into the curriculum. By using many nonfiction as well as fiction books, teachers and librarians help students build an understanding of the time period in which a novel is set. Students are encouraged to find out about the everyday lives of the people; how they lived, what they ate, what they did for recreation, songs they sang, who the writers were who influenced their thought and behavior, and what the major current events of the period were. In investigating these questions with my own students, I fill the classroom with historical fiction and nonfiction books as well as art, music, maps, and films. In this way, I help my students develop a richer understanding of the historical period explored in the story.

Exploring Historical Fiction in the Classroom

Group discussions offer learners a forum for testing their ideas about plot and characters in a story. Since expressing an opinion helps a person know what he or she thinks about an issue, I encourage children to respond to each other's views in an interchange of opinions.

Character and Setting

During the reading of *The Witch of Blackbird Pond*, by Elizabeth George Speare, I ask students to respond to the question: why did Kit Tyler encourage Prudence to meet her regularly at Hannah Tupper's cottage to learn to read? Some students, concerned about disobeying parents, say that Kit should have known better than to help Prudence; others argue that Kit did the right thing because both Kit and Prudence needed friends. My students express concern about the child's right to an education and have trouble understanding the limited opportunities open to females in that historic period for learning to read and write. They argue that Prudence was an additional companion for Hannah, a character with whom they empathized. Group discussions encourage children to interact with ideas presented in the story, to formulate opinions, to share them aloud, and to hear how others react to the same situation. This gives them the chance to reflect and solidify or modify their own position.

Discussions can take many forms although I often focus on the literary elements of setting, characterization, and plot when creating questions. I also provide numerous maps so that students can extend their knowledge of the setting beyond the author's description. The students locate the site of the story using the map and a globe, relating the setting to our current location. If the story takes place in the United States we look at a world map, a map of North America, one of the U.S.A., and perhaps one of the state or city in which most of the action occurs.

In studying *The Witch of Blackbird Pond*, we found an issue of *Cobblestone* magazine devoted to the history of Connecticut. It contains a simplified map of the state and pinpoints Wethersfield and Old Saybrook so children can trace the Dolphin's slow progress up the river from Long Island Sound. A world map or globe helps them to locate Kit's native land, Barbados, to see how far it is from Connecticut. This helps them understand that Kit's move from the open and relaxed tropical island to the harsh and restrictive home of her Uncle Matthew was extremely difficult. Books such as Edwin Tunis' *Colonial Living* contain drawings of colonial houses, both inside and outside elevations, which allow students to visualize the "great room" of the Woods' home. As they see how small these dwellings were, they begin to understand why the addition of one more person to the household was a hardship.

Historical fiction provides the opportunity to connect with many strong characters, although elementary age children sometimes need help in understanding their personalities, motivation, and behavior. Clarification often occurs during group discussions as readers discover the true nature of a character by looking at what others think or say about him or her. How would Judith and Mercy Woods, from *The Witch of Blackbird Pond,* have characterized Kit Tyler? How did Matthew and Rachel see her? What were Nate's feelings about her? How did she affect William? Why was Goodwife Cruff so upset with her? What were Prudence's perceptions of Kit? What did Kit think of herself and her behavior? How did Kit's values differ from those of people in Wethersfield at that time? When discussion reaches this point, students begin to investigate other resources to help them understand the time period more fully.

Audio-visual resources can be used to provide students with an overview of a particular era or to help them understand specific events. For example, a video tape, *The Witches of Salem,* sheds some light on the belief system of New England settlers during the late seventeenth century. The early settlers were particularly susceptible to the idea that "bad persons" in their midst had to be rooted out in case their aberrant behaviors were the cause of the hardships and grief that members of the colony suffered.

The tape is a reenactment of scenes that might have occurred in Salem, Massachusetts, in 1692. The young ladies of Salem acted as though they had been bewitched by members of their own community. Viewing and discussing the tape helps middle graders understand the hysteria prevalent during that period. As a result, they can better deal with the treatment Hannah Tupper and Kit herself received from the members of their community. This video tape is also used effectively with *Witches' Children* and *Mercy Short.*

Theme

Reading a number of historical fiction novels that explore a similar theme is another way of helping children grow in their understanding of human behavior. The theme, man's inhumanity to man, is starkly addressed in many novels set before, during, and just after World War II. These stories present some of the atrocities of the Holocaust within the framework of fiction, thus softening the harshness of the reality of history. *Friedrich* and *I Was There*, both by Hans Peter Richter, are an effective pair of titles because of their differing points of view. In the former, the reader sees through the eyes of his friend the vicissitudes of the life of Friedrich, a young Jewish boy, growing up in Germany from 1925 to 1942. *I Was There* allows the reader to experience Hans Richter's own preadolescent and teen years as a member of the Hitler Youth.

Other novels set in the same period extend understanding of theme. Barbara Gehrts' *Don't Say a Word* shows children that not all Germans were Nazis and that all individuals suffer during war, no matter what their beliefs. In Roberto Innocenti's *Rose Blanche* this point is made dramatically through a simply told story and exquisite paintings. The naive child, Rose Blanche, in an attempt to assuage the hunger of children in a concentration camp near her home, saves food from her lunch and secretly delivers it to them daily. Rose, the penultimate innocent victim, loses her life in a fog-shrouded battle between retreating German soldiers and the attacking Russians.

Yoshiko Uchida, in *Journey to Topaz,* and Jeanne Wakatsuki Houston, in *Farewell to Manzanar,* have shown readers that Americans, too, treated innocent persons in an inhumane fashion during World War II. Both stories tell of Japanese-American families stripped of their civil rights and made to suffer psychological and financial hardship during their years of internment. Students who read books with a similar theme can construct comparison charts (described in other chapters) to display graphically similarities and differences between the experiences of important characters.

Dramatic activities are another way to involve students in a deeper interaction with a novel. As students plan how they will role-play a scene, they must go back to the book to check what really happened. They decide how they will interpret their character's feelings during the action and discuss what might have been said at a specific point in the plot. Sam Meeker's court martial is an example of an event in the story that is not reported firsthand; it is an event that requires suppositions about behavior and feelings of characters based on the outcome of the event.

During discussions of historical fiction, students often ask, "Which parts are true?" When the plot of a story turns on a specific event, such as a war, part of the question can be answered easily by reading factual accounts. An author's note also helps to distinguish fact from fiction. If further clarification is necessary, it is possible to place a conference telephone call to the author, allowing the children to ask their questions directly. To arrange this experience, it is necessary to write to the author to set a definite time for the call. Students feel more comfortable in speaking if they have prepared their questions in advance, perhaps reading them from a large piece of chart paper. Followup thank-you letters to authors for their time also enrich students' reading and writing experience.

When students read historical fiction in a school setting, parents have the opportunity to participate in the learning experience. Themes discussed in school often become topics of dinnertime conversation. Parents and grandparents can tell of their own experiences in living through what is now history for today's children. As students read World War II novels, I urge them to ask older relatives how the war affected them. Sharing anecdotes and souvenirs with classmates is an enriching experience for all. Friends, relatives, and community members may be a source of speakers for classes that have been engaged in a study of World War II novels.

Parents can also provide assistance in locating items that could be included in a student's Jackdaw, a collection of realia suggestive of an historical period. Parents may also plan family vacations to settings of historical novels their children have read in school. Readers of Peter Spier's *Tin Lizzie* who visit the Henry Ford Museum and Greenfield Village in Dearborn, Michigan, will see many models of early cars on display. Walking Boston's historic Freedom Trail helps students move back in time to the days when Paul Revere and Sam Adams were active in the Sons of Liberty.

Extending Understanding of Historical Fiction through Response Activities

Students' responses to the stories they have read may take many forms. In planning response activities, my primary goal is for the readers to interact with the story once again and to gain a deeper appreciation of it. I encourage response activities that cause them to seek out sources that provide additional information to round out their understanding of the period in which the book is set.

As students read a book, it helps for them to create a time-line of the story events and, using nonfiction, add the actual historical events occurring in the same period. The search to locate clues to build the time-line excites the detective nature in children. During Chapter 1 of *My Brother Sam Is Dead,* Sam mentions that there was a skirmish between the British and the Patriots up around Lexington, an oblique reference to the battles of Lexington and Concord. Reading aloud Henry Wadsworth Longfellow's poem "The Midnight Ride of Paul Revere" with its vivid description of the events of April 18, 1775, anchors the start of the Colliers' story.

Creating a time-line of real events, paralleling the story's actions, often leads to the discovery of historically important speeches, books, or documents such as The Declaration of Independence or Thomas Paine's *Common Sense.* Paine's treatise helps us to understand why young men like Sam joined the Revolutionary Army when that action was diametrically opposed to his parents' beliefs. Students reading World War II novels understand the period better if they can listen to President Roosevelt's declaration of war on Japan or one of Winston Churchill's wartime speeches.

Students enjoy learning when activities involve their tactile/ kinesthetic senses in two- or three-dimensional art projects. My students draw maps of the community in which the Meekers lived as well as maps that show the towns through which Tim and his father passed on their way to Verplank's Point. Most of these communities still exist and can be located on modern maps.

In a search through Edwin Tunis' *The Tavern at the Ferry,* students decide what the Meeker Tavern might have looked like, both inside and out. This information is translated into a model of the building or a mural showing Redding, Connecticut, as it might have looked during the Revolutionary War.

We examine Shirley Glubok's *The Art of Colonial America* to see how wealthy children of that period were regarded as miniature adults. Their elaborate clothing, contrasted with the simple garments of the ordinary colonial children and adults, is shown in Edwin Tunis' *Colonial Living.* My students create paper doll figures and dress them in clothing appropriate to a character's station in life.

The simplicity of pioneer life is brought into focus when students read Anne Colver's *Bread and Butter Journey*. Barbara chooses carefully the treasures she will pack when her family migrates to western Pennsylvania: her doll Ariminta, her silver candlestick, six ivory buttons from her Mama's wedding cloak, her school reader, a pebble from the brook, a curl of birchbark, Shadow's feather, and an acorn. I often suggest that she might also have taken an ox-yoke puzzle, which each child assembles from precut wood, string, and two large wooden beads I provide. As children use trial and error to solve the puzzle, it becomes clear to them that pioneer children could have enjoyed such a simple toy.

Cooking always generates enthusiastic responses to historical fiction when students research recipes and prepare food eaten by book characters. What clearer way for students to internalize the meager food available to crew and slaves in Paula Fox's *The Slave Dancer* but for them to eat hard tack. On the other hand, preparing a jolly, colonial-style, covered dish meal is a meaningful culminating event when reading books set in that period.

My students also like to create newspapers that might have been written during the time in which a story is set. To produce the papers, I give students 12×18 inch sheets of drawing paper, which they divide into three 4×16 inch columns, with a two-inch space at the top for the masthead. They write their articles on four-inch strips of lined notebook paper, which they then mount to the drawing paper with rubber cement. They may write news articles, human-interest pieces about book characters and events, or report actual events of the time. They fill small spaces with advertisements or vital statistics — announcements of births, deaths, or marriages. Students also include political cartoons or an advice column.

Middle grade students appreciate opportunities to take charge of their own learning and to make choices in fulfilling assignments. I offer students a list of response activities from which they choose a number to create, locate, or reproduce. They often create a literary Jackdaw in response to reading an historical novel; it serves to deepen their understanding of a chosen book and its time period.

Students collect or create facsimile items of the period and include them in a box appropriately decorated. One fifth-grade girl who had read *The Witch of Blackbird Pond* placed her Jackdaw items in a small cardboard carton decorated to look like one of Kit Tyler's small trunks. When she shared her work, she showed the class a pair of Kit's gloves, a hand-dipped candle, a facsimile of a hornbook made from cardboard and waxed paper, a drawing of the Woods' home in Wethersfield, Connecticut, an enlarged drawing of a postage stamp that might have been issued in the late 1600's, a hand-drawn map of Wethersfield that included the field where Matthew grew his onions and the area around the pond, Hannah's house, and the house William was building. The student also shared her colonial newspaper, which discussed the mysterious disappearance of the Connecticut Charter and the implications that the event might have on Great Britain's control of the colony. To the delight of the class, she also served them a blueberry cake similar to Hannah Tupper's.

Objects that do not fit into the Jackdaw box may accompany it. One boy brought a two-dimensional model of a Brown Bess rifle (all five feet of it), made of cardboard and colored paper. Two girls who worked on a Jackdaw together taught their classmates a folk dance as their contribution to the group's understanding of our country's early days.

Children gain a deep appreciation of historical fiction when they actively interact with a writer's ideas and when they investigate the fabric of society during the period in which a novel is set. As they synthesize their new knowledge and create products to share with classmates, their own experience becomes even richer. Students and their parents affirm the positive nature of these educational investigations, which help the children grow in understanding by using the strengths of their individual learning styles.

Summary

Using historical fiction in the classroom stimulates indepth investigation of historical time periods; it provides role models for students, and gives them opportunities to exercise judgment and decision making. Response activities involve discussions of the literary qualities as well as the historical settings, people, and events. Exploring themes through historical fiction helps students see how a similar theme can be realized in several different ways. Drama, art, and music are natural extensions of historical fiction which can lead to a full humanities curriculum.

References

Connecticut State Map from Ebenezer's Atlas. (1981, January). *Cobblestone: The History Magazine for Young People*, 2(1); 24–25.

Paine, Thomas. (1953). The American Crisis: I. *Common sense and other political writings.* New York: Macmillan. (*Common sense*, originally published in 1776.)

The Witches of Salem: The Horror and the Hope. (Videotape). From the series "The Shaping of the American Nation". Learning Corporation of America. Coronet MPI, 1972. Deerfield, IL.

15

Living Close

to History

Mollie Hunter

"You Scots live so close to your history!"

This remark, a somewhat astonished one, came from a visiting American friend who had met two storytellers in the course of one morning in my home area. Both were ordinary working men, casually encountered, and just as casually retelling incidents that had happened a millenium before their own time. As I pointed out to my friend then, however, there was nothing really remarkable about that.

Scotland, after all, is a very small country, and even today its population is only five million. Its long history is a highly colourful one, and the Celtic influence on our culture inclines us naturally towards storytelling, so much so, that implications of story occur even in conversational terms.

To say admiringly of someone, for instance, that he "has the heart of Bruce" is to hark back directly to the fourteenth century story of King Robert the Bruce and the persistent bravery that made him a legend even in his own lifetime. For centuries past, too, we have had a strong tradition of literacy, something that has combined easily with story to make communication flow as easily from one generation to another as it does among those of the same generation.

The ballad — the story in song — has also always been part of our culture. *Oh, cold is the snow that sweeps Glencoe/and covers the grave of Donald*. . . To hear the plaintive notes of that particular ballad is always, for me, a most moving experience that recaptures completely the feeling I had when I wrote *The Ghosts of Glencoe,* the book that centres around that bloody seventeenth century event, the Massacre of Glencoe. Taking all this together, I find small wonder in the fact that writing in Scotland has so often been in the form of the historical novel.

All these advantages of heritage have to be balanced, of course, against the fact that the history of Scotland is largely unknown outside its own borders. The technical skill that achieves the point of entry into a story must, therefore, include in it the ability to do so in combination with some easily recognisable reference to its time and setting, especially so when one is writing for a youth audience. Long before that problem arises, one has to face the three questions that, as I see it, must be asked by any historical novelist.

What happened? *Why? How?*

One turns to research, of course, for the answer to "what," but research for a novel still needs more than a scholarly knowledge of any given period. To recreate actual figures from history, one must have the ability also to ferret out the kind of detail that instantly sharpens focus on them; and such ability must be furthered by the imagination to deploy one's findings in ways that will portray these figures as the three-dimensional people they were in real life rather than the photographic representation that is all that emerges from any coldly recorded account of their actions.

The locale of a story is something that should also be intimately known, not only for the bearing that its terrain may have on the events one has in mind. To have a sense of the place is also all-important for how else can one convey the actuality of the feelings created by having to flee for one's life through mountain country, as Connal Ross did in *A Pistol in Greenyards?* Or those evoked by a dangerous foray through the canyons formed by the tall, crooked buildings lining the narrow streets of eighteenth century Edinburgh, as happened with Sandy Maxwell in *The Lothian Run?*

Why? Motivation is what this question seeks to uncover — the thoughts behind the deeds of historical figures; and it is only by means of a combination of applied insight and imagination that one can even begin to do so. Further to this, of course, one has to recognise the type of society in which one lives as being always a determinant factor in one's behaviour. Thus, for both real and imagined characters in a historical novel, a detailed knowledge of the social patterns of their day is similarly important to establishing motivation for their actions.

What if one's sources of research are limited, as mine were in *The Stronghold*, to a situation that offers no known historical figures and a past so remote that only informed guesswork can assess the effect of its social structure? It is here, as I found, that intimate knowledge of locale can really come into its own — my intimacy, in that case, being with the group of islands called the Orkneys.

Isolated off the north coast of Scotland, windswept and treeless, these islands have a timeless atmosphere in which the present merges easily with the past; in which one can just as easily drift through the barrier between the natural and the supernatural. It can send cold shivers up one's back, that atmosphere, or, as we would say here, it can "gar ye grue." Yet still I spent much time on Orkney accepting that feeling, allowing it to pull me back, back, through the centuries since my characters had lived until, wholly absorbed at last into that timeless atmosphere, I had what I felt was my first clear insight into their thoughts, their emotions. It was only then that I was able to start writing that book.

How? To answer that question is also to determine the structure of the book because this is where the craft of the storyteller must merge with that of the writer to produce a story line clear and strong enough to impact vividly on the reader's imagination. For example, to take the basic facts behind my novel *You Never Knew Her As I Did,* the beautiful and young Mary, Queen of Scots, has been imprisoned by rebellious nobles, with Sir William Sinclair of Lochleven Castle as her jailer. Sir William's younger brother, George, falls in love with her, tries to effect her escape, but fails in the attempt and is banished from the castle. Another escape plan, previously proposed by Sir William's page, the sixteen-year-old Will Douglas, is then tried. That, too, fails, and Will is also banished from the castle. Will, however, succeeds in regaining his position there, and it is then by the most daring of stratagems that he does finally effect the Queen's escape.

A true tale, a very simple one known to every Scottish schoolchild, but to develop from it the structure of a novel, I had first to learn from "what" that young Will Douglas was a bastard bred by Sir William on an unknown mother, which meant, probably, that his position in the castle household was a somewhat uneasy one. Whether or not this was so, it was still clear that he was a bright, inventive boy. It was equally clear, however, that he was also boastful, careless, and self-centred, in spite of all which his banishment from the castle did not lead to his taking off on his own concerns.

Instead, he loitered miserably in its vicinity until he had the chance to free the Queen by a method that, had it failed, would have meant his certain death. Furthermore, he stayed in her service until her own death almost twenty years later, all that time, too, at continuing risk to his life.

Why? What had stripped from that boy all those characteristics that were perhaps only the mask for his own insecurity? What had so changed him? Had he, too, been smitten by the charm that was legendary to Mary Stuart? Or was it even more than that? Could it have been that he, at the vulnerable age of sixteen, had fallen so hopelessly in love with her that he had not only dared death for her sake but had given her his whole life as well?

I decided that he had, that there was no other explanation for that change. That was how I structured the book — as the story of a scrapegrace boy surprised into love for a young queen who, in his eyes, was much more sinned against than sinning; in effect, an escape story that was also a love story. So also, I hope, I made it what I have always thought a historical novel should be — a book that can stand in its own right as a book because it links past to present in a story of real people with real emotions that touch some chord universal in human nature.

It can and often does take "the heart of Bruce," mind you, to achieve that goal. But tell me now, am I not the fortunate one to have my roots in a culture that gives so much inspiration towards it?

16

Knowing Poetry:

Choosing Poetry

for Children

Rebecca L. Thomas

Clapping, moving, laughing, joining in are some of children's responses when they hear poetry read aloud. Reflecting, caring, appreciating, enjoying are also responses from children when they hear poetry read aloud. Good poetry captures the essence of experiences and emotions; it allows children to nod in recognition of a shared moment, to think about possibilities, and to celebrate feelings. It also invites adults who work with children to share in the complete range of feelings and experiences by using the many fine volumes of poetry that are available.

Sharing poetry with children involves them in language as they absorb its sounds and patterns. They develop an appreciation for the poet's careful use of words and images and become more creative in their own use of language.

Poetry for children gained critical attention in the 1980s with many volumes receiving awards and recognition. In 1982, for the first time ever, a book of poetry was awarded the John Newbery Medal from the American Library Association. *A Visit to William Blake's Inn* (Willard, 1981) was selected by the Newbery Committee as "the most distinguished contribution to American literature for children." The 1987 Notable Children's Books, chosen by a committee from the Association of Library Services for Children, included five collections of poetry and verse while the "Children's Choices, 1987" list from the International Reading Association, selected by children, included four poetry titles. With all of the acclaimed poetry for children, teachers and librarians have a wealth of resources to choose from to bring children and poetry together.

Poetry Preferences

Knowing the kinds of poetry that children enjoy helps teachers and librarians develop their own poetry resources to share. Poetry preference studies conducted throughout this century (e.g., MacKintosh, 1924; Bradshaw, 1937; Kyte, 1946; Avengo, 1956; Terry, 1974; Fisher and Natarella, 1982) produced amazingly consistent results. Terry's (1974) research focused on the poetry preferences of students in grades four through six while Fisher and Natarella (1982) used the same schools to examine the preferences of primary grade children. Both studies were based on a national sample.

Terry (1974) found that students in grades four through six preferred poetry that rhymed and had a definite rhythm. They preferred limericks most with narrative poems, particularly humorous narratives, running a close second. Students preferred contemporary poems over traditional ones. The types of poetry they preferred least were haiku, free verse, and poems that used imagery and figurative language. By analyzing preferences by grade level, Terry found that fourth graders preferred poetry more than students in grades five and six. Also, girls expressed a higher degree of preference for poetry than boys.

Fisher and Natarella (1982) extended Terry's study to the primary grades, with similar results. The younger students also preferred limericks and humorous poems about animals, childhood experiences, and the fantastic or strange. Similar to the older students primary grade children liked poems with rhyme and rhythm and disliked haiku, lyric poetry, and free verse as well as poems using metaphor, simile, or personification.

An interesting fact about the findings of both studies is the consistency of the preference patterns with those of earlier studies. Two recent regional surveys (Ingham, 1980; Simmons, 1980) updated the poetry selections used and reported similar findings. Students still preferred humorous poetry and poems about familiar experiences. In Ingham's study, the poems of Shel Silverstein and Dennis Lee were among the most preferred poems, and contemporary poems (those published since 1972) were preferred over traditional ones.

These surveys of student preferences provide teachers and librarians with valuable information to use when selecting poetry. A core collection of poetry will include choices that students enjoy hearing and will want to read on their own. Humorous verses, like those from Shel Silverstein, Jack Prelutsky, and Dennis Lee, will attract students to poetry. So, too, will poems about familiar everyday activities, such as going to school, playing with friends, skating, climbing trees, and staying home. Poetry books need to be purchased regularly so that the collection is kept up-to-date; poetry anthologies should include some of the popular poems reported in these surveys. For example, in addition to limericks, the students in grades four through six (Terry 1974) selected the following as their favorites: "Mummy Slept Late and Daddy Fixed Breakfast," by John Ciardi; "Fire! Fire!"; "Little Miss Muffet," by Paul Dehn; and "Hughbert and the Glue," by Karla Kuskin (Terry, 1974, p. 15). The most popular poems of primary grade children were "The Young Lady of Lynn"; "The Little Turtle," by Vachel Lindsay; "Bad Boy," by Lois Lenski; "Little Miss Muffet," by Paul Dehn; and "Cat," by Eleanor Farjeon (Fisher & Natarella, 1982, p. 339).

Sharing popular poetry provides teachers and librarians with a successful beginning for their poetry activities. Enthusiastic reponses from children encourage others to share more poems and to extend their knowledge about poetry.

Moving Beyond the Preferences

Studies of student preferences provide a starting point for selections of poetry to share. One possible reason for the consistency of poetry preferences is that many children do not hear or read much poetry. In fact, Terry (1974) questioned teachers about their use of poetry and reported that it received very little attention in the classrooms surveyed. Poetry was read only occasionally or once a month in approximately three-fourths of the classrooms. Short-term poetry units, often just one or two weeks over the course of a school year, are also common (Craven, 1980; Hecht, 1978). Certainly we cannot influence student preferences unless we give them experiences with poetry more often than once a month or two weeks a year.

Children who share the fun of poetry develop an appreciation for more complex poetry topics and forms. Contemporary poets include many of the features that are popular with children, such as rhyme, rhythm, and sound, but they also include inventive use of language and creative views of the world. More than appealing to a child's sense of humor, they often touch on more sensitive feelings. Excellent poetry challenges children with a variety of poetic styles and presents different ideas, moods, and perspectives.

Excellence in Poetry for Children

Some of the poets whose work exemplifies the best in poetry for children have received the Award for Excellence in Poetry for Children from the National Council of Teachers of English. This award, established in 1977, has been presented to David McCord in 1977, Aileen Fisher in 1978, Karla Kuskin in 1979, Myra Cohn Livingston in 1980, Eve Merriam in 1981, John Ciardi in 1982, Lilian Moore in 1985, and Arnold Adoff in 1988. Looking at some of the titles from these poets provides guidance in selecting books for classroom and library collections.

For more than thirty years, children have been enjoying the poetry of David McCord. *One At A Time* (McCord, 1980), a collection of poems that originally appeared in five previous titles, displays McCord's range in content and style. From the rhyming and very popular "The Pickety Fence" to the challenging examples of poetic forms, such as "The Tercet" and "The Ballade," *One At A Time* provides poetry that appeals to different ages and interests. The natural world is the subject of many of the poems in this collection. McCord writes about insects, flowers, birds, and trees, but he also touches on the feelings of respect and wonder that come from observing this world. Another recent collection of McCord's poems is *All Small* (McCord, 1986). The short poems and small size of this book make it especially appealing for younger children.

Aileen Fisher's poetry celebrates nature and living things. Several titles, designed as picture books, show her poetic narratives interpreted by a variety of artists. *Listen, Rabbit* (Fisher, 1964), *In the Middle of the Night* (Fisher, 1965), and *I Stood Upon a Mountain* (Fisher, 1979) describe the beauty of the natural world. Fisher takes a close look at what many people take for granted. Her poems encourage children to be more observant and to find delight in the world around them. *Out in the Dark and Daylight* (Fisher, 1980) is a collection of 140 poems arranged around the seasons; they present different images of animals, weather, and feelings about nature throughout the year.

The nature poems of David McCord and Aileen Fisher provide an opportunity to look at how poets present different images of the same topics. For example, both poets have written about crickets. In *One At A Time* (1980), McCord has two poems. The first shows the crickets "all busy punching tickets, clicking their little punches" (p. 231). The movement and noise in this poem are contrasted by the subtle mood of his cinquain:

> Do you
> care for crickets?
> I love their summer sound
> Late fall I like one in the house
> Chirping
> (McCord, 1980, p. 480).

Three of Aileen Fisher's poems in *Out in the Dark and Daylight* (1980) provide factual information about crickets. "Cricket Jackets" tells that crickets regularly shed their shells, "Chirping" describes how they rub their wings to make sounds, and "Cricket Song" discusses the way they hear through their legs. Comparing Fisher's poems with McCord's demonstrates how poets look closely at ordinary things but present different images. Looking at other poems about crickets, such as "Cricket" by Mary Ann Hoberman in *Bugs: Poems* (1976) or "Left-Winged Cricket" by Norma Farber in *Never Say Ugh to a Bug* (1979), extends the discussion. Children also want to look at how crickets are presented in nonfiction, such as Seymour Simon's

Discovering What Crickets Do (1973), and in fiction, such as *The Cricket in Times Square* (Selden, 1960), to see different images of crickets.

"Hughbert and the Glue" and "I Woke Up This Morning" are two humorous poems from Karla Kuskin that consistently receive positive responses from children. Children laugh at the image of Hughbert stuck to his mother, his brother, the floor, and the door. They relate to the frustration of the child who wakes up and is confronted by adults instructing, correcting, and admonishing. Both poems appear in *Dogs & Dragons, Trees & Dreams* (1980). This collection not only introduces children to Kuskin's poetry, but it also provides some background information from Kuskin about her writing. Karla Kuskin encourages children to paint with words, to surprise themselves and to be keen observers of life. She writes:

> If there were a recipe for a poem, these would be the ingredients: word sounds, rhythm, description, feeling, memory, rhyme and imagination. They can be put together a thousand different ways, a thousand, thousand . . . more. If you and I were to go at the same time to the same party for the same person, our descriptions would be different. As different as we are from each other. It is those differences that make our poems interesting. (Kuskin, 1980, p. 78)

Near the Window Tree (1975) is also a combination of poetry and philosophy about poetry. Knowing some of the ideas and feelings that a poet uses when writing helps children learn more about the writing process. Kuskin's poem "Where do you get the idea for a poem?" answers this question with more questions. After reading this, children begin to understand that poems come from the world around them and the feeling within them.

Myra Cohn Livingston has published more than twenty volumes of poetry. She has also written two important books about children and poetry: *When You Are Alone/It Keeps You Capone* (1973) and *The Child As Poet: Myth or Reality?* (1984). Two of her recent poetry books demonstrate the wide range of appeal of her poetry. *A Song I Sang to You* (1984) collects poetry that reflects the interests of younger children, while *Worlds I Know and Other Poems* (1985) has images and ideas that reach older children. In *A Song I Sang to You,* there are poems about roller skating, shaping clay, visiting the zoo, and celebrating Halloween. Children climb trees; they fly kites; they are pestered by their little brothers. There is a sense of activity in many of the poems, but there are also poems of reflection — finding a dead bird, looking at trees in November, and dreaming about flying.

Livingston's clear images capture the variety of feelings and moments of childhood. *Worlds I Know* also contains poems for many moods. There are poems of remembrance tinged with sadness — "Aunt Ruth" speaks of a relative whose health is failing and "The Hill" tells of visiting the cemetery and sharing the sense of loss. Other poems recall moments of joy — "Kittens," "May Day" and "Aunt Evelyn." There is a feeling of nostalgia in these poems that brings a response from children old enough to look back on special times and people in their lives. Over the last few years, Myra Cohn Livingston has collaborated with Leonard Everett Fisher on *A Circle of Seasons* (1982), *Sky Songs* (1984), *Celebrations* (1985), *Earth Songs* (1986), and *Sea Songs* (1986). Livingston's poetic images are extended by Fisher's paintings.

Can there be a poem about junk mail, an artichoke, a new pencil? Yes, there can; they appear in the book *Fresh Paint*, by Eve Merriam (1986). This collection of new poems also tells of "Flying for the First Time," "Peeling an Orange," "Fudging the Issue," and "How to Solve a Problem." As Merriam has described in an earlier poem

> It doesn't always have to rhyme,
> but there's the repeat of a beat, somewhere
> an inner chime that makes you want to
> tap your feet. . .(Merriam, 1964, p. 3)

Many of the poems in *Fresh Paint* (1986) have an internal rhyme that is even more apparent when the poems are read aloud. Merriam also includes a new kind of poetry — "A Throw of Threes." Each of these poems consists of three descriptive images; for example:

> Anticipations
>
> a crocus tip in the snow
> the plume of a steam locomotive
> an unopened letter
> (Merriam, 1986)

Teachers who use poems as models for student writing will want to share these with their classes.

Other recent titles from Eve Merriam include *Blackberry Ink* (1985) and two titles in paperback: *Jamboree: Rhymes for All Times* (1984) and *A Sky Full of Poems* (1986). Many of the poems in these books invite participation. Their refrains and repetition encourage children to join in — chanting and clapping along with "Swish, swash, Washing machine" (1985) and "Bam, Bam, Bam" (1984). "A Round" (1986) repeats the word "spaghetti" sixteen times, a great follow up

FRESH PAINT

New Poems by Eve Merriam

Woodcuts by David Frampton

to reading Tomie de Paola's *Strega Nona* (1975). Other poems promote movement, like tumbling and swooping with the "Autumn Leaves" (1984) or imitating a cat along with "Cat's tongue" (1985). Children enjoy looking through these books to find more poems that they can interpret.

John Ciardi, well-known for his commentary about word origin and usage, made regular broadcasts for National Public Radio on the origins of language. *Doodle Soup* (1985) was his last book of poetry for children. Ciardi died in 1986.

The poems in *Doodle Soup* (1985) humorously portray situations when we find the unexpected in the ordinary. In "The Chap Who Disappeared" a forgetful man goes upstairs, which is simple enough. The problem is that he lives in a tent that has only one level. "Doing A Good Deed" tells of helping an ice cream truck that is stuck in the mud, and, of course, the load must be lightened first. "A Lesson in Manners" gives some guidance to children who are contemplating being bad. This is an excellent choice to read with Karla Kuskin's "I Woke Up This Morning" (1980) or "Rules" (Kuskin, 1980). Or, how about a poem where a guest is encouraged to play with these pets — a crocodile, a grizzly bear, a wolf, a tiger, and a shark? No wonder the title of the poem is "I Made Him Welcome But He Didn't Stay."

One of Ciardi's most popular poems, "Mummy Slept Late and Daddy Fixed Breakfast," gives a child's point of view of what it is like to eat Daddy's cooking. This poem is in the book *You Read to Me, I'll Read to You* (1962). In this book, every other poem is printed in black, alternating ones are printed in blue. Children enjoy taking turns reading these poems and meeting characters like "Arvin Marvin Lillisbee Fitch," Jimmy James in "About Jimmy James," and "Chang McTang McQuarter Cat."

Lilian Moore, in an interview in *Language Arts*, said, "When I'm writing a poem, I feel as if I'm working all the time" (Glazer, 1985, p. 649). Her work has resulted in seven poetry collections, including *I Feel the Same Way* (1967), *See My Lovely Poison Ivy* (1975) and *Think of Shadows* (1980). One collection, *Something New Begins* (Moore, 1982), contains fifteen new poems with selections from six previous titles. The new poems develop a common theme of dealing with change. "The Whale Ghost" laments the slow destruction of the natural world. "Hurricane," "December 21," "Stampede," and "Fog Lifting" show the changing weather. Many of the poems in this collection are in free verse. In each, Moore carefully chooses words and images that provide insight into experiences. "Bike Ride" uses action words — "ride," "glide," "roll," and "spin" — to capture the feeling of a bike ride on a sunny day. "New Sounds," places the words in a thin column to demand a staccato reading that imitates the crisp sound of walking on leaves in the fall. This collection helps us examine the variety of styles and subjects a poet can use.

Moore's collection, *See My Lovely Poison Ivy*, is subtitled "And Other Verses About Witches, Ghosts and Things" (1975). Imagine what a witch's child would want for "Bedtime Stories," or how "Little Ugh," the witch's daughter, behaves when she goes Trick or Treating. There is a poem about a city witch on a vacuum cleaner, a thing on the stair, and a teeny tiny ghost. Some poems are filled with humor, such as the witch at the supermarket who cannot find the ingredients for her spell. The surprises in other poems make them perfect for sinister sounding whispered readings on Halloween.

Arnold Adoff selects words and images that he carefully places on the page to intensify their impact. "The Apple" in *Eats: Poems* (1979) illustrates his technique.

The Apple
       is on the top
branch
     of the tree
        touching
the
sky
     or the apple is
         in
     the
     sky
touching
     the top branch
       of the tree

and i am
   me on the ground
   waiting
      for
       a
   good
   wind

The words in this poem are suspended, like the apple in the tree, and then they fall down the page, reinforcing the message of the poem. Adoff describes his writing by saying, ''I must do things in my poems to help you understand the meanings and feel the rhythms. And what I do then is to shape and space and control and polish and give my poems structure. So the three S's — if you're going to remember — about my work are what the poems say, and how they sing, and the structure or shapes, how they're shaped'' (Chapman, 1985, p. 236).

All the Colors of the Race (Adoff, 1982) is a collection of poems that celebrates the cultural diversity of Adoff's family. *Tornado!* (Adoff, 1977) captures the power and destruction of the Xenia, Ohio, tornado of 1974. *The Cabbages Are Chasing the Rabbits* (Adoff, 1985) is a whimsical fantasy where vegetables chase rabbits and dogs chase hunters while birds just sit and wait for food to come to them. In addition to writing his own poetry, Adoff has edited several poetry collections, including *I Am the Darker Brother* (Adoff, 1968), and *My Black Me* (Adoff, 1974).

Summary

As children hear and read great quantities of poetry, they become more discerning about poetic elements, topics, and styles. They feel the many moods of poetry. The poetry from the recipients of the NCTE Award for Excellence in Poetry is funny, touching, somber, loud, active, thoughtful, and sad. It delights and challenges. Reading and discussing outstanding poetry allows children to develop an appreciation for quality writing.

Charlotte Huck writes "Appreciation for poetry develops slowly. It is the result of long and loving experience with poetry over a period of years. Children who are fortunate enough to have developed a love of poetry will always be the richer for it" (Huck, Hepler, & Hickman, 1987, p. 452). Those of us who work with children have both the opportunity and the responsibility for enriching their lives with poetry. As teachers and librarians, we can be guided by the words of Charlotte Huck as we provide children with a "long and loving experience with poetry" (Huck, Hepler, & Hickman, 1987, p. 452).

References

Avegno, S. (1956). Intermediate-grade children's choices in poetry. *Elementary English, 33*, 428–432.

Bradshaw, R. (1937). Children's choices in the first grade. *Elementary English, 14*, 168–76.

Chapman, D.L. (1985). Poet to poet: An author responds to child-writers. *Language Arts, 62*, 235–242.

Craven, M.A. (1980). *A survey of teacher attitudes and practices regarding the teaching of poetry in the elementary school.* Unpublished doctoral dissertation, Lamar University.

Fisher, C., & Natarella, M. (1982). Young children's preferences in poetry: A national survey of first, second and third graders. *Research in the Teaching of English, 16*, 339–355.

Glazer, J.I. (1985). Profile: Lilian Moore. *Language Arts, 62*, 647–652.

Hecht, S. (1978). *The teaching of poetry in grades seven and eight: A survey of teaching practices and materials.* Unpublished doctoral dissertation, Boston University.

Huck, C.S., Hepler, S., & Hickman, J. (1987). *Children's literature in the elementary school.* (4th ed.) New York: Holt Rinehart & Winston.

Ingham, R. (1980). *The poetry preferences of fourth and fifth grade students in a suburban setting in 1980.* Unpublished doctoral dissertation, University of Houston.

Kyte, G.C. (1947). Children's reactions to fifty selected poems. *Elementary School Journal, 48*, 331–339.

Livingston, M.C. (1973). *When you are alone/It keeps you Capone: An approach to creative writing with children.* New York: Atheneum.

Livingston, M.C. (1984). *The child as poet: Myth or reality?* Boston: Horn Book, Inc.

MacKintosh, H. (1924). A study of children's choices in poetry. *Elementary English Review, 1,* 85–89.

Simmons, M. (1980). *Intermediate-grade children's preferences in poetry.* Unpublished doctoral dissertation, University of Alabama.

Terry, A. (1974). *Children's poetry preferences: A National survey of upper elementary grades.* Urbana, IL: National Council of Teachers of English.

17

Poetry in the School:

Bringing Children and

Poetry Together

Amy McClure, Peggy Harrison, and Peg Reed

A poem is a living thing, given first breath by its creator, the poet. Although it owes its creation to the poet, it owes continued life to its readers and listeners: those who hear its song and are touched by the ideas and messages it presents. It does not tell about experience as much as it invites participation in the experience (Huck, 1987). From this perspective the task of bringing children and poetry together must be viewed as an artistic endeavor, one in which an emotional connection is forged between literature and listeners.

Common Approaches to Poetry Instruction

Unfortunately, many teachers do not view the teaching of poetry in this way. Rather than stressing enjoyment and love of poetic language, they tend to equate their task to the teaching of biology: just as one dissects a frog, they dissect poems to see what makes them jump. Or they require memorization for later class recitation and testing. Unfortunately, when such activities are the focus of poetry instruction, something vital and alive is lost: the poems no longer jump for the listener.

Critical Interpretation Approach

Traditionally, literary response theory has focused on text or author with the influence of reader virtually ignored. As a result, research on response to poetry has been concerned with student ability or inability to discover the "correct" meaning of text. Children are first taught to recognize significant poetic elements, forms, and common poetic devices. It is only after receiving extensive drill on these elements that they are considered ready to study poetry. Children are then shown a course they must follow in order to uncover the "true" meaning inherent in a particular poem. They analyze words and lines as well as search for poetic devices they have been taught to recognize. The teacher acts as arbitrator of what constitutes a correct interpretation, controlling both the procedures followed and the nature of the response. The children are neither expected nor encouraged to bring their personal perspectives to the response process.

Although teachers have long favored the interpretive approach, it is commonly cited as one of the most salient factors contributing to the dislike of poetry. Evidence for this assertion comes from many surveys, Craven (1980) and Baskin et al. (1984).

For example, Verble (1973) in a survey of elementary students asked the children why they did not like poetry. The majority of responses were "because I can't understand it" and "because my interpretation is never right." Their dislike seemed to be directed less at the poetry itself than what they were expected to do with it in class.

Use of Commercial Materials and Language-Arts Exercises

Teachers often use commercially published or prestructured materials. These booklets and kits usually include paintings, photographs, or drawings, all designed to motivate the writing of poetry. Frequently, these materials print the beginning of a poem or verse, then ask the child to complete it. Predetermined questions as well as suggested answers to these questions are also often provided.

Advocates of these materials contend they provide necessary guidance and support for teachers who would otherwise neglect poetry. When one considers the inadequate preparation teachers have in teaching this genre, it seems that many teachers may need such structured guidance. However, these materials allow children no opportunity to create their own images or to go beyond the conventional boundaries established for them. In discussing such an approach, Livingston (1976) queries:

> What of the child who does not wish to write about a zoo or sunset? What of the child who has never seen the ocean or the tall buildings of a metropolitan city? What if there is no meaningful page or picture which elicits some thought or feeling from the child?

Frequently language arts texts and workbooks use fill-in-the-blank exercises, which ask children to respond to various predetermined forms and grammatical structures. For example, students create similes and metaphors by providing their own associations as in "the pillow is as soft as _____," "red is _____," or "freedom is _____." Students are also taught formulae for writing various poetic forms like haiku, limericks, couplets, and the like. The diamonte (Tiedt, 1969) is typical of these. With this form children are asked to supply nouns, adjectives, synonyms, and antonyms at predetermined points in the poem in order to describe something. Little provision is made for spontaneity or intense emotion about the object being described.

Advocates of this approach contend that this structure provides needed support for teachers and children who have little experience with poetry and need some direction. Others like Livingston (1976) and Larrick (1971) concede that some good creative efforts can result from these exercises if a teacher is skilled in stimulating a child's imagination and understands the art of poetry. However, in their opinion creative and highly imaginative responses, characterized by strong emotional feelings, do not usually evolve from this approach.

Freedom From Conventional Form and Pattern

Another method provides children with general patterns while simultaneously freeing them from the conventional boundaries of rhyme, meter, and form. The approach is exemplified by the work of Kenneth Koch (1970, 1974), who believes the strict emphasis on rhyme, meter, and correct spelling places severe limits on children's ability to be imaginative. Another barrier he sees is a common belief that poetry is remote and difficult to understand. Koch suggests that this feeling can be avoided by presenting poetry simply without reference to formal literary terms like "metaphor" or "iambic pentameter."

With these concerns in mind, Koch developed an approach in which he first suggests some ideas (comparisons, wishes, dreams, etc.) to students. He then introduces several related activities that provide examples to help make the idea clear and create a mood for writing. For example, the procedure for a color poem begins with children closing their eyes and listening to Koch clap his hands. The children are then asked to tell what color this sound represents to them. This activity is repeated and children make additional associations between colors and words. The object is to encourage divergent, free association in preparation for imaginative written responses.

In his later book, *Rose, Where Did You Get That Red?* (1974) he incorporates the use of contemporary and traditional adult poetry into the basic procedures. This is done so that children are surrounded by fine poetry that is worthy of their attention, providing them with ideas about poetic elements which they can incorporate into their own pieces. Proponents of Koch's program argue that his methods do not disregard poetic craft but rather focus on it deliberately and imaginatively (Western, 1977). His approach does provide an alternative to the heavy reliance on commercial materials and emphasis on discovering correct interpretation and form used by many teachers.

However, critics such as Livingston (1976, 1978), X.J. Kennedy (1981) and others argue that although Koch offers a viable alternative for facilitating response to poetry, his methods only offer children beginnings. Because children are not required to conform to standards, these critics contend that children receive the false idea that real poetry is totally a personal product, unbounded by convention.

Freedom Within Form: An Alternative Method for Fostering Poetic Response

Concerned with maintaining the integrity of poetic form, Myra Cohn Livingston (1976) suggests an alternative method, one in which children are encouraged to write and respond freely to poetry yet are expected to conform to certain poetic conventions and forms. Livingston believes that children cannot be taught to write through formulae and structured exercises. Rather, teachers can only develop children's sensibilities so their unique voices come through in their writing. This is accomplished through a combination of insistence on adherence to both convention and form as well as exposure to fine poetry.

Specifically, Livingston begins by sharing many poems with children. Poems selected for sharing are those that stimulate and arouse the imagination while also providing a fine example of a particular form under scrutiny. She believes that humorous poetry is particularly good for initial sessions because it serves as an ice-breaker and also helps to counteract the prevailing notion that poetry can only be about "Truth," "Beauty," and other sentimental ideas.

Next, children are given an observation sheet on which they record objective responses ("What I saw") and subjective responses ("What I thought about what I saw") as they observe. These sheets are designed to provide a bridge between fact and feeling, necessary for the writing of good poetry. The sheet can be used to record not only observations of concrete objects but also responses to abstractions like sounds, smells, and tastes. Thus, for example, Livingston might bring in a bag of potato chips and get children to taste, smell, and enjoy their crunching sound. Or she might ask them to listen to a passing fire engine and describe its siren. She also suggests that teachers have children keep a daily observation journal in which ongoing feelings and observations can be recorded.

The next step is to get children to turn these observations and feelings into a poem. The teacher's role is to encourage children to use the subjective feelings they have recorded. This is necessary because often a child who makes insightful metaphorical statements or creates unusual turns of a phrase in the observation book will forget to use these when writing the poem.

Livingston works with the children through individual conferences to help make their writings more like poetry. In these meetings, she will first point out good features of the work. Then she begins to gently probe about various aspects, pointing out parts of the work that do not quite work; a rhyme used poorly, a meaning unclear. She also has students find poetry they enjoy to share with the group. This provides an additional opportunity to discuss how poets use rhyme, meter, and form to express their intense feelings. The ultimate objective of this approach is to achieve a critical balance between the discipline required to use poetic elements and the child's own voice.

Bringing Children and Poetry Together

Myra Cohn Livingston presents an intriguing alternative to the poetry teaching practices commonly used in schools. However, are her ideas practical for busy teachers to implement with "real" children? We believe the answer is a resounding "Yes!" Teachers can provide experiences with poetry that help children become sensitive to words, images, and the world around them. In the process the children's own creative voices can be recognized and nurtured.

The following is a description of a poetry program created by two teachers, Peg Reed and Peggy Harrison, who have combined the ideas of Livingston encountered in Charlotte Huck's poetry course with their own extensive knowledge of children to create a program where students eagerly seek out poetry.

Both teachers strongly believe that involvement with poetry (reading, hearing, writing) increases sensitivity and awareness. It helps children become more observant, causing them to look deeply within themselves and to reach far beyond themselves to universal truths. Additionally, they feel that experiences with reading and especially writing poetry help children become better writers. Their prose becomes more poetic, more fluent, and more to the point. They learn to say what they mean in a few words; to be concise. They also learn to appreciate the nuances of language involved in creating a fine piece of literature. Thus, for these teachers, poetry is not a vehicle for objective dissection or analysis. Rather, it is conceived as a source of enjoyment and an artistic venture. The following description of their classroom will provide insights into how they achieve these goals.

It is the beginning of the school day early in November. While the daily chores of lunch count and attendance are being completed Peg has an opportunity to watch and listen to what is going on around her. Many children have chosen books from the poetry display. A few have gone off by themselves to read alone while others are forming small groups around the room to share together. Some occasionally drift back to the poetry bookcase to exchange books and to peruse the "front cover forward" display. Others leaf through pages of a book, stopping to read an old favorite or to experience the enjoyment of a new find. The room is filled with the music of poetry. It's such a pleasant way to start the day!

Rafe, a fourth grader, and his friends have claimed the couch for their reading and sharing place.

"Here it is: *Words With Wrinkled Knees*," Rafe signals to the boys waiting for him on the couch. "It's the one I was telling you about." He holds up Barbara Juster Esbensen's book for them to see. He then wiggles in among the group of third and fourth grade boys who are busily sharing poems together.

"Listen to this," he calls out when there is a break in the sharing, "This one's about a crow. All the poems in this book play on the name of a thing." He continues leafing through the book, "I like this one about the spider. I think I'll read it first today." His voice joins the others as the music of poetry flows in rhythmic waves throughout the room.

When Peg finishes her duties, she assembles the class in a circle at the rug area to participate in the delight of those who have been asked to share special poems. The children tell about poems they have discovered or rediscovered, poems that remind them of something they have observed and experienced, or poems they feel compelled to share with the whole class. Insights, observations, and questions — threads that give meaning to the pattern of the classroom tapestry — interweave themselves among the poems being shared.

Lars shifts the focus of the group when he states, "I have an idea for a poem. Can I have time to write in my poetry journal right away this morning?" Other children comment that they also would like time for this activity. Soon many move to other parts of the room to make entries in their poetry journals. A few remain to continue reading and sharing.

Next door, Peggy has pulled out her brand new book, *Roomrimes* by Sylvia Cassedy. She has noticed that two children, Lauren and Jamie, have written poems about a closet. Since *Roomrimes* looks at everyday rooms (including closets) from different perspectives, she thinks this is the perfect time to share it. To introduce the book, she reads some of her favorites, asking the children to tell how each poem is different. The children seem particularly fascinated by "Fire Escape."

"I like the way she personified the sun," comments Anne after Peggy reads the poem.

"Yea, it's neat how you think the sun is a prisoner and you hold the keys. I never thought of it like that before," says Josh.

"I like the way she said the sun skins its sides going between the buildings. That's kind of like it really is," Anne adds.

Soon several voices chorus, "Read 'Fire Escape' again!" The children listen intently as Peggy rereads the poem. Occasionally, she stops to comment on an unusual image or play on words.

Tony had momentarily left the group but returns, poetry journal in hand. "I wrote one kind of like this poem. It's about my bedroom." He reads the poem aloud to the appreciative audience.

"You might like to try writing your own poems about rooms and spaces like Tony did," she suggests. Several children enthusiastically decide to do this, and the group breaks up to begin the day's various activities.

How do the teachers begin with these children? How do they get to the point where they eagerly choose poetry as a favorite daily activity? One of the most important things they do is share many fine examples of poetry written for children and encourage the children to do the same. This is usually done in teacher-led large groups. In these sessions, the teachers perceive their role as providing children with ideas and exposure to unusual kinds of poetry so as to help them experience pieces that are conceptually beyond what they might normally pick up on their own. Thus, they share poetry by poets like Walt Whitman, Langston Hughes, and Carl Sandburg, then discuss how poets can evoke strong emotions and sway public opinion. Or a poem like Masters' "April" will be read aloud, and the children will be asked to comment on how the poet has used unusual images such as a lawn mower going through a "waterfall of grass." Soon they come to know the voices of individual poets. By the middle of the year the teachers will often read a poem, then ask the children to identify the poet. Invariably, they can.

Sharing of fine poetry is also done more informally. The teachers often make special books visible and accessible by arranging them on the chalkrail or in a prominent position in the poetry center. Sometimes poems read aloud in large group sessions will be left casually on a table so they are available for rereading. Often the teachers will link poetry with other units of study or subjects. Thus, when Peggy's class studied milkweed, Harry Behn's book, *Crickets,*

Bullfrogs and Whispers of Thunder was displayed and read. Children were then encouraged to find related poems. In the fall, she brought in zinnias and placed Valerie Worth's "Zinnia" poem next to the arrangement. The children were encouraged to find similar poems.

As the children acquire experience with poetry, they are encouraged to experiment regularly with their tentative understandings of poetic elements by trying them out in their own writing. The teachers firmly believe the writing phase should not be neglected as it is the experimentation involved in writing and then revision of one's initial efforts that deepens insights and understandings.

How do the teachers make this happen? First, they help children become aware of the lilt and flow of words in all that they hear. For example, Peg will share a poem like Eve Merriam's "Summer Rain" and then discuss how the poet has used words to create the musical sound of a gentle summer shower. She asks the children to pay attention to how the words "play against each other, sound with each other, bounce against each other," then suggests they try to do this with their own poems. They also experiment with ways of "lining" a poem, with word order, and with discovering unique ways of expressing their ideas. All this is done not only by reading the work of published poets but sharing pieces done by the children as well.

The teachers do not stop with praising the children's initial efforts. Over the year their role gradually shifts from that of motivator and cheerleader to questioner and facilitator. They strive to do what Charlotte Huck continually suggested: "lift the children beyond where they are to reach new insights." Thus, they constantly look for the unusual, the kernel of a unique thought that lies within a seemingly ordinary piece. To stimulate thinking they frequently ask children questions like the following:

"You've done something very special here. How would you describe it?"

"How could you use what you know about poetry to make your piece more interesting?"

"Have you looked closely at that thing you're describing? Have you become a part of it so you really see it?"

"Did you notice that spring (winter, fall, etc.) is coming? What makes you feel it? Something's different? What is it?"

"Listen to my poem. Do you know what I'm struggling to say? Will you help me with this part?"

Thus, when Chelsea decided to explore seriously what she could do with words, she chose to write about a particular word expressing how it affected her personally. She revised the entry in her poetry journal seven times. However, she actually reworked it many more times in her head and while discussing it with her writing community peers and her teacher. After days of thinking and writing, she brought it to Peg, stating triumphantly, "It says just what I wanted it to say FINALLY!" Peg encouraged her to share it with the rest:

CROWDED

I don't like the word crowded.
    It's packed too tight,
      Always full,
Sometimes popular (but never with me).
      It presses me
When I want to be free.

Chelsea Rice
Grade 4

Although all of this revision is not demanded, it is strongly encouraged. The teachers believe that experimentation with poetic language, playing with ideas and how to express them best, is important. To show their students how to do this, both teachers model the revision process by sharing pages from their own poetry journals. The process of revision is compared to "using a scalpel." With a pencil, unnecessary verbiage is cut away to create a piece that uses the most succinct, appropriate words to describe the essence of something. Rafe has dubbed this process "getting rid of the excess baggage." His intense interests in the revision process as well as his interpretation of Eve Merriam's "How to Eat A Poem" (which he valued enough to copy on the back of his poetry journal for constant reference) inspired him to write the following:

Writing a poem
Is like piloting a plane
If it's not flying smoothly
Throw out the extra baggage.

Rafe Kasumi
Grade 3

Poems are never viewed as finished in this classroom. Rather, children are encouraged to view the writing process as analogous to baking bread, "kneading, punching it down and kneading some more" until satisfied that a unique statement has been made. When a poem reaches this point, it is "checkmarked," indicating that the writer, for the moment, is satisfied with what he or she has written; that the entry makes sense; and that it is edited so it can be used for display. However, children are encouraged to return to a checkmarked poem to consider it from a new perspective or to change a word or lining pattern so the piece conveys the intended meaning even more clearly. In short, emphasis in this classroom is on both process and product. Product is deemed important, but process, in which the true thinking and experimentation takes place, is seen as critical.

Children sometimes initially complain that they cannot think of anything to write. Mutterings of "I can't do that" or "You can't make me a poet" are occasionally heard, particularly at the beginning of the year. When this occurs, the teachers guide the children to look through the extensive classroom poetry collection. They help them discover that indeed anything can be the "stuff" of poetry. Soon the children are seeing the poetic in even the simplest everyday phenomena. For example, Erin got the idea for the following poem while lying spread-eagle in the snow:

I lie
In the soft
Snow
The night
Is silent,
With only
The sound
Of a car
Slowly passing.
What a lovely
Winter world.

Erin Murphy
Grade 5

Anne wrote this poem after studying metamorphosis and change in science:

Silk Wings

What metamorphosis
Are you going through —
From a caterpillar
To a mysterious chrysalis?
With silk wings,
To the naked eye
Stretch out that silk,
Butterfly

Anne Langford
Grade 3

Even such common objects as gym shoes and coat hangers can
stimulate children to create a poem as the following pieces attest:

Nikes

An old pair of Nikes,
Full of holes,
Sit talking to the
New shoes in the closet,
Hearing stories of the
Girl who left them.

Jamie Turner
Grade 5

Sagging Shoulders

Coat hangers hang
In the closet
All year round,
In winter
Their shoulders sag
From the weight
Of heavy winter coats.

Lauren Pritchet
Grade 5

The children are encouraged to ''say something new'' or ''say
something old in a new way'' when they take everyday phenomena
as the subject of their poems. Thus, the use of unusual phrases, unexpected comparisons and fresh images are supported and praised. Lars
embodied these ideas in his creation of the following poem:

Vroom!
Vroom!
Cars
Go
Whizzing
By me.
I
Slow
Them
With
Yellow. . .
I
Catch
Them
With
Red . . .
I
Free
Them
With
Green.

The people in a hurry say,
"Hurry up you old traffic machine."

Lars Mahler
Grade 4

By the end of the school year Peg and Peggy's teaching of poetry merges with their teaching of writing. When the children write, they see themselves as a community of writers that extends beyond their classroom to include the poets who have created pieces they savor over and over again. When they read, they bring an awareness of the struggle involved in creating, as well as depth of response that is shaped by their experiences as writers.

Poetry lives and breathes in Peg and Peggy's classrooms. The children see and feel it in everything they do. They read it, chant it, act it out, write and illustrate it. In the process, they begin to develop a sense of the common and endeavor to make the common come alive, breathing new spirit into worn ideas.

Summary

Poetry does not tell about experience; it invites participation in the experience. Earlier methods of poetry study included the interpretive approach which sought one "correct" interpretation, extensive use of pre-packaged commercial materials with structured lessons, and introduction to the general patterns of poetry while freeing children from its conventional boundaries of rhyme, meter and form. An alternative method, freedom within form, fosters a more creative response in that children are encouraged to write and respond freely to poetry yet respect its conventions and forms. When children are deeply immersed in hearing, reading, and writing poetry, they become more observant, reach beyond themselves to universal truths, and become better writers.

Favorite Poetry Sources
(suggested grade levels are listed in parentheses)

Adoff, Arnold. *All the Colors of the Race.* Lothrop Lee & Shepard, 1982. (3–6)

  Eats: Poems. Lothrop Lee & Shepard, 1979. (3–6)

Amon, Aline, Adapt. *The Earth is Sore: Native Americans on Nature.* Atheneum, 1981. (4–6)

Atwood, Ann. *Fly with the Wind, Flow with the Water.* Scribner's, 1979. (4–6)

Cassedy, Sylvia. *Roomrimes.* Crowell, 1987. (3–6)

Cummings, e.e. *Hist, Whist, & Other Poems for Children.* Liveright, 1983. (5–6)

DeRegniers, Beatrice Schenk, *et al. Poems Children Will Sit Still For: A Selection for the Primary Grades.* Citation Press, 1969. (K–6)

Dunning, Stephen, et. al., Comps. *Reflections on a Gift of a Watermelon Pickle & Other Modern Verse.* Scholastic, 1966. (5–6+)

Farber, Norma & Myra Cohn Livingston. *These Small Stones.* Harper & Row, 1987. (2–6)

Foster, John, Comp. *First Poetry Book.* Oxford University Press, 1982. (K–6)

  Comp. *Second Poetry Book.* Oxford University Press, 1982. (1–6)

  Comp. *Third Poetry Book.* Oxford University Press, 1983. (2–6)

  Comp. *Fourth Poetry Book.* Oxford University Press, 1983. (4–6)

Frost, Robert. *You Come Too.* Holt, Rinehart and Winston, 1959. (5–6)

Hoberman, Mary Ann. *Bugs.* Viking, 1976. (1–6)

  Yellow Butter/Purple Jelly/Red Jam/Black Bread. Viking, 1981. (K–5)

Hopkins, Lee Bennett, Sel. *Dinosaurs.* Harcourt Brace Jovanovich, 1987. (1–6)

  Sel. *Crickets, Bullfrogs, and Whispers of Thunder.* Harcourt Brace Jovanovich, 1984. (4–?)

  Sel. *To Look at Anything.* Harcourt Brace Jovanovich, 1978. (3–6+)

Hughes, Ted. *Season Songs.* Viking, 1975. (4–6)

  Under the North Star. Viking, 1981. (4–6)

Hughes, Langston. *Selected Poems of Langston Hughes. Don't You Turn Back.* Edited by Lee Bennett Hopkins. Knopf, 1969. Random House (Vintage Books) (5–Adult)

Kennedy, X.J. *Knock at a Star.* Little, Brown, 1982. (3–6)

Kuskin, Karla. *Dogs & Dragons, Trees & Dreams.* Harper & Row, 1980. (1–6)

  Near the Window Tree. Harper & Row, 1975. (K–8)

Larrick, Nancy. Sel. *Piping Down the Valleys Wild.* Dell, 1968. (2–6)

Latham, Edward, Ed. *The Poetry of Robert Frost: The Collected Poems, Complete and Unabridged.* Holt, Rinehart and Winston. (5–Adult) n.d.

Livingston, Myra Cohn. Sel. *Cat Poems.* Holiday House, 1987. (3–6)

  Celebrations. Holiday House, 1985. (1–6)

Lobel, Arnold. *The Book of Pigericks.* Harper & Row, 1983. (K–6)

Mayer, Mercer, Coll. *A Poison Tree.* Scribner's, 1977. (4–6+)

McCord, David. *One at a Time.* Little, Brown, 1980. (K–6)

McGovern, Ann, Sel. *Arrow Book of Poetry.* Scholastic, 1985. (3–6)

Merriam, Eve. *Jamboree. Rhymes for all Times.* Dell, 1984. (3–6)

Moore, Lilian. Coll. *Go With the Poem.* McGraw Hill, 1979. (4–6)

  Think of Shadows. Atheneum, 1980. (2–6)

O'Neill, Mary. *Hailstones and Halibut Bones.* Doubleday, 1961. (1–6)

Prelutsky, Jack, Sel. *The Random House Book of Poetry.* Random House, 1983. (1–6)

Sandburg, Carl, *Early Moon.* Harcourt Brace Jovanovich, 1930. (4–6)

  Wind Song. Harcourt Brace Jovanovich, 1960. (4–6)

Saunders, Dennis, Sel. *Magic Lights and Streets of Shining Jets.* Greenwillow, 1977. (1–6)

Starbird, Kaye. *The Covered Bridge House.* Four Winds Press, 1979. (1–6)

Thurman, Judith. *Flashlight.* Atheneum, 1976. (1–6)

Werner, Isabel, Comp. *The Poetry Troupe.* Scribner's. (1–6) n.d.

Worth, Valerie. *All the Small Poems.* Farrar, Straus & Giroux. 1987. (3–6)

References

Baskin, B., Harris, K. & Sally, C. (1984). Making the poetry connection. In P. Barron and J. Burley (Eds.), *Jump over the moon: Selected professional readings.* New York: Holt, Rinehart and Winston. 77–87.

Craven, M.A. (1980). *A survey of teacher attitudes and practices regarding the teaching of poetry in the elementary school.* Unpublished doctoral dissertation, Lamar University.

Huck, C.S., Hepler, S. & Hickman, J. (1987). *Children's literature in the elementary school.* (4th ed.). New York: Holt, Rinehart and Winston.

Kennedy, X.J. (1981). Go and get your candle lit: An approach to poetry. *The Horn Book, 42,* 273–279.

Koch, K. (1970). *Wishes, lies and dreams: Teaching children to write poetry.* New York: Vantage.

Koch, K. (1973). *Rose, where did you get that red? Teaching great poetry to children.* New York: Random House.

Larrick, N. (1971). *Somebody turned on a tap in these kids.* New York: Delacorte.

Livingston, M.C. (1976). But is it poetry? *The Horn Book, 52,* 24–31.

Livingston, M.C. (1978). Beginnings. *Language Arts, 55,* 346–354.

Tiedt, I. (1969). A new poetry form: The diamonte. *Language Arts, 46,* 588–589.

Verble, D. (1973). *A road not taken: An approach to teaching.* Nashville: Tennessee Arts Commission (sponsored by the National Endowment for the Arts).

Western, R. (1977). A defense of Kenneth Koch. *Language Arts, 54,* 763–766.

An upcoming book on this topic, entitled *Sunrises and Songs: Reading and Writing Poetry in an Elementary Classroom*, is being published by Heinemann Publishers, Inc., Portsmouth, N.H.

18

A Bouquet of Poems

About Poetry

for Charlotte

Eve Merriam

Eve Merriam is one of the outstanding authors who visits The Ohio State University campus often. Even on the first visit her poetry had preceded her; her work was well known before she arrived. Charlotte Huck had read from her work so often that every member of the audience could recite a verse or two.

Eve Merriam loves to write poetry and loves to hear Charlotte Huck read poetry aloud. Since Eve Merriam is one of Charlotte's favorite poets, she often chooses her work to read aloud.

The results of this cyclical process paid high dividends when we asked Eve Merriam to write about poetry from a poet's viewpoint. Eve Merriam went beyond that and gathered a bouquet of poems about poetry for Charlotte.

—Editors' Note

A Bouquet of Poems
About Poetry for Charlotte
with everlasting affection
from Eve

BAD ADVICE TO GOOD CHILDREN

What do you need?

A roof over your head,
shoes,
and bread.

Rules to go by,
not fools.

If you go poking holes in the moontop sky
and dabble your toes in the starry spray,
and dawdle with verses the livelong day,
you will never arrive at the straightened way —

but oh the kiss of bumping in the street
and laughing when you curving meet!

(previously unpublished)

THE POET'S CRAFT

To grasp the word
to pluck that great clumsy blossom
and not blear its creamy petals

to trace its sticky texture to the bough
to bend it down
and feel it spring away recalcitrant

to press apart the weight of leaves
drooping like udders

to tussle for its lemon ginger scent

to pull it off

(previously unpublished)

"I," SAYS THE POEM

"I," says the poem arrogantly,
"I am a cloud,
I am a tree.

I am a city,
I am the sea,
I am a golden
mystery."

How can it be?

A poem is written
by some someone,
someone like you
or someone like me

who blows her nose,
who breaks shoelaces,
who hates and loves,
who loses gloves,
who eats, who weeps,
who laughs, who sleeps,

an ordinary she or he
extraordinary as you or me

whose thoughts stretch high
as clouds in the sky,

whose memories
root deep as trees,

whose feelings choke
like city smoke,

whose fears and joys in waves redound
like the ocean's tidal sound,

who daily solves a mystery:
each hour is new, what will it be?

"I," says the poem matter-of-factly,
"I am a cloud,
I am a tree,

I am a city,
I am the sea,

I am a golden
Mystery."

But, adds the poem silently,
I cannot speak until you come,
Reader, come, come with me.

(From *It Doesn't Always Have To Rhyme* © Eve Merriam 1964)

SKYWRITING

1.

Fireworks!
They shower down as verbs,
and come to rest as nouns.

Fountain in reverse,
words that delight take flight,
flash like fireworks in the air,
blazon and remain there.

2.

Adjectives like leaves
palpitate the trees.
Yearly the seasons must renew
as April's green and singing sound
falls to silent winter ground.

A poem shapes the landscape,
holds the singing green.
Leaves that do not die,
planted in the poem sky.

3.

Birds write verses in the sky;
swift verbs that fly,
slow nouns in their downy nest.
Wingbeat repeat, repeat
the symmetry of birds, of words.

The flight soaring,
the song outpouring.

The flight dying,
the song still flying.

(From *It Doesn't Always Have To Rhyme* © Eve Merriam 1964)

MONA LISA

"You'll mean what I say," tells prose.
"Say what I mean," smiles the poem.

If you can, if you can.
Catch me if you can.
If you can catch yourself, you can.

(From *It Doesn't Always Have To Rhyme* © Eve Merriam 1964)

WHAT DID YOU SAY?

A poem rarely has to shout,
for even when it is addressing a crowd

it is speaking only to you
and to me.

So when the syllables repeat,
it is sheerly for the music,
clearly.

(From *It Doesn't Always Have To Rhyme* © Eve Merriam 1964)

SOME USES FOR POETRY

to paint without a palette
to dance without music
to speak without speaking
to feel the strangeness between hot and cold
to feel the likeness of hot and cold
to plunge into both at the same moment

(From *It Doesn't Always Have To Rhyme* © Eve Merriam 1964)

WAYS OF COMPOSING

typewriter:
a mouthful of teeth chattering
afraid to be quiet

a pencil
can lie down and dream
dark and silver silences

(From *Rainbow Writing* © Eve Merriam 1976)

THE POEM AS A DOOR

A door
is never
either/or.
A door
is always
more.

You cannot skip over,
you cannot crawl under;
walk through the wood,
it splits asunder.

If you expect it to be bolted,
it will be.

There is only one opening:
yourself as the key.

With a sigh of happiness
you pass through
to find on the other side
someone with a sigh of happiness
welcoming you.

(someone = Charlotte)

(From *Rainbow Writing* © Eve Merriam 1976)

REPLY TO THE QUESTION:
"How Can You Become A Poet?"

take the leaf of a tree
trace its exact shape
the outside edges
and inner lines

memorize the way it is fastened to the twig
(and how the twig arches from the branch)
how it springs forth in April
how it is panoplied in July

by late August
crumple it in your hand
so that you smell its end-of-summer sadness

chew its woody stem

listen to its autumn rattle

watch as it atomizes in the November air

then in winter
when there is no leaf left
                              invent one

(From *Rainbow Writing* © Eve Merriam 1976)

DOORS FOR CHARLOTTE

Three Locked Doors
tomorrow
the heart of love
yourself

Three Open Doors
tomorrow
the heart of love
your self

(From *Fresh Paint* © Eve Merriam 1986)

Part III

Patterns: Developing Literature-Based Programs

Introduction

Teachers and librarians implement literature programs in diverse ways. The first two chapters in this section offer general as well as specific descriptions of ways to start programs. In the lead chapter, Joan Glazer gives a behind-the-scenes description of the real journey one school system is making toward a literature-based program. As a participant in the journey, Glazer helped with the initial planning and implementation of the program, which included the development and testing of teacher-made study guides for numerous trade books. Continuing this theme, Susan Hepler reviews some of the ways to get a literature program started. She advises people to start small, gather support, and keep their goals in mind. She suggests sustained silent reading, reading aloud, focused discussions, discussions over time, and thematic units as ways to extend literature across the curriculum.

Next, Steve DeLapp, an administrator, addresses the assumptions underlying curriculum change. These are based on a deep-rooted respect for each child as a unique learner and a commitment to the role of teacher as decision maker. Given these essentials, DeLapp outlines the features of the literature-based programs in his schools.

Diane Driessen, an elementary school librarian, shows how the librarian can be a key figure and partner with teachers in a literature-based program. By working with teachers, she shows how the library literature curriculum both supports and extends the experiences students have in their classrooms through read–aloud programs, book fairs, author visits, book discussion groups, and most of all, by making the library as accessible as possible.

Barbara Peterson, who has been both a public librarian and a teacher of teachers, describes ways to enrich the resources needed to make literature available to teachers and students. She suggests using personal networks, professional organizations, and printed materials in the search for new books and new ways of using them.

19

Moving Toward

a Literature-Based

Program

Joan I. Glazer

This is the description of a journey one school system is making, a journey still in progress. We hope what we are learning may help you plan one of your own or, if you are already on the road, let you sit back and fondly reminisce. To describe how Scituate, Rhode Island, is moving toward a literature-based program means telling a bit about the place it left as well as where it is going. Whereas a short trip to a similar locale requires scant planning and little adjustment, a long trip to a new area takes quite a bit more planning and demands far more adjustment. For Scituate, the move to a literature-based program is a continuation of a journey — in some ways long; in others, short, but eased by the fact that it is being undertaken by seasoned travellers.

At the Start

Scituate is a rural community in northwestern Rhode Island. It has three elementary schools. Teachers and principals have moved from school to school within the system, worked together regularly on curriculum development projects, and, in general, come to know each other well. They are professionally active. At the beginning, the teachers in kindergarten and grade one used the language experience approach to reading instruction, gradually moving the children into basal readers. They worked with Dr. William Oehlkers of Rhode Island College, both to improve their own skills and to help in the education of preservice teachers. Teachers in grades two through six used basal readers for reading instruction, read orally to the children, and encouraged the regular reading of trade books for recreation. They, too, worked with preservice teachers.

Each school had its own media center, staffed by a full-time librarian. The school system had in place a policy for the selection of materials in media centers, a policy that included affirmation of the American Library Association *Library Bill of Rights* and the *Freedom to Read Statement* "within the boundaries of community values." There was an established procedure for citizens to request reconsideration of a book or other media.

Deciding to Move

Deciding to move toward a literature-based program was just that — deciding. The impetus for a school system to make a move may grow out of a desire to escape an unsatisfactory situation or from a desire to be someplace better. Scituate had no real need to move. Test scores showed children were performing above the national average in reading, and there was no pressure from outside to make a change. What the teachers did was read a whole series of "travel brochures" — *Becoming a Nation of Readers* (Anderson, *et al.* 1985); the work of Donald Graves (1983), Marie Clay (1982), Kenneth Goodman (1986); in short, the works referred to in the earlier sections of this book —

and decide to go someplace better. The brochures were acquired by Sharon Capobianco, a reading specialist and director of reading for the schools, who shared them with the assistant superintendent for instruction and with the superintendent, who in turn shared them with the entire faculty. The reading was exciting.

Sharon and two other reading specialists, Mary Cerullo and Lois Oehlkers, began talking with the classroom teachers about the possibilities. The reading committee, made up of the three specialists and several classroom teachers, began exploring ways they might make literature more central in the curriculum, especially for reading instruction. Rather than adopt a new basal series for the above average intermediate grade readers, the committee decided to purchase sets of trade books and to implement what was termed a ''reading enrichment curriculum.'' They had made the downpayment on their trip.

Now it was time to do serious planning. Where exactly did they want to go? The teachers decided on three basic destinations. They wanted to use trade books for reading instruction for all children. They wanted to integrate the teaching of content areas with the teaching of reading, writing, and literature. They also wanted to employ selected whole language strategies.

Deciding What to Pack

They knew that there were some prized possessions that they wanted to take with them. One was their participation in the statewide Young Authors Conference; another was their Young Authors Conference. At the statewide conference, one child from each grade level in each system may attend. At their own, every child who elects to write a book may attend. They wanted to continue to have authors of children's books speak to the pupils. They wanted to continue the use of language experience techniques in kindergarten and first grade. They also wanted to continue to establish goals and objectives to guide their curricular planning.

The goals for the use of trade books at the intermediate level were clear. They were

1. To foster in students a love of reading.
2. To assist students in moving towards more mature levels of moral awareness.

3. To develop and extend a reader's understanding of people, their values and their way of living.

4. To develop in students an awareness of the variability in style, pattern, and worth among various pieces of literature.

5. To develop in students a discerning attitude towards literature.

Under each goal were the specific objectives. The objectives under the goal of fostering a love of reading were

A. Students will be provided with books appropriate to their interests

B. Books will be displayed attractively in the classroom

C. Students will be given ample time to read for pleasure

D. Students will be read to on a daily basis

Changes in the curriculum and in the approach to teaching would continue to be guided by stated goals and objectives.

Planning the Trip

The next question was how these teachers and this school system would get where they wanted to go. Certain travel arrangements seemed to make sense. One was to invite some guests to come along, guests who could contribute their expertise to the endeavor. Sharon asked Joan Glazer, the guest who is writing this description, to meet with the teachers who were going to select the trade books for the intermediate grades and who would develop study guides for them. Together we assessed the quality of books available in paperback, looked at how they could be paired or grouped to elicit deeper understanding of themes and literary aspects, looked at commercially developed guides to assess the state of the art, and made a general outline of the type of guide we wanted to develop.

Our list includes such pairings of books as Smith's *A Taste of Blackberries* and Babbitt's *Tuck Everlasting*, for discussion of death; *Homecoming* and *Dicey's Song*, for continuation of a story and a study of Cynthia Voigt's writing; and *The Cricket in Times Square* by Selden and *Getting Something on Maggie Marmelstein* by Sharmat for the theme of friendship. There are guides for the individual books and a guide for comparing them. Each guide follows the same format.

- Summary (usually one paragraph or less)
- Objectives (which of the reading/literature objectives are addressed in the guide)
- Journal writing (suggestions for journal writing keyed to the reading of the book)
- Prereading discussion/activities
- Discussion questions/activities (listed by whatever chunk of reading is planned, usually two to four chapters)
- Follow-up activities (from which teachers select)
- Further reading (suggested titles on a similar theme, with a similar style, or by the same author)

There is focus on the text itself and on the transaction between reader and text. Within each guide are questions and activities designed to enhance literary understanding and others designed to elicit personal responses. Teachers using the guides are to select from both categories.

The development of guides will be ongoing, an open rather than a closed system. New titles will continually be added. Teachers will select titles so that the children have a balance of genre, writing styles, mood, and authors. Because we were developing a systemwide curriculum, we assigned certain books to certain grade levels. The expectation is that each teacher doing book discussions will use those titles at or below his or her grade level. Children's records will show which titles they have read and discussed as part of a classroom group. Thus a teacher can plan using grade level or below titles or any others not reserved for a higher grade.

Probably our most important understanding as we began our work was that we would be willing to reassess and make changes as we went along. Our original list, therefore, does not match our current list. Some titles went out of print, some titles we rethought, some did not fit as well once we made other changes, and some we added when they appeared in paperback. We revised the format for the guides midyear to include the suggestions for journal writing.

As is often the case, good company and stimulating conversation made the guest reluctant to go home. My way of being able to extend my stay was to apply for a sabbatical leave from my college to continue work on the project. By the beginning of my sabbatical in September, books had been purchased, guides for more than twenty books had been developed, and several teachers were using sets of trade books in the classroom. During that semester I pilot tested guides in nearly all of the intermediate grade classrooms.

The work with children was great fun. They had insights that went beyond the questions they were asked. One group reading Walsh's *The Green Book* summed up this science fiction story of beginning life anew on another planet as "Laura Ingalls Wilder of the future." Another group when asked, after having read *Dicey's Song,* if they thought that "life was simple like a song," answered in similes of their own. "Life is not simple like a song. It doesn't keep a steady rhythm like a song, and you never know when the chorus will come." "If life was a record, it would have a lot of scratches." There were also the comparisons volunteered by thoughtful readers. *"The Indian in the Cupboard* [by Banks] is fast all the way through, from one good part to another. It's not like *Tuck Everlasting.* That one started out so slow . . . but once you got to the middle, you couldn't put it down."

Pilot testing the guides served a dual function. It helped us in revising the materials, and it gave the teachers a chance to watch another educator work with their children. For some it was an opportunity to observe the responses of their students. For others it was an introduction to how this kind of lesson could be structured and to the enthusiasm of the children as they participated. It was like showing a video to those who had not been sold by the printed brochures.

Also in September, grant monies from the state for which Sharon had applied became available. The Rhode Island Department of Education had instituted a K–3 Student Literacy Project, with a "Special Demonstration Grant Program" for school systems that had solid proposals for teaching literacy skills through the content areas in the primary grades. While intermediate grade teachers began using trade books for supplemental reading instruction and kindergarten and grade one teachers began using big books, language experience, and shared reading and writing, the teachers in grades two and three began meeting to select science and social studies topics that they would use as vehicles in teaching literacy skills. They, too, began by determining goals and objectives and then looking at teaching materials and strategies.

The third grade teachers planned a year-long curriculum focusing on local history and activities. It includes content dealing with water and the water cycle, as Scituate is located near a huge reservoir that provides water for it and the major cities in the state. The town was moved and rebuilt when the reservoir was constructed and the original site flooded. Children learn about the history of Scituate, interview local residents, and visit the sites of mills left from earlier times when the textile industry flourished. They visit apple orchards, talk with the farmers about changes in agriculture, and watch and record the growth of apples. They are surrounded with books about the topics. They read the work of local authors, looking at *Mill* by David Macaulay, listening to the books of Chris Van Allsburg, and reading many of the stories of Scott Corbett. They write what they are seeing, what they are learning, and what they are thinking. They take surveys and show information in graph form.

The second grade teachers decided to use animals as the central theme. They began with habitats of New England animals, which spread to animals of other places, to books about real animals and toy animals, and about animals that talked. They brought materials to the workshops, making copies for their colleagues or suggesting purchase. They added to the list of good books, shared the writing and the projects of their students, and combined their knowledge and their resources to create for each of them a classroom of exciting materials.

For both second and third grade teachers, the time to meet together was essential. The regularly scheduled workshops gave time for them to share their successes and their concerns, to plan together, and to revise and restructure. It was a time they could tell Sharon and me what they needed so that we might help. It was a time we could bring materials and ideas to them for review and discussion.

Checking the Itinerary

Important in the journey was the fact that those using these ideas had elected to do so. They were not the victims of forced relocation. In fact, teachers initially worked after hours and during the summer to get materials prepared. The verbal support of the administration grew into financial support, with released time provided during school hours for committee work and in-service workshops. Sharon was given a reduced teaching load so that she and I could spend time working more directly with the teachers, planning workshops, gathering possible materials, and addressing problems as they arose.

We have been trying to observe the speed limit. We do not want the move toward a literature-based curriculum to go so fast that we lose passengers, run over bystanders, or get stopped by a disgruntled policeman. Thus the use of trade books began with the advanced readers in the intermediate grades and in conjunction with a basal reader. They are now being used in certain second and third grade classrooms as well and with groups other than the above average readers. Eventually, trade books will supplant the basal. The integrated approach is being used in the primary grades now and will spread to the upper grades. Process writing is being used throughout, but not by every teacher. At some point, although we do not have a target date, the curriculum will be entirely literature-based.

Moving a system, even one with only three elementary schools, is slower than moving a single class. Instead of one driver hopping in the U-Haul and taking off, it is more like hiring Allied Van Lines and having everyone ride along, with the added challenge of having encouraged everyone to backseat drive. We have also felt it important to let the community know where we are going. There have been evening presentations for parents, newsletters to parents, a newsletter that circulates to the public, and word-of-mouth, which in a small, close-knit community is amazingly effective. Letters to parents, such as one at the holiday season suggesting titles of books that would make good gifts, have included the rationale for a strong reliance on trade books.

In our discussions with other travellers, we have come to realize the importance of a good driver. Sharon has been available to provide maps, discuss either short cuts or scenic routes, and even to get others to pay for part of the gas. When several teachers are working together, it is useful to have someone serve as a coordinator.

Advising Fellow Travelers

If you embark on this journey toward a literature-based curriculum, your questions are likely to be the same as ours. Why should we go? What should we take with us from our old home? What route should we follow? How fast should we drive? How will we know if the journey was worth it? That last question is one we are still working to answer. Teachers have responded on a questionnaire that they see children reading more, reading and writing with understanding, and coming eagerly to discuss books and projects that involve books. We will need to do more with evaluation, probably not only through behavioral checklists but also through some appropriate measurement of reading skill.

Perhaps we can encourage others to make the move toward a literature-based curriculum by advertising in the style of Burma Shave. For those of you whose childhood did not include travelling rural highways in the Midwest, a quick explanation is in order. Burma Shave had advertisements which consisted of a clever rhyming saying, with the phrases appearing on signs spaced far enough apart that they could be read as one drove by. Our signs might read

Give children time

To read real books

And you'll see faces

With happy looks.

After all, it is what we read, as well as saw and heard, that made us want to move.

Summary

This description of one school system's journey toward a literature-based program reports our traveling conditions as well as our progress. Good schools wanted to be better. They planned ahead, established goals, and invited a consultant (this writer) to come along. In looking back over the route we have followed, several things stand out — the commitment of teachers and administrators, the cautious pace we have maintained in making changes, our efforts to include parents, and the importance of a good coordinator. Although we have not yet reached our destination, it has been a satisfying trip.

References

Anderson, R.C., *et al.* (1985). *Becoming a nation of readers: Report of the commission on reading.* Washington, D.C.: National Institute of Education, U.S. Department of Education.

Clay, M.M. (1982). *Observing young readers.* Portsmouth, NH: Heinemann.

Goodman, K. (1986). *What's whole in whole language?* Portsmouth, NH: Heinemann.

Graves, D. (1983). *Writing: Teachers and children at work.* Portsmouth, NH: Heinemann.

20

A Literature Program:

Getting It Together,

Keeping It Going

Susan Hepler

Suppose you already have something going in a literature program. Perhaps, like Ramona Quimby's teacher, Mrs. Whaley, in Cleary's *Ramona Quimby, Age 8,* you have a near-daily "DEAR" (Drop Everything And Read) spot. Or you may be reading aloud several times a week from books you think your class would like (or should know). Or maybe you have a file of teaching guides for books and periodically you turn your fifth graders loose on individual projects. Or, perhaps any of this would sound wonderful if you could just get time to do it, given all those million curriculum goals you have to fulfill before June. What options should you consider in designing a classroom program? How could you augment your current program to make it even better? If you have not started yet, where should you begin?

Gathering Support

You are not alone. For the past few years, there has been immense public interest in helping children become enthusiastic, knowledgeable, and competent readers who love books. Parents have been nudged by authors such as Jim Trelease (1985), Andrea Cascardi (1985), Margaret Mary Kimmel and Elizabeth Segel (1983) to take an interest in books. The State of California has developed the California Reading Initiative to insure that all grade levels are exposed to quality literature and other states are sure to follow. Publishers have reissued excellent titles in paperback; others have offered ''Teacher Guides'' to support literature in the classroom.

Magazines and books have featured articles by teachers who are evolving a literature program. Liz Waterland (1985) writes about her switch from the kind of teacher who feeds students knowledge to one who regards students as apprentices — active and already partly competent sharers in the task of learning how to read. Linda Henke (1988) details her whole district's gradual conversion to a literature-based reading program when faced with the purchase of a new basal system. Marcia Burchby (1988) contrasts basal teaching with a whole language literature approach to the teaching of reading in her primary classroom. Joelie Hancock and Susan Hill (1988) demonstrate *Literature-Based Reading Programs at Work*.

Common features of these writings include teacher delight with enthusiastic readers; how much children know, remember and apply what they read; how much readers reveal about their reading, thinking, and writing abilities; and the parent support that grows as teachers explain what they are trying to accomplish.

However, nearly all of the teachers moving toward a literature-based reading program say how much time they spend planning, gathering materials, and learning something themselves before embarking on an author or a thematic study, or an in-depth study of a novel. All mention keeping parents clearly informed. In a ''Teacher Feature'' of The WEB (Hickman & Huck, 1983), two teachers discussing their developing literature program revealed that they had never worked so hard. They said it took a lot more organization, remember-ing, preplanning, and trying things out than just opening up a manual and following it. Both mentioned, too, the support they received from each other.

If you are just starting out, find someone to talk to and to work with. Locate one of these articles to sustain you in the frustrating moments with the thought that the rewards are worth the effort. Then, make a modest beginning.

A Modest Beginning

Start small. Pick some aspect of a literature program and imple-ment it in the classroom. For instance, most children welcome the chance to read if they are given some school time to do it. Instead of saving Sustained Silent Reading (SSR) or DEAR time for "when all the other work is done," make twenty minutes three to five times a week when everyone reads. Let younger children read in pairs (we all know how talk can help pre-readers make sense of the pictures and the words).

Then, add something to the small start. Children are often the best reader advisory service to each other. If you provide another short time following SSR when you invite several readers to share an inter-esting part of the book they are reading, other children will want to have that book next. Let the "community of readers" work for you (Hepler & Hickman, 1982). Or you might add a changing classroom display of books so that when readers finish a book, they can go right over to the reading corner and browse for a new book.

Another small start is to agree to read aloud to children each day. Kimmel and Segel (1983) give actual reading-aloud times for a number of titles in *For Reading Out Loud*. Decide how much time you can devote per day to the title you select. Suppose you read Mary Norton's *The Borrowers* to a fourth grade class. The reading time is approxi-mately 3 hours, which you could spread out over three weeks of fifteen-minute sessions. If you added some discussion about who is more afraid of whom, the Boy or the miniature Borrowers, or made a list of the many everyday items that the Borrowers put to interesting use, you could add another hour. Then, you might add a kind of celebration of the book at the end when your class could choose to make a museum of artifacts important to the story, create a room used by Borrowers, or write the newspaper article reporting the alleged sighting of miniature people (Hepler, 1987). In this way, you would have introduced them to a wonderful book and you would have given them reason to go back to the book once again as they worked on their projects.

Where Are You Heading?

Charlotte Huck has often spelled out the purposes of the elementary school literature program as helping children: discover delight in books; interpret literature; develop literary awareness; and develop appreciation (Huck, Hepler, & Hickman, pp. 630–633). Needless to say, the foundation upon which these four rest is the first one: discovering delight. In addition, Huck has outlined the five components of a fully developed literature program as time for reading aloud each day, provision for wide reading (an SSR or DEAR time), in-depth or sustained discussion of books or poetry, provision for many types of response to books, and literature as central to all parts of the curriculum (Huck, 1977). If teachers wish to "get this all in," they need some careful initial planning so that what is begun in September can be built upon all year and "raked up" in the spring.

Foundations and Springboards

Sustained Silent Reading

I described above a modest start on an SSR time. Suppose you added to that a record keeping system that children above third grade might keep, a monthly list on 6×8 cards of "Books I have read this month." Then you could see at a glance a child's preferences for genre or author, whether the child is having trouble finding satisfactory books to read, or across-the-class reading patterns. One teacher used these cards for a monthly chat with each reader. As the year progressed, she asked questions such as "I see you have read three books by Betsy Byars. How are they alike?" Or she called three readers who had read many "animal stories" to her table to talk about "patterns in animal stories." She also let children use their cards to advise each other. Student readers value evidence of their own progress, and while we adults recognize that quantity of books read may not compete with quality, a child likes to see that "I only read five books in October but in December, I read seven." You can see that what you have set up, then, can have multiple uses as the year progresses. The time it takes to talk with or advise individual students can be taken from the twenty-minute SSR time you set up in September.

Reading Aloud

Let's take the same approach with reading aloud. In the best of all possible worlds, you could read many books aloud given twenty-five minutes each day of unfettered time. Classroom realities, fragmented time slots, and other demands, however, often make it difficult to any but the most committed teacher to read more than eight or ten novels. Primary teachers fare a little better because picture books fit into so many small timeslots, and it is not uncommon for a first grade teacher to read ten to twenty books aloud in a week. So, given the limitations of eight novels, or about one per month, what are you going to consider?

There are many reasons for choosing a particular book to read aloud. Speare's *The Sign of the Beaver* might introduce your sixth grade's study of historical New England; Fleischman's ''Prince-and-the-Pauper'' funny fantasy, *The Whipping Boy,* would make even the most jaded fifth grade group sit up and listen; and Thomas's *The Comeback Dog* is a beautiful but short book you could finish with your third and fourth graders before vacation begins! Notice, though, that the teacher has made very specific choices and has not wasted those four or five classroom hours on mediocre literature. Children may want you to read aloud the books they love and at the primary level, where you may read three or four books a day, certainly one ''scratch and sniff'' or grocery store book read by you will not hurt. Since you are building a literature program with what you choose to put in the classroom, however, it makes good sense to use some care in choosing what you will spend your and their time with.

What to choose and why? Start with what you think children will enjoy. If it is Curious George, Paddington Bear, and Ramona, you will have reinforced some children's idea of the joy that literature holds while you introduce a new friend to other readers. If science fiction has your group in its grip, *My Robot Buddy* by Slote would win friends for this popular author among fourth graders; Daniel Pinkwater's silly titles would do the same for fifth and sixth graders. Consider balance during the course of the year. If your class loves *The Borrowers*, resist the urge to read the next one in the series and move along, perhaps to another genre. Or move around in fantasy and read L'Engle's *A Wrinkle in Time* or Cooper's stirring *The Dark is Rising*.

Some teachers introduce an author study by reading aloud several titles by that author. For instance, Jane Yolen's *Piggins* and its sequel, *Picnic With Piggins*, are funny Victorian mysteries set in the elegant mansion of the Fox family. Her signature word play and tongue-in-cheek humorous tellings win immediate second grade fans. A teacher might read these aloud to introduce a thematic unit on the books of Jane Yolen.

A fifth grade teacher planning a study of life on the American prairie might begin by reading aloud Turner's quiet picture book, *Dakota Dugout*. The poetic text is full of inference and would help children feel the loneliness, excitement, and distance yet nearness in time of our pioneer ancestors. This, in turn, would set a mood for an in-depth reading of Patricia MacLachlan's *Sarah, Plain and Tall*. (See below for more on thematic units).

Obviously, it is helpful to have a loosely planned list of possibilities for reading aloud to a specific grade, but this may change as you become more familiar with your class. What worked wonderfully last year may fall flat this year. It is usually not helpful to assign certain titles to be read each year at a particular grade level. Not only does this practice insure boredom in teaching the same titles over and over; it encourages the use of a canned curriculum, worksheets, and projects that repeat yearly. Then, good ideas become so encrusted with age that all the life is drained out of what was once fresh and exciting.

In-Depth Discussion

Thus far, I have mentioned informal discussions teachers may have with the whole class following SSR, and focused discussions teachers may have with small groups of students. But what about planning sustained discussions over time? Many teachers starting out have no trouble with finding books to read aloud but falter over what to emphasize and how to lead children to greater depth of understanding.

There are many guides currently on the market that help teachers develop questions and activities to help children reexamine books. Teachers will have to weigh the merits of each guide's format, tacit assumptions about what a reading program should be, and classroom usability.

Figure 20-1.
A new classic, *Sarah, Plain and Tall*.

For instance, compare three guides for *Sarah, Plain and Tall*. The first, by Barbara Chatton, is two pages long, has seventeen questions emphasizing inferential thinking, personal but substantiated opinions, and the craft of the author. Six activities reflect on the book's content. The second, by Sonia Landes and Molly Flender, (1987) is a forty-seven page guide for this fifty-eight page book. Four sections encompass an introduction of the book, chapter-by-chapter questions and activities, worksheets to be duplicated, and follow-up activities. Emphasis is on character, style, structure, theme and setting, and children are led to a close reading of the text. The third is "A Web of Possibilities" (Hickman & Huck, 1987), which sets *Sarah, Plain and Tall* in the context of a thematic unit. Questions and activities moving children into the book and out into the world are grouped by idea or theme. Many other titles are suggested for further reading either about prairie life or by this author. Each of these three guides may be useful to a fourth or fifth grade teacher. But, all imply different things about individual and whole group work, a book seen as a literary work and as part of the curriculum, the amount of time spent on this title, and the teacher's role in fostering student response.

There are guides that support the primary teacher as well. Here are two for Arnold Lobel's *Frog and Toad Are Friends*. The four-page one from Sundance's (1984) "Alert" series presents five generic questions about main characters, setting, problems, and solutions. Two duplicatable pages feature a cloze ("fill in the blanks") test, a retitling exercise, suggestions for letters, model homes, and writings about friendship or sleeping. Doris Roettger's (1987) thirty-two page guide for the same book presents an exhaustive exploration of this book: author information, pre- and postreading questions, vocabulary words, bulletin-board ideas, cut-out puppet templates, numerous art, drama, writing and research activities, learning centers, and a partial bibliography.

Once again, teachers need to evaluate these guides according to their own needs. Do you want to spend several weeks on a "Frog and Toad" story with first graders? Do you want to quiz them on "facts" from the book? Is it helpful to put isolated vocabulary words up front before you have read them in context? Most guide makers would state that their guides simply suggest some ideas to get you started. Perhaps it is most helpful for schools to have a variety of guides to encourage staff to begin. However, it is wise to avoid the trap of overkill by using these guides judiciously and buying into no single series exclusively.

Eventually, teachers who understand childrens' preferences and typical responses to books, who have a sense of higher level thinking skills and the activities that bring those about, and who understand something about children's literature will want to develop their own guides. (For some suggestions based on Hoban's *Bread and Jam for Frances*, see Hepler (1988).

Thematic Units, or Literature Across the Curriculum

One of the most exciting ways to teach is to begin with a large idea and then plan ways children, books, ideas, and activities may interact. I have already suggested above such thematic units as a study of prairie life, author, or genre studies. Our elementary school curriculum is full of these larger ideas — the how, why, and what of state history; living together cooperatively; minorities; life in other lands; ecology; the industrial process; traditional literature; seasons; and on and on. It is easy enough for a district to take one of these topics, begin to loosen it up, and enrich it with literature. Often teachers at a particular grade level can plan a unit together. Starting, for instance, with Spring Weather, one group of primary teachers developed a list of concepts they hoped children would grasp. At the same time, they used existing bibliographies (found in the "Subject Guide to Children's Books in Print," and in this case a WEB called Spring Weather). They added books and ideas to categories such as Storm Coming; Cloudy Skies; Windy Weather; Becoming a Weather Expert; Celebrating Spring. The categories emerged from the books they knew or found.

Joy Moss (1984) in *Focus Units in Literature: A Handbook for Elementary School Teachers* presents thirteen such units in a helpful narrative format. She shows how teachers began such thematic studies as The Sea, Japan, Dragons, or Folktale Patterns. Each narrative also has objectives, annotated titles, actual children engaged in real discussion and project work, and a sense of how teachers evaluated children's work. Another helpful book for teachers seeking jumping-off points is Mildred Laughlin's (1986) *Developing Learning Skills through Children's Literature.* She and co-author Letty S. Watt develop more than sixty units from author studies of Pat Hutchins, Mercer Mayer, Leo Lionni, Betsy Byars, or Myra Cohn Livingston to themes such as Clever Cats, Friendship, and Sensory Exploration. These, too, proceed from a specific title with suggestions for activities and discussion to a general list of ideas. Both books imply that students are working as a whole group but also in small group or individual projects related to the overarching topic. While it makes some teachers nervous to have five small group projects humming along in the same classroom, students can learn to work cooperatively and quietly if given practice in ever-increasing doses. Remember that what you build in the fall pays dividends for the rest of the year.

These purposeful plans for thematic teaching are one kind of literature across the curriculum, but there is another as well. It is the incidental book that informs something else going on in the classroom. Suppose the second grade has just hit big numbers in the math text. Then, it is a natural to share Steven Kellogg's *How Much is a Million?* Of course, if the group previously studied ''Steven Kellogg's Characters Come to Life'' (Laughlin and Watt, 1986), they would be delighted to recognize this author/illustrator again. The science teacher trying to train sixth graders to be close observers begins by reading aloud from John Moffitt's poem, ''To Look at Any Thing.'' Or perhaps the art teacher shows marbleized paper examples from two Grimm folktales illustrated by Nonny Hogrogian before letting children try the craft.

Obviously literature experiences of this sort need to be planned for. Unless teachers of all subjects talk to each other, seek the advice of the children's librarians at the school or public library, and enlist the aid of children in relating books to each other and to topic areas, many opportunities for rich and integrated learning can be lost.

Summary: Getting It All Together

How does a year look when you have a full-blown literature program? The answer is, of course, it depends. You would have set aside time for reading aloud, SSR, and group work, whether reading with you, working independently, or working in small purposeful groups. You would have decided on an author or two to study and a thematic unit or two to develop in concert with another teacher. You would have in place some form of record keeping that would include what children have read, heard read, and have made in response to books. And you would have a repertoire of experiences you would wish children to have — delight in rhyme and repetition of Mother Goose and discovery of the cumulative pattern in folktales for the kindergarteners, or appreciation of figurative language both in poetry and in the books of Byars for fifth graders.

Your classroom would show that children love books. There would be a reading corner, displays of books currently being worked with, perhaps a chart of books read aloud so far this year with stars by the ones most favored by the class, and bulletin boards not of canned and preprinted posters but of children's work. Of course, there would be no book report forms. Instead, writing in many modes — explanations, first-person accounts, letters, "next chapters", poetry — as well as a variety of projects would reflect the teacher's understanding of how to help children organize their literary experiences.

Most importantly, children would be brimming with enthusiasm to tell visitors to the classroom or each other about the books they are enjoying and what they are discovering. Their ability to discuss what they read would be expanding with practice so that literary terms and patterns would be an easy part of their vocabulary. They would know and love some authors and illustrators. And they would see themselves as readers. So would you.

References

Bennett, J. (1985). *Learning to read with picture books.* (3rd ed.). South Woodchester, Stroud, Glos., Great Britain: The Thimble Press.

Burchby, M. (1988). Literature and whole language. *The New Advocate, 1,* 114–123.

Cascardi, A. (1985). *Good books to grow on.* New York: Warner Books.

Chatton, B. (1987). Teacher's guide to *Sarah, Plain and Tall.* Hartford: H.P. Koppelmann, Inc.

Hancock, J., & Hill, S. (1988). *Literature-based reading programs at work.* Portsmouth, NH: Heinemann.

Henke, L. (1988). Beyond basal reading: A district's commitment to change. *The New Advocate, 1,* 42–51.

Hepler, S. (1988). A guide for the teacher guides: Doing it yourself. *The New Advocate, 1,* 186–195.

Hepler, S. (1987). Teacher's guide to *The Borrowers.* Hartford: H.P. Koppelmann, Inc.

Hepler, S., & Hickman, J. (1982). "The book was okay. I love you" — Social aspects of response to literature. *Theory Into Practice, 21,* 278–283.

Hickman, J., & Huck, C.S. (Eds.). (1983). Spring weather web. *The WEB, 7,* Spring.

Hickman, J., & Huck, C.S. (Eds.). (1987). *Sarah, Plain and Tall* web. *The WEB, 11,* Winter.

Huck, C.S. (1977). Literature as the content of reading. *Theory Into Practice, 16,* 363–371.

Kimmel, M.M., & Segel, E. (1983). *For reading out loud! A guide to sharing books with children.* New York: Delacorte.

Landes, S., & Flender, M. (1987). *A book wise curriculum guide to Sarah, Plain and Tall*. Cambridge, MA: Book Wise, Inc.

Laughlin, M., & Watt, L.S. (1986). *Developing learning skills through children's literature: An idea book for K–5 classrooms and libraries*. Phoenix, AZ: The Oryx Press.

Moss, J. (1984). *Focus units in literature: A handbook for elementary school teachers*. Urbana, IL: National Council of Teachers of English.

Roettger, D. (1987). *Reading beyond the basal: Guide for Frog and Toad Are Friends*. Logan, IA: The Perfection Form Company.

Sundance Publishers. (1984). *Teacher's Guide for Frog and Toad Are Friends*. Littleton, MA: Sundance Publishers.

Trelease, J. (1985). *The read-aloud handbook*. (Rev. ed.). New York: Penguin.

Waterland, L. (1985). *Read with me: An apprenticeship approach to reading*. South Woodchester, Stroud, Glos., Great Britain: The Thimble Press.

21

Administrative

Support for Literature-

Based Reading Programs

Steven R. DeLapp

A great deal of attention is focused on whole language and literature-based programs, and, as is the case with any curricular change, administrators will play a critical role in determining their overall success. This chapter explores the attitudes and knowledge base to guide administrators in developing literature-based programs and focuses on the support they need to provide teachers to work effectively in implementing them.

Some Guiding Principles

Educational programs that place literacy experiences at the heart of the learning process are guided by two enduring curricular values: a deep-rooted respect for each child as a unique learner; and a strong commitment to the role of the teacher as a curriculum decision maker. The educational policies, guidelines, and curriculum materials in our schools are mediated through this dual commitment to child as learner and teacher as a professional decision maker. This means, in a practical sense, that children are permitted to learn in different ways and teachers are encouraged to teach in different ways.

Several assumptions about curricular change underlie a whole language perspective. Administrators who work effectively with literature-based programs accept them willingly. The first assumption is that educational goals are formed as well as executed within the educative process. Education itself is a process of discovering which values are worthwhile and ought to be pursued. Curriculum planning, therefore, is perceived as a joint effort between teacher and child, one that cultivates shared responsibility for nurturing learning.

A second assumption is that those who face the complex, interactive, and highly unpredictable events of classroom life, namely teachers, have a leadership role in designing educational programs. What works for one teacher may not work for another; therefore, teachers cannot be passive recipients of someone else's curricular ideas. Instead they make thoughtful and informed decisions about curriculum when they collect information to indicate changes are needed and assume a role in designing appropriate actions.

A third assumption about curricular change is that a literacy curriculum is an ongoing process to be reviewed and revised regularly. Curriculum itself is viewed as a changing and growing set of possibilities rather than a fixed set of required outcomes.

Although the characteristics of a literature-based program may vary from school to school, there are essential features that administrators need to understand if they are to support teacher growth in this curricular area. These features include the following:

1. *Children are read to on a daily basis.* The read aloud program incorporates variety in the literature shared — poetry, picture books, informational books, fantasy, folktales, historical fiction, realistic fiction, biography and the like. The read aloud experience is not limited to once a day. Teachers share a variety of books for a range of purposes throughout a school day.

2. *Children have time to read books of their own choosing.* The amount of time can be increased as the year progresses and children demonstrate they can sustain interest for longer periods of time. During this quiet reading time, teachers can read books themselves or hold conferences with individual children about the books they are reading.

3. *Children discuss and reflect upon the books they read.* Discussion occurs in large groups (e.g., from books read aloud), in small groups that are teacher planned or child initiated, and in teacher-child conferences. Children reflect upon their reading in dialogue journals with the teacher or in more personal reflective record keeping.

4. *Children respond to books through writing, art, drama, music, and talk.* The major function of book response is to make certain books memorable for children and to deepen their experiences with literature.

5. *Children write on topics of their own choosing.* Teachers welcome individual responses during writing time in topic choice, style, length of work, form, and purpose. They encourage children to do a lot of writing, some of which they may not even read. Writing grows out of real interests and experiences that the children have within and outside of school. Much of their writing grows from their reading, so the literature program has a profound effect on children's selection of topics and styles in writing.

6. *Children share their reading, writing, and art products with the entire class.* These sharing experiences provide opportunities for delighting in a child's efforts and the opportunity to think critically and reflectively about one's efforts. Teacher comments and peer comments are an important component of deepening a child's understanding of his or her work efforts.

7. *Children use a variety of good books as an essential part of any theme or unit of study.* Some themes may be directly related to literature (e.g., African folktales or books by Ezra Jack Keats). Other themes incorporate books to deepen children's learning, but the books themselves are not the focus in the unit of study. In either case, literary experiences are a very important dimension in curriculum planning.

8. *The daily schedule is flexible.* Both the amount of time and curricular focus vary. This flexibility makes it possible for children to sustain themselves with reading, writing, and exploring thematic experiences. Having the time to pursue an interest in depth is a critical feature of the literature, language arts environment.

Ongoing Learning for Teachers

Administrators of elementary schools with literature-based reading programs have a unique opportunity to become vital partners in the ongoing learning with teachers, children, and parents. In order to fulfill this role successfully, they need knowledge in several areas. The first of these is knowledge of reading and language learning itself; the second is knowledge of the practical dimensions of school administration that often present roadblocks to innovation; and the third is knowledge of the people with whom they are working — teachers, parents, and children.

Teachers, like any other group of people, will be at different stages in their own learning and understanding of literature at any given time. It is critical for the administrator to be aware of this and not expect that the entire school must move toward a specific program at the same time. To attempt a consistent program schoolwide does little more than achieve uniform mediocrity. Rather, the administrator must be willing to allow teachers to do as much as they are able to do. For some, this will mean prompt development of an outstanding program; for others, it may mean watching from the sidelines for a year and then beginning to integrate more literature into whatever approach they have used in the past.

In any event, opportunities must be given for all teachers to extend their knowledge of children's literature and language learning and to apply in a practical way such theories in the classroom. Often, colleagues provide much of the needed support. Other more traditional possibilities include university courses and in-service sessions.

The attitudes administrators hold about teachers and themselves as professionals and learners are critical in this process. Literature-based programs work when teachers are empowered to make curricular decisions for their own classrooms. One of the difficulties in making the transition to literature-based teaching is that there are

no specific formulas and guides to follow. There are general characteristics of literacy environments, but packaged programs designed
to get us there are viewed with skepticism. On the other hand,
teachers explore a variety of teaching practices as they work to extend
their knowledge of literature-based programs. For example, movement toward a literature-based program may initially involve asking
teachers to become more thoughtful and committed to the decisions
they make about what is worth reading aloud to children. Exposing
children to a range of genres is seen as critical. There emerges a growing recognition that poetry and picture books need attention
throughout the elementary years.

Teachers moving toward literature-based programs are committed
to creating multiple and varied response opportunities for literary
experiences. These include experiences such as discussion and story
telling, visual and model displays, writing, drama and puppet plays,
and comparison charts. The possibilities grow as teachers become
more knowledgeable about books, the art in books, and how connections between books build literary understandings for children.

Teachers who use literature as the heart of their programs search
for ways to support children's own choices as independent readers.
They do this through teacher-child conferences, response journals and
in-depth book discussion groups. They keep track of what children
read as they plan and develop record-keeping strategies. They also
help children make satisfying appropriate choices in regard to interests, levels of difficulty, and genre.

Teachers using literature-based programs look for ways to use
literary experiences to support themes and to integrate books with
all curriculum areas. Knowledge of books is essential to good unit planning and for some teachers is seen as the starting point. Science
themes call for informational books as well as poetry and fiction.
Social studies themes incorporate a wide selection of historical fiction and folk literature. Many classroom themes have literature itself
at the center of study; for example, author studies, folktale or fantasy units, or myths and legend studies.

Administrative support for teachers, as they move in any of these
curricular areas, is a personalized process. The administrator's
awareness of the specific strengths and needs of each teacher is
gathered from classroom observations and teacher conferences. It is
dependent, too, upon a collegial and collaborative relationship
between the administrator and the teacher so that discussions of

growth areas can be explored honestly by each individual. For some teachers, the support may initially focus on the overall read aloud program. Is there a range of literature shared? Are children encouraged to reflect upon the stories read aloud and make connections with other literary experiences? Are children encouraged to consider character development, narrative styles, and language itself as they respond to books shared aloud?

For other teachers, instructional input may focus on the kinds of strategies teachers use to support individual readers. For example, what books do teachers choose for children that assist and support the child-initiated efforts? Are children reading material of appropriate levels of difficulty? What strategies are teachers using to build reading independence in children? How often is the teacher able to work individually with each child in the room?

The overarching point is critical: good supervisory support recognizes that the teachers have *different* needs and strengths. Growth occurs when our feedback to teachers is sensitive to these differences. We respond to the knowledge base and understandings each teacher brings to the teaching/learning environment rather than expecting teachers to have the same professional growth needs.

Helping Parents Understand the Program

Successful administrators are also aware of the expectations that parents have regarding the school reading and language program. They commmunicate clearly the theory undergirding the program and respond to the concerns of parents. To do these things effectively, administrators must have a solid, if not extensive, understanding of the research into children's language learning. In addition, administrators must understand the reading process and be familiar with many of the children's books used in the classrooms. This may require additional inservice or university work for the administrator along with teachers. Difficult or time consuming as this might seem to be, it is critical to the effective administration of a school with a literature-based program.

A frequent question asked by parents who have children in a literature-based program is whether or not teachers use the "phonics method" for teaching beginning reading. The question is reflective of how important language knowledge is for the administrator if teachers are to have the support they need to continue using litera-ture. The response to this question might be phrased: No, we do not use an isolated phonics method. The methods we use are designed to assist readers in developing a variety of strategies in an integrated way. Phonics is one of these strategies and it is an important one. Kindergarten and first grade teachers help children build an under-standing of letter-sound relationships but never to the point where this strategy is overemphasized to the exclusion of others.

Phonics, despite much of the popular literature, is not a method of learning to read. On the contrary, it needs to be viewed by parents, teachers, and administrators as one of several strategies readers use as they begin to unlock meaning in words. Phonetic knowledge means being able to use cues from letter-sound relationships to figure out words. Used by itself, it is a cumbersome and inefficient way to read. When it is integrated with other strategies, it becomes an important and essential tool for developing real skill in reading.

Debates have raged in this country since the 1950's concerning the "phonics" method versus "sight word" or some other method. Published materials for teachers frequently swing back and forth between these varying perspectives. The problem with these peren-nial shifts is that the debate has been an inappropriate one; in fact, the debate itself has been a major reason for much of the confusion that still exists about the role of phonics in education. From reading and language research in the 1970's and 1980's, we recognize clearly that young readers need support in using and integrating a variety of strategies to get at meaning. Phonics is only one of these strategies, although it is an important one. It is a tool that needs to be developed alongside others — predicting on the basis of meaning, predicting on the basis of sentence structure, and knowing a basic sight vocabulary.

Perspectives on phonics instruction and the role of phonics in the literature-based reading program is only one example of how the administrator's understanding of the reading process becomes a critical component in building parent and teacher support for the overall literature curriculum. Administrators communicate this knowledge through parent newsletters, open houses, individual parent conferences, and through parent education meetings. Given the conventional assumptions that guide most parent thinking about reading and writing instruction, this role is essential if literature-based programs are to be successful ones.

Overcoming Obstacles

Anytime we undertake a new venture we encounter roadblocks. Evaluation perspectives (e.g., testing and report cards) and materials and budget considerations each present potential difficulties for a school engaged in movement toward an integrated, literature-based program. School administrators are the key individuals in helping teachers progress beyond these practical constraints. They need to know how to reallocate money budgeted for workbooks to spend on real books for reading. Furthermore, they must use their knowledge of the parts of a quality literature program to ensure that available monies are spent effectively. They understand the need for multiple copies of a variety of books — not enough for the entire fourth grade to read the same book simultaneously but enough for a small group to read and discuss a book in depth. They recognize the need for a wide range of books to be available at all reading levels — historical fiction, fantasy, realistic fiction, poetry, and informational books. They also know that the emergent readers in the youngest classes require books especially designed for children at this stage, allowing them to develop the strategies they need to move into fluency and the reading of quality children's literature.

Administrators also need to work with teachers in developing evaluation instruments that reflect the kinds of reading skills that are valued in a literature-based program, in contrast to the inordinate amount of attention typically given to decoding skills. A primary level report card that evaluates the following reading skills is making an important statement to parents and children concerning the major goals of the reading program:

- Enjoys and responds to literature
- Selects appropriate reading materials
- Uses a variety of reading strategies
- Comprehends a variety of fiction and informational texts
- Makes good use of reading time

A major roadblock for implementing literature-based reading programs continues to revolve around the ways we use and misuse standardized reading tests. Administrators need a thorough understanding of the limits of reading tests so that parents and teachers are able to put these evaluation tools into perspective. Norm-referenced tests can be particularly troublesome for us in a society that deifies numbers as the primary way to measure learning. Although norm-referenced test scores can give us comparative rankings of children as readers for one particular test, they tell us nothing about how a child ought to have performed, nor do they tell us what a specific child knows or does not know about reading. Administrators play a key role in communicating to parents and teachers the kinds of evaluation strategies that help us understand children's growth as readers and the role that standardized assessment can play in this process. What needs to be reinforced continually with parents is the important role teacher observation plays in understanding the reading strategies a child employs, the kinds of books he or she selects, and the levels of understanding that are brought to the literary experience. These teacher insights can typically get lost in our preoccupation with measuring the parts of the reading act.

Summary

Amidst the conflicting forces in our society that contribute to both a technological and skills oriented view of reading and reading assessment, it is essential for administrators to hold on to a view of reading that focuses on how children learn and what literature can do for children in this process. Children should be helped to learn to read using the initial skills and processes that they find most effective. They should also be allowed to experience and appreciate the significance and functions of reading, and to read with enjoyment and fluency appropriate to their stage of development. Finally, children should be given opportunities to experience the full range of what literature has to offer us as human beings. Support for literature-based reading programs is ultimately built upon administrators, teachers, and parents working together to these ends so that all children can experience the power of literacy learning in their lives.

22

Librarians and Teachers

Working Together

Diane Driessen

After I had taught kindergarten, first and second grades, and been both a school librarian (K–12) and a children's librarian in a public library, I had seen children interacting with books in a variety of ways. This experience, in a dozen schools and three states, helped me build my own theories about children, reading, books, and literature. Unfortunately, my observations did not match what I had been taught in college or what I was seeing practiced in the schools.

At that point I heard Charlotte Huck speak at a workshop in Ohio. She talked about the importance of reading real books. She advocated reading aloud, reading widely, reading across the curriculum, and providing time for children to read, discuss, and respond to literature.

I studied with her and felt liberated in finding the theories, research, and practice that made sense with what I had observed. I have applied these concepts to my work and to my approach to librarianship.

Creating an Inviting Atmosphere

At this writing, I am a librarian in a school with grades kindergarten through five. When I took the position one of my goals was to create a library with a warm, inviting atmosphere. We moved shelving and furniture to create cozy places to read and added beanbag chairs and floor pillows to provide comfort. This type of portable seating is inexpensive, flexible, and well-used by the students. At the end of the day I like to see where the pillows are left because it shows the pattern of children reading alone, in pairs, or in groups.

Children's work adds a great deal of cheerfulness so I decorate the library with it. The displays include work done both in the classrooms and library. For example, this year two- and three-dimensional folktale projects, Jackdaws, weather instruments, and Indian villages have been displayed.

Activities initiated in the library include both whole group and small group extensions. For example, after hearing and discussing *Old Henry* by Joan Blos, third and fourth grade students wrote letters to Henry. A smaller group met for a week each afternoon to paint, mount, and organize the display. First and second grade students heard and discussed Eve Bunting's *Ghost's Hour, Spook's Hour* as a class. Then in groups of five they came to the library to hear the story again and discuss it in depth before writing about their own frightening experiences. They illustrated their stories in their classrooms. The final projects were mounted and displayed on bulletin board paper attached to the wall in the library. A group of fifth grade students from two different classrooms met with me to read L'Engle's *A Wrinkle in Time*. One of their extensions was to create and write about a favorite character. These creations were mounted and displayed as a collection. A three-dimensional model Calvin O'Keefe sat on top of a fiction bookshelf for weeks.

Some of our activities have reflected more general themes. After winter break I spent time with several classes reading poetry about the new year. This lead to a discussion about resolutions and the children writing "I resolve to . . ." Their resolutions were mounted collage-fashion and placed in the hallway. I would see children and adults reading our "graffiti" wall. Other displays were a result of preparation for a major event — the school's visit from author Jane Yolen. The children made drawings with markers of their favorite Yolen characters; then these were cut out and displayed. Some were mounted as a collage and hung in the hallway with the caption "Do You Know These Jane Yolen Characters?" Of course, many stopped to name them. I had inquiries when a character was not recognized, and then I was able to introduce a book new to that student. Another display was done by placing similar characters together. Portraits of Piggins, the proper butler, made an attractive display.

Children are interested in seeing their work and their friends' work. One addition to the student work this year was a collection of teachers' poetry and chalk drawings. The children thought it was great to see their teachers' work, too.

Plants and commercial posters advertising books and authors are also placed around the library. The book posters entice children to ask for the book. One popular poster shows photographs of the authors published by one publisher. The children love talking about how the authors' looks meet (or do not meet!) their expectations. The Caldecott and Newbery posters provide an opportunity for the children to talk about the books they have read and lead them to new ones.

Maintaining a Flexible Schedule

In addition to making the library physically attractive, I have a goal of wanting children to be welcome in the library at all times, not just with regularly scheduled classes. I believe that students and staff should have ready access to the library and its resources. I invite students to come to the library whenever their teacher says it is all right. The children like to do sustained silent reading in the library as well as preview audiovisual materials. At one point this year several third grade girls spent their free time watching videos of the *Just-So-Stories*. The library is always open. At times, every inch of space is used while I am conducting a scheduled class. This calls for cooperation and flexibility by everyone involved.

In order to move in the direction of a better use of my time and the library's resources, our staff changed the library schedule from every class meeting weekly to biweekly. Instead of seeing twenty-six classes weekly, I see thirteen. The classes are scheduled before one o'clock so that I am able to meet with students, staff, and parents on a flexible basis during the afternoon. This also gives me time to do library-related chores.

Since I believe that a library needs to be available to everyone who has a need for its resources, I am a proponent of flexible scheduling. "Library" should not be treated as a separate subject. Its use should be integrated into the curriculum. To do this it is necessary for the librarian and teachers to plan together. This could mean that the librarian would work with students every day for several weeks or introduce and bring to closure a study in a single session. Experiences with children are planned according to need. Some of these experiences may include producing learning materials, such as posters, slides, filmstrips, videos, puppets, and dioramas. Also, working with reference material is important. An introduction to using *The Reader's Guide to Periodic Literature* needs to be done when students are doing research and followed by a trip to the public library to put into practice the skill learned and to retrieve articles of use to them. Other library related topics, such as the card catalog, Dewey Decimal System, indexes, encyclopedias, and almanacs are taught in context. The traditional practice of scheduling a library time weekly or biweekly could be eliminated with completely flexible scheduling. This would allow more time for the librarian to help individual students with book selection. When an entire class comes to the library at the same time, it is difficult to help everyone in the allotted time.

I envision the school librarian planning programs in ways similar to those planned in public libraries. The school library could also be the site for storytimes, puppet shows, and speakers. Of course, the librarian needs time to plan such diverse experiences in addition to routine library duties. Collection development, weeding, ordering, vertical, picture, and author files are all important aspects of a librarian's job.

Working with Teachers

An important part of the school librarian's job is working with teachers, not only to plan for curricular needs but also to provide staff development opportunities. Most of all, teachers want to know and see new books. During my first year at Windermere School, we had monthly "Literature and Lunch" programs in which I planned a variety of experiences, such as book talking, showing films and videos, and providing speakers. We viewed and discussed the film "What's a Good Book?" (Weston Woods Studios) and several of Caroline Feller Bauer's videos. Kathy East, the Children's Services Coordinator at the Public Library of Columbus and Franklin County, who was on the 1986 Caldecott Committee, brought possible winners for us to examine and allowed us to keep the books for a week so that children had a chance to respond to them. One of the books I read to several classes was *Hey, Al* by Arthur Yorinks and Richard Egielski. The children felt smug when the 1987 Caldecott was announced several months later. We already knew it was a good book. An exciting extension of the "Literature and Lunch" program was a weekend trip to see the Dr. Seuss exhibit at the Carnegie Museum in Pittsburgh.

A good way for teachers to become familiar with authors and new books is by reading *The Horn Book, Booklist,* or *School Library Journal.* I ask them to initial the reviews of the books they would like ordered. Teachers also like to see the new books that come into the library. Keeping these books on display for several days before allowing them to circulate gives more teachers (and children) a chance to see what's new. Also, having an afterschool new book party with refreshments is a way to show off new acquisitions.

Another way a librarian can help teachers is by locating materials for them. Teachers will often inform me about classroom units of study so that I can gather the pertinent materials from our collection. I frequently call public librarians in the area to ask their help in filling teachers' requests. This also assists the public librarians in letting them know which materials will be popular in the coming weeks.

Librarians can also help teachers plan for special events, such as author visits. The four elementary librarians in our system planned a Jane Yolen workshop for teachers when we learned that she would visit our schools. We arranged for two consultants who spoke about Jane Yolen's work during an in service day. Not only was this an enjoyable day, but it provided opportunities for teachers from different buildings to interact, to become familiar with Yolen and her work, and to begin planning experiences for their students.

Author visits are annual events, and we have learned that teacher input is important during the planning. One year we asked students to make banners to hang from the ceiling of the multipurpose room. This year, because Jane Yolen visited in February, we used a heart theme, "Getting to the Heart of Jane Yolen," and children made heart-shaped posters. To help us become familiar with Jane Yolen's books as we prepared for her visit, I borrowed hundreds of her books from the Columbus Public Schools and the Public Library of Columbus and Franklin County. The librarians who made arrangements for the book loans were so cooperative we invited them to meet and have lunch with the author.

Literature is an important focus at our school. Many teachers in the past few years had expressed an interest in learning more about using it in their classrooms. When my principal asked who would be the best person to teach such a course for the staff, I naturally recommended Charlotte Huck. We were fortunate that arrangements could be made for Charlotte to teach a weekly class called Using Literature in the Classroom during a ten-week term. As always, Charlotte planned an exciting course that was extremely practical. On the last night, we had a walkabout in which we went from classroom to classroom to see children's work displayed and hear how the work was accomplished. Charlotte reminded us that when she goes into a classroom, she always asks the question, "What is valued in this room?" We were able to see that our colleagues valued literature that evening.

Fostering Cooperative Relationships

I believe it is important to make friends with area public and school librarians in order to encourage cooperation. The school librarians in our district meet with area public librarians to discuss how we can help each other. In addition, one teacher at our school has a partnership with the area public library. The children visit the public library on a regular basis and create book extensions to display there.

Friendships with other people in the community can also be helpful. Two graduate students in the School Library Media Program at The Ohio State University used Windermere School as their project one winter term. They developed a floor plan for integrating the collection. I have also worked with a student intern from The Ohio State University who needed practical school library experience. These cooperative efforts benefit all involved.

Parents are also good resources. At our school they volunteer in the library to help with daily routines or to do special projects. For instance, a parent working on an advanced degree in journalism wrote press releases to send to the media before our author visit. Another parent in the printing business printed bookmarks as a remembrance of the authors' visits, one year with an original design by visitor Steven Kellogg and another year with the poem Jane Yolen wrote for us.

Our Parent Teacher Organization supports our library program. They sponsor our author visit and provide money for special events. This year, in honor of the 50 years of the Caldecott Award, they purchased a collection of the winning books. These noncirculating books are shelved in a special browsing section. They also purchased a secretary's chair for the circulation desk. In return, the library welcomes members of the community. This year our visiting author planned an evening presentation for the public. In preparation for the event, I conducted an evening "Meet Jane Yolen" program the week before her visit.

Some Personal Goals

I believe that the library should be integrated into all aspects of the curriculum. I also believe that the collection should be integrated within the library, that is material on the same topic should be shelved together regardless of format. This means that all of the information on birds would be found together. A patron would not have to go to one place to look for books, another place for filmstrips, another place for records and still another place for videos. If the library owned a video of Bemelmans' *Madeline*, it would be shelved with the *Madeline* books, records, and cassettes. This type of arrangement makes it easier for patrons to find what they want, gives students access to a variety of formats, and helps match type of material to the student's needs.

I keep library skills in proper perspective since the most important library skill I hope children master is that of enjoying reading. The most important thing that I do to help children toward this goal is to read aloud to them. I read new books by familiar authors, books by new authors, and many by the same author. When possible, I integrate poetry, fiction, and nonfiction, and help the children to see connections between books and authors.

I think it is important for children to borrow books that they choose for themselves. Some books are related to classroom work but I want children to be able to get things they want. Sometimes the ones they select may seem too difficult, too easy, or too familiar. Yet I cannot imagine telling adults that *Scientific American* is too challenging or that *People Magazine* is below their reading level. Similarly I would not say those things to children about their choices. Our collection is large enough so that arbitrary limits do not need to be placed on the number of books that children may borrow. I also hope to be able to allow children to borrow nonprint materials such as filmstrips, records, cassettes and videos as well as books. In addition, I would like to have portable equipment that could be circulated.

Summary

As a school librarian I try to meet the needs of my patrons, both children and adults. Flexibility is the key to providing good library service. If the library is to be the center of the curriculum and not a separate special area, an open door policy and a friendly, relaxed, service-oriented atmosphere is necessary. I have tried to show here that a school librarian is much more than that — an advocate of reading, a guide to experiences with literature, and an important resource for teachers.

23

Enriching Your

Literature Resources

Barbara Peterson

I am somewhat bewildered as I ponder how to write about "enriching your resources." From my perspective, my office would be a useful departure point. Paddington Bear stands at attention next to my printer, gazing in the direction of a motley assortment of bookshelves. The room bulges with books, an accumulation of years of passion as well as of study.

I wish you were here. Then I could find out what you have read, what you have liked, and where you would like to go. I could watch your eyes for a spark of excitement as we rediscover a favorite book. I could note signs of disinterest or boredom as I mentioned another, and perhaps I would try to convince you otherwise. I would ask if the book were for you, for a single child, or for a whole classroom. Are you looking for something to read aloud, or is your interest directed to literature related to curriculum? Our exchange could be lively and the floor covered with books as we pull them off the shelves and spread them around to get a better look. I might even show you my beloved 1932 edition of *A Child's Garden of Verses* by Robert Louis Stevenson, a gift from my grandparents when I was four.

Alas, this scenario is unlikely, and a more practical approach is needed to advise you on how to enrich your resources. The place to begin is with yourself, with what you know and love best. Jot down the titles of your favorite children's books. Next, think about the direction you wish to pursue. There are many ways in which you can extend your knowledge. You have already made important discoveries by reading this book, and you may have rushed to the library to borrow at least one book that has sparked your interest.

Now let us explore three broad areas of recourse — personal networks, professional organizations, and printed materials. All are related, and each will lead you onward. Think of these areas not as specific categories but rather as places to start developing effective strategies for finding out more about good books.

A Community of Readers

Begin with people, your friends and colleagues who read. In a short time you will discover your own personal "community of readers" (Hepler, 1982), people eager to share their knowledge and experiences with children's literature. Talk to teachers, librarians, and students about your interests. Inevitably, the mention of one or two books among friends brings forth a chorus of offerings that will expand your reading repertoire.

As a children's librarian, I know firsthand that one of the greatest joys of the profession is matching people to books. Visit classrooms where children are actively engaged in reading children's literature and extending their understandings through writing, art, and drama. Talk to teachers and ask them to recommend a few books that have been successful with their classes. Invite children to tell you about their favorites. The possibilities are many, and you will quickly find that you are a contributor, too.

Libraries and Bookstores

Where else can you find out more about good children's books? Explore the resources of the many institutions and organizations that feature literature for children. Begin with a public or school library, preferably one alive with children eagerly searching for books and an enthusiastic librarian who is knowledgeable about the library's book collection. There are many strategies for approaching the children's department, and the one you choose at a particular time will depend on your current needs.

Librarians are accustomed to requests from both children and adults who have just finished a wonderful book and want another one "just like it." For example, you notice a dog-eared copy of *My Side of the Mountain* by Jean George making the rounds among your fifth graders, so you decide to read it. Intrigued, you wonder if there are other books about resourceful children who learn to survive away from their parents. Ask the librarian, and do not be surprised if you are presented with an armload of books.

Another approach to expanding your resources is to search the library's card or computer catalog methodically for books on a particular topic. Suppose you want to introduce your class to life in the Middle Ages but find the social studies text sketchy and uninteresting in comparison to the rich heritage of the era. You may have some students with special interests in castle architecture, daily life, or holidays and celebrations. By searching the catalog entries under "Middle Ages" or "Medieval Life" you would find *Castle* by David Macaulay, *The Luttrell Village* by Sheila Sancha and *Medieval Holidays and Festivals* by Madeleine Cosman, as well as many other appropriate titles.

Another strategy for gaining access to children's literature in the library is to browse through shelves of books. This approach is helpful when you want to learn more about a general topic such as poetry or folklore and are not looking for a specific title. Simply check the card catalog for the classification number (most poetry books are in the 811's and folklore in the 398's), find the proper shelf, and begin to read.

In addition to books for children, most libraries maintain separate professional and reference collections of books about children's literature, authors, and illustrators. In response to frequent requests, librarians often compile bibliographies on popular topics such as adventure, mystery, monsters, humorous stories, and sports stories. If you know of a book that ought to be in the library's collection, make your wishes known. Most libraries are eager and willing to respond to patron requests.

Irresistible delights are also available through bookstores that specialize in children's literature or devote attention to developing a children's collection. Chances are your passion for providing children with real books will not be satisfied only by borrowing from libraries. When you find yourself reluctant to return some treasured items to the library because you can not bear to part with them, you know the time has come to start building your own collection. Acquaint yourself with your bookstore's offerings, and if you are unable to find something, ask if you can place a special order.

Professional Associations

By now you have probably discovered many people who share your interest in children's literature and your list of what you have read is probably growing quickly. Your dilemma now is how to incorporate literature into the ongoing activities of your classroom and you need some practical advice. You would love to abandon dull texts and stimulate your students' curiosity by having them delve into good books. You need to enrich your resources within a community of teachers and other educators who are knowledgeable about literature and classroom practices.

Many professional organizations and associations provide resources through workshops, conferences, and publications that can assist you in making connections between literature and classrooms. At the local level, grassroots organizations of teachers interested in literature and whole language have sprung up in many communities. The Literacy Connection, based in Columbus, Ohio, is one example. This group sponsors several programs and workshops each year and publishes a newsletter featuring organizational news, school activities, and children's work.

Formal studies in children's literature can be pursued through college and university courses. Programs that emphasize the child as well as literature will probably meet your needs more than those that focus exclusively on the content of a few books. At many colleges and universities, annual conferences have grown out of the enthusiasm and interests of graduate students and faculty. Such gatherings provide more opportunities for expanding your personal community of readers.

There are also several national organizations concerned with children's literature and classroom and library programs. Many national organizations also have regional and state affiliates, and most sponsor conferences and publish journals and newsletters. Some organizations also have divisions or special interest groups devoted to children and literature for them.

The National Council of Teachers of English (NCTE) and two affiliated assemblies, the Children's Literature Assembly (CLA) and the Assembly on Literature for Adolescents (ALAN), feature programs and workshops on using children's literature in the classroom at NCTE's national conferences. A variety of articles about children's literature and reviews of new books appear in *Language Arts* (NCTE), *The Bulletin* (CLA), and *The ALAN Review* (ALAN). NCTE also produces many other related publication, including *Reading Ladders for Human Relations* (Tway, 1981), *Shadow and Substance: Afro-American Experience in Contemporary Children's Fiction* (Sims, 1982) and *Adventuring With Books: A Booklist for Pre-K–Grade 8* (Monson, 1985).

Children's literature in the classroom reading program is also promoted through publications and conferences of the International Reading Association (IRA). *The Reading Teacher* features a monthly review of new children's books. A recent IRA publication, *Children's Literature in the Reading Program* (Cullinan, 1987) provides inspiration, information about books, and practical suggestions for teaching through literature.

Several other organizations provide publications and services that promote and contribute to knowledge of books for children. The American Library Association (ALA) is probably best known for the sponsorship of the annual Newbery and Caldecott Medal Awards, which honor distinguished writing and illustration in children's literature. *The Journal of Youth Services in Libraries* is a joint publication of two ALA divisions, the Association for Library Service to Children and the Young Adult Services Division. While the articles within do not focus on classrooms, many pertain to children's literature and would be of interest to teachers.

The United States Board on Books for Young People (USBBY), the U.S. section of the International Board on Books for Young People (IBBY), publishes a newsletter that includes articles and reviews covering the international scene in children's literature. The Children's Book Council (CBC), a professional association of children's book publishers, produces a biannual newsletter called *CBC Features* that will keep you advised on how to obtain posters, bookmarks, bibliographies, and such.

Remember to cruise the publishers' exhibits when you attend professional conferences. Publishers' booths are lively places where you can sample and savor and delight in the newest books before you read about them in reviews or see them in libraries or bookstores. To entice you further, authors and illustrators are often available at scheduled times to autograph their books. Best of all, you will enjoy the camaraderie of kindred souls while enriching your resources.

Journals: Reviews, Articles, and Bibliographies

I have already mentioned professional associations as one source of publications related to children's literature. It would also be helpful for you to read from review journals regularly. There are many journals that have the common purpose of exploring books for children. Generally speaking, most journals include both reviews and articles, although each has a distinctive style with a different proportion of reviews and articles. All include publisher information, cost, and age range of the books reviewed. Information about national and international conferences and book awards may also be found.

Some journals are designed to be comprehensive and review all recently published books; others select only works considered significant to the field. Length of the reviews varies also. Some reviews are relatively short and describe only the essential features of the book; others are longer and may include reviewers' explicit opinions. To get you started, I will discuss a few journals most likely to be available from school, public, and university libraries. Many journals have traditionally been written for an audience of public and school librarians. While we all have the ultimate goal of getting children involved with good books, classroom teachers are choreographers of children's reading over the course of a year and consequently have slightly different needs from librarians. First, I will discuss two journals that specifically attend to teachers and classroom settings. Then I will highlight other important sources.

The WEB strives to entangle teachers and children with *W*onderfully *E*xciting *B*ooks, and features extended reviews written in a lively, informal style with an emphasis on children as well as on books. Reviewers often include anecdotes of how a book was used in their class, how children responded, and suggestions for extending book experiences through writing and other activities. Central to each issue of *The WEB* is a real web of possibilities for incorporating literature into the ongoing life of the classroom. A web is a graphic display, somewhat like a map, that presents a network of ideas for linking books and study around a particular theme, a single book, or several works by one author.

Enriching classroom reading is also a primary goal of *The New Advocate*, which brings together the multiple perspectives of writers and artists, teachers, children, school administrators, and researchers. Critical issues related to the content and teaching of reading are explored through a diverse range of articles. Books are reviewed in a regular feature called "Book Review Sampler."

The Horn Book Magazine approaches children's literature from many perspectives, including the voices of authors, illustrators, librarians, teachers, and publishers. Each issue includes in-depth articles and shorter, regular feature columns. One column I always look forward to is "News from the North," which highlights literature from Canada. Reviews of individual titles are well developed and may include segments of a book's language and comments on illustrations.

School Library Journal (SLJ) also features a variety of articles, annotated bibliographies, and regular columns that address aspects of literature and related professional matters. I think of *SLJ* as a quick scan that covers a lot of territory. Reviews are succinct and provide an overview of the book's content. Less tangible characteristics are captured through the use of descriptive phrases such as "briskly moving," "frank discussion," or "poignant and revealing reminiscence."

Booklist reviews cover a wide range of materials typically purchased by public libraries, and each issue features sections on children's books and young adult books. Reviews vary in overall length but generally include an extended description of the content and a comment or two on a book's unique strengths or weaknesses. *Booklist* produces many annotated bibliographies, including children's books in other languages, special topics, and "Children's Editor's Choice" for the year's most outstanding books.

There are many other sources of reviews, articles, and bibliographies. Local newspapers sometimes carry reviews. Professional organizations not specifically oriented to reading and literature often review children's books related to certain content areas. The National Council for the Social Studies–Children's Book Council Joint Committee produces an annual annotated bibliography of "Notable Children's Trade Books in the Field of Social Studies" that appears in the April/May issue of *Social Education.* "Outstanding Science Trade Books for Children" is a similar compilation prepared by the National Science Teacher's Association-Children's Book Council Joint Committee that appears in the March issue of *Science and Children.*

Awards and Prizes

It seems that everyone has a favorite book or two, and in order to honor special and unique contributions to children's literature, various organizations bestow awards. The Newbery and Caldecott Awards probably come first to mind; however, according to the Children's Book Council, there are approximately 125 awards currently given in the area of children's literature. You can check your library's reference collection for *Children's Books: Awards and Prizes,* a comprehensive list compiled by the Children's Book Council. Remember that awards, like beauty, rest in the eye of the beholder. The needs and interests of you and your children may be different from the purposes of a committee making an award.

Textbooks, Reference Books, and Collections of Articles

Another source of helpful information about children's literature can be found in a vast array of books. Currently available are several volumes designed for use in children's literature courses that provide a comprehensive overview of the field. One of the best known is Charlotte Huck's *Children's Literature in the Elementary School* (1987), now in its fourth edition. Filled with rich detail about genres of literature, individual books, children's response to literature, and the development of a literature program, the scope of this book is like a symphony.

Other kinds of resources that you will find useful are indexes, bibliographies, and directories found in the library's special reference collection. Reference books tend to be rather formidable in appearance, but that is primarily because their purpose is to provide a lot of information that you can find quickly. Most are updated and revised periodically.

Books such as *A to Zoo: Subject Access Guide to Children's Picture Books* (Lima, 1986) and *Fantasy for Children* (Lynn, 1983) are invaluable aids in guiding you to resources on specific topics. Poems and fairy tales often appear in larger collections and may be difficult to find. You can find assistance from the *Index to Poetry for Children and Young People* (Brewton, Blackburn, & Blackburn, comps., 1984) and the *Index to Fairy Tales, 1973–1977: Including Folklore, Legends and Myths in Collections* (Ireland, comp. 1979). Subject specialists have selected and annotated exemplary science books in *Best Science Books for Children* (Wolff, ed., 1983).

Children's Books in Print is an annual, comprehensive list of children's books currently in print, arranged alphabetically by author, illustrator, and title. In another volume, *Subject Guide to Children's Books in Print,* titles are arranged according to more than 6,000 subject entries. Publishers' addresses are included.

Once hooked on children's books, readers inevitably become curious about the people who create those books. One way to pursue this interest is to consult *Something About the Author,* a series devoted to biographical information about contemporary authors and illustrators. Poets are featured in *Pass the Poetry, Please!* (Hopkins, 1987).

Collections of speeches and articles by individual writers such as Mollie Hunter (*Talent Is Not Enough*) and Katherine Paterson (*Gates of Excellence*) allow you to ponder and savor dimensions of experiences that influence their writings. Stimulating also are volumes of critical essays such as *The Marble in the Water: Essays on Contemporary Writers of Fiction for Children and Young Adults* (Rees, 1980) and *A Sounding of Storytellers: New and Revised Essays on Contemporary Writers for Children* (Townsend, 1979). In addition, you will find appropriate articles in many of the journals previously mentioned. To facilitate your search, check the last issue of each volume to an index to articles for the whole year.

Summary

At this point in our travels together, I can think of many superb resources that I have left out. Consider this chapter as a sampler, and use the information as a way to begin. Remember to consult with colleagues and friends who are willing to share their enthusiasm for books. Tap into professional organizations, and be a regular reader of journals and other publications concerned with children's literature. By now you ought to be amazed at how much knowledge you have. The thrill comes in recognizing your strengths and then moving ahead by continuing to make links. Action is the key: share your discoveries with a kindred spirit, and prepare yourself for new adventures. Think of enriching your resources as a lifelong journey, and enjoy!

References

Brewton, J.E., Blackburn, G.M. III, & Blackburn, L.A. (Comps.). (1984). *Index to poetry for children and young people — 1976-1981: A title, subject, author, and first line index to poetry collections for children and young people.* New York: Wilson.

Children's Book Council. (Eds.). (1986). *Children's books: Awards and prizes.* New York: The Children's Book Council.

Children's books in print 1988–89. (1988). New York: Bowker.

Commire, A. (Ed.). *Something about the author.* Vols. 1–50 Detroit: Gale.

Cullinan, B.E. (Ed.). (1987). *Children's literature in the reading program.* Newark, DE: International Reading Association.

Hepler, S.I. (1982). *Patterns of response to literature: A one-year study of a fifth- and sixth-grade classroom.* Unpublished doctoral dissertation. Columbus: The Ohio State University.

Hopkins, L.B. (1987). *Pass the poetry, please!* New York: Harper & Row.

Huck, C.S., Hepler, S., & Hickman, J. (1987). *Children's literature in the elementary school (4th ed.).* New York: Holt, Rinehart and Winston.

Hunter, M. (1976). *Talent is not enough.* New York: Harper & Row.

Ireland, N.O. (Comp.). (1979). *Index to fairy tales, 1973–1977: Including folklore, legends and myths in collection.* Metuchen, NJ: Scarecrow Press.

Lima, C.W. (1986). *A to zoo: Subject access to children's picture books* (2nd ed.). New York: Bowker.

Lynn, R.N. (1988). *Fantasy literature for children and young adults: An annotated bibliography* (3rd ed.). New York: Bowker.

Monson, D. (1985). *Adventuring with books: A booklist for pre-k–grade 6.* Urbana, IL: National Council of Teachers of English.

Paterson, K. (1981). *Gates of excellence: On reading and writing books for children.* New York: Elsevier/Nelson Books.

Rees, D. (1980). *The marble in the water: Essays on contemporary writers of fiction for children and young adults.* Boston: Horn Book, Inc.

Sims, R. (1982). *Shadow and substance: Afro-American experience in contemporary children's fiction.* Urbana, IL: National Council of Teachers of English.

Subject guide to children's books in print. Annual (1986). New York: Bowker.

Townsend, J.R. (1979). *A sounding of storytellers: New and revised essays on contemporary writers for children.* New York: Lippincott.

Tway, E. (Ed.). (1981). *Reading ladders for human relations,* 6th ed. Urbana, IL: National Council of Teachers of English.

Wolff, K. (Ed.). (1983). *Best science books for children: Selected and annotated.* Washington: American Association for the Advancement of Science.

Professional Organizations

American Library Association (ALA)
50 East Huron Street
Chicago, IL 60611

The Children's Book Council (CBC)
67 Irving Place
New York, NY 10003

International Reading Association (IRA)
800 Barksdale Road, P.O. Box 8139
Newark, DE 19714-8139

National Council of Teachers of English (NCTE)
Children's Literature Assembly (CLA)
Assembly on Literature for Adolescents (ALAN)
1111 Kenyon Road
Urbana, IL 61801

United States Board on Books for Young People (USBBY)
(U.S. Section of the International Board on Books for Young People — IBBY)
c/o International Reading Association
800 Barksdale Road, P.O. Box 8139
Newark, DE 19714-8139

Journals

Booklist
c/o American Library Association
50 East Huron Street
Chicago, IL 60611

CBC Features
c/o The Children's Book Council
67 Irving Place
New York, NY 10003

Journal of Youth Services in Libraries
c/o American Library Association
50 East Huron Street
Chicago, IL 60611

Language Arts
c/o National Council of Teachers of English
1111 Kenyon Road
Urbana, IL 61801

School Library Journal
P.O. Box 1978
Marion, OH 43305-1978

The ALAN Review
c/o National Council of Teachers of English
1111 Kenyon Road
Urbana, IL 61801

The Bulletin
c/o National Council of Teachers of English
1111 Kenyon Road
Urbana, IL 61801

The Horn Book Magazine
Park Square Building
31 St. James Avenue
Boston, MA 02116

The New Advocate
Christopher-Gordon Publishers, Inc.
P.O. Box 809
Needham Heights, MA 02194-0006

The Reading Teacher
c/o International Reading Association
800 Barksdale Road, P.O. Box 8139
Newark, DE 19714-8139

The WEB
Martha L. King Center for Language and Literacy
Department of Educational Theory and Practice
29 W. Woodruff Avenue
Columbus, OH 43210-1177

Epilogue

In the Words of

Charlotte S. Huck

The following article, first printed in 1979, is based on an address presented to the general session of the International Reading Association at their 1976 national convention in Anaheim, California. It was influential in encouraging members of that organization to give more attention to the role of children's literature in the reading program. Although in these pages you will not find references to the latest in children's books or to the most recent research studies, you will discover an enduring philosophy, eloquently stated, as true and moving today as it ever was.

No Wider than the Heart Is Wide

Charlotte S. Huck, *The Ohio State University*

The common use of the term *literacy* in this country is usually prefaced by the word *mere* — we talk about mere literacy or a kind of minimal or functional ability to read and write that will enable an individual to just barely survive in our modern society. This definition of literacy has grown out of despair and failure on the part of teachers. We haven't been successful in teaching some children to read and so in desperation we try to provide a little survival kit for life; we teach them to read street signs, help wanted ads, and recipes and to fill out job applications and welfare notices. Certainly we want to go beyond this kind of functional literacy.

There is another group of students who are literate, who know how to read but just never do, for they have never found any pleasure in reading. In England they refer to these students as ex-literates and I have called them our "illiterate literates." Certainly we want to go *beyond* this kind of literacy.

An older use of the term literacy, which is still very current in certain parts of the world, refers to the fully literate person: the autonomous reader who reads widely on a variety of subjects; who makes rational decisions based upon an enlightened view of all sides of a controversy; the humane man or woman of letters who can entertain new ideas, accept different points of view and through reading can enter into the joys and hopes, the sorrow and despair of the world across time and space. In a very real sense it is impossible to go *beyond* this definition of literacy, but we can make it our goal. There is only one way to achieve it and that is through developing a love of good books. Children will never become fully literate persons unless they discover delight in books. The route, then, to full literacy is through literature.

The purpose of this article is twofold. First, I hope to help the reader discover the power of literature to educate the human heart and to develop the fully literate person. Second, I hope to convince the reader of the power of literature to help children to learn to read, to become readers.

Literature and Life

All of us can remember reading books that have made a difference in our lives, that have changed us as human beings, changed how we look at life and the world and the nature of things.

Two adult books that I read last year made me aware once again of the power of the written word to shock and to strengthen. The first one was a research report titled *The Mountain People* written by an English anthropologist, Colin Turnbull (1972). It was first published in 1972 but I came to it late through the great and glorious boon for reading, the paperback. *The Mountain People* is a detailed account of the dehumanization of an African tribe in less than three generations. It is the terrifying story of a people appropriately called "The IK" whose only purpose in life is individual survival.

> They steal from each other,
>> Snatch food out of the hands of the sick and dying.
>>> One couple walled in their own five-year-old
>>>> And went away for the weekend while
>>>>> she died of starvation.
>>> Another family refused to allow their father
>>>> to die in their hut, for they would then have had
>>>>> to provide a funeral.

This is a compelling and frightening book that made me realize how very fragile that which we call our humanness really is.

Then I read Margaret Craven's moving short novel, *I Heard the Owl Call My Name* (1973). Some of you may have seen the truncated version of it on television. It is the story of a young Anglican priest who has only three more years to live. His Bishop knowingly sends him to the Northwest Indian village of Kingcome to learn the meaning of life and death. At first the Indians treated him with respect but left him alone and Mark was desperately lonely and afraid. Slowly he was absorbed into the life of the village.

> He played with the children
>> fished with the men
>>> officiated at weddings and funerals
>>>> ached with them when their youth went off to the city
>>> and suffered with them when
>>>> a mother of six died in childbirth.

Slowly he learned what his wise Bishop had sent him to the village to find: "Enough of the meaning of life to be ready to die." In their quiet perceptive way the Indians ask Mark to remain in the village until "The Owl calls his name" and death has to come.

Two very different books — one a research report, the other a novel — made me ponder the meaning of life, to consider the question of what makes us human. How would the anthropologist account for the difference between these two groups of people: one almost a subspecies of humanity, the other, a representation of all we respect in human beings — courage, dignity, and compassion?

I will never visit ''Kingcome'' on the Northwest Pacific Coast nor the mountain tribe of Africa. But my mind has been stretched, my heart educated by the experience of reading about them. No one can live long enough to see all of life clear and whole. But through wide reading, as well as living, we can acquire a perception of life and literature; and, on this fragile green world, a tiny globe of humanity must learn compassion and cooperation or cease to exist.

Edna St. Vincent Millay (1917) said it best in the last verse of her long poem, ''Renascence.''

> The world stands out on either side
> No wider than the heart is wide;
> Above the world is stretched the sky —
> No higher than the soul is high.

Most of what children learn in school is concerned with *knowing;* literature is concerned with *feeling.* We cannot afford to educate the head without the heart. The parallel between the Mountain People who have abandoned their humanity and our own society's headlong rush towards destruction is frightening.

Now it would be naive of me if I suggested that *only* literature or that *all* literature is capable of educating the human heart. Certainly we know that the values of the home, the school, and peers, the influence of TV and mass media all have a profound effect on the ideas and feelings of children.

In fact that is one of the problems. How do we reach the hearts of this television generation who all their lives have been receiving such mixed messages about values that Coke has become the real thing,

> Ideal is a dog food
> Joy is a liquid soap

and they've been asked to believe in peanut butter!

The quiet times that you and I spent curled up with a book, today's children spend sprawled in front of a TV set. Statistics are frightening as we learn that most children average five hours a day of viewing time. In fact, Nancy Larrick (1975) reports that a child of today will spend a total of *ten years* of his life, watching TV.

Books can't compete with that, but they can offer children options, give them freedom to choose how they will spend their time and with whom. The autonomous reader is never limited by the offerings of the TV channels. Once children have discovered delight in books, the knowledge of the world is theirs — free and as accessible as their nearest library.

Books can create feelings, and they can educate feelings even in the very youngest child. We have many stories that explore the theme of sibling rivalry, particularly children's reactions to the arrival of a new baby sister or brother. One of my favorites is Eloise Greenfield's *She Come Bringing Me That Little Baby Girl.* Kevin asked his mother to bring him a little baby brother from the hospital but she came home instead with a baby sister. At first Kevin didn't like her at all. She cried too much and was all wrinkled. Besides that his mother and father looked at her like she was the only baby in the world. It just made Kevin sick the way they fussed over her and the presents everyone gave her. Then Kevin's mother told him that she used to be a baby girl and her big brother used to help take care of her. "Uncle Roy said, 'That's right, I wouldn't let nobody bother my little sister.'" Kevin looks at the baby with new respect and decides that she really isn't so ugly any more; in fact, she's even a little bit cute. He shows her off to his friends, "watching closely to see that they don't squeeze her too hard!"

The Russian poet Chukovsky, in his remarkable book titled *From Two to Five* (1963), tells us that the goal of the storyteller

> Consists of fostering in the child, at whatever cost, compassion and humanness — this miraculous ability of man to be disturbed by another being's misfortunes, to feel joy about another being's happiness, to experience another's fate as your own.

One book that will help children develop empathy for others is *The Bears' House* by Marilyn Sachs. This is the story of Fran Ellen who is ten-years-old and still sucks her thumb. The other girls in her class tease her telling her that she is dirty and smells. Fran Ellen retreats into her own fantasy world by doing her school work quickly so that she may play with the Bears' House, an old doll house that had belonged to her teacher when she was a little girl. The Bears' House becomes a real house in Fran Ellen's fantasies. Here Mamma Bear cooks and cleans and gives Fran Ellen a beautiful dress, while Papa Bear holds her on his lap and tells her that she is his good little girl. Fran Ellen's fantasy world contrasts sharply with her real world where her father has deserted the family and her mother is ill. Fran and her little brother are trying to take care of their baby sister, Flora, in shifts and somehow hold the family together. This is honest, realistic fiction and Fran Ellen can't cope without adult assistance. Miss Thompson, her teacher, discovers the family's plight and goes for help, but the reader never knows if the family is separated or not.

When you read this story to children and ask them how they think the problem is resolved, they always make up a happy ending for they want Fran Ellen to be able to stay with Flora and her brother. They have suffered enough *with* her to care *about* her.

One of the most popular books among the boys in a sixth grade class where I visit is *Hang Tough, Paul Mather* by Slote, the story of a twelve-year-old boy who was a top baseball player, but who is now dying of leukemia. A young compassionate doctor helps him play out his short season with dignity and tremendous courage.

James Baldwin (1963) said:

> You think your pain and your heartache are unprecedented in the history of the world, but then you read. It was books that taught me that the things that tormented me the most were the very things that connected me with all the people who were alive, or who had ever been alive.

Nothing connected David Ullman to the rest of his Jewish family for he was the lone survivor; the rest, including his twin brother, had been gassed or died in the German concentration camps. This grim story, *The Survivor* by James Forman, seems to speak of every known form of human cruelty. When David is finally freed, he has little strength and seemingly nothing left to live for. But then he finds the key to his future in a remarkable letter which his Grandfather had hidden behind a tile in their old home in Amsterdam. Knowing what any survivor of the family would have been through, the Grandfather's first words were of the goodness of life:

> Life is a wonderful gift. Like the tropic sun, it can strike you blind, but it is magnificent. Never despair. . . At the bottom of all human renunciations, buried under so many ''no's,'' there is that last indestructible ''yes,'' and it sufficient to rebuild everything.

Whether for adults or for children, great literature illuminates living — the light may shine as readily from fantasy as from realistic fiction. In fact, fantasy has always allowed us to view ourselves from a unique and special perspective. Alan Arkin has written a wry and amusing tale, titled *The Lemming Condition*, which appeals to both adults and children. One day for no apparent reason there is much excitement on the plains where the lemmings live as the word is spread that it is time for "the great march." One young lemming is full of questions. He wants to know where they are going and why. He even has the audacity to ask if they can swim — an unheard of question that somehow casts doubt on the whole race of lemmings! Finally, Bubber seeks the advice of an old lemming who has little to do with the rest of the herd. Their conversation is very funny indeed as the youngster reports that everyone is underground packing.

"Packing?" says the old lemming, incredulous.
"What do you take along for a mass suicide?"

When Bubber returns to the plains, the great march has begun. Caught up in the powerful surge of small bodies, our critical thinker is powerless to act. He does save himself in the last instant, however, by falling in a crevice between two rocks. After the madness is over, he walks over the silent barren plains and is startled to meet four young lemmings who are bemoaning the fact that they missed the whole show. They had stayed up to see it and then slept through the moment that made their species unique. They ask Bubber to join them, but he is beginning to understand how the mystique of the great lemming leap is passed on from one generation to the next and he wants none of it. Like the rats in O'Brien's *Mrs. Frisby and the Rats of NIMH*, he is determined to change his basic behavior. Alan Arkin's unstated metaphor is that we too could change the course of our seemingly mad determination to eliminate ourselves in periodic wars of greater and greater magnitude. "The Lemming Condition" is obviously ours, and we need more young, critical lemmings to question its sanity.

Literature for children is not just entertainment, although it may entertain. Literature for children is essential for their education. Edgar Dale says that good books may inform, great books transform.

Fine literature will create an awareness of living — a sensitivity to beauty that we have not observed before. In Mary Ellen Chase's *A Goodly Fellowship* (1939), she describes a clear crisp night in Maine when her father awakened the entire family and took them out into the back yard to observe the brilliant Northern lights. After they had watched in awe for some ten minutes, he led them back into the house with only one brief comment, "Don't ever forget it."

Let's give children literature that will help them see more, be more, feel more. White's *Charlotte's Web* can be read for many layers of meaning — a funny barnyard story; or an account of the meaning of friendship, its vicissitudes and loyalties; or as social commentary as to why Wilbur received the prize for Charlotte's work. I love the characters, the geese that speak in triplicate, the gloomy sheep, Templeton the rat who had to be bribed to be helpful and then wanted to take full credit, and Wilbur innocently eating his slop until told of his final destination. Yet my real joy in this book is White's marvelous ability to recapture the sights, the sounds, and smells of rural living. You remember the passage near the end:

> Life in the barn was very good — night and day, winter and summer, spring and fall, dull days and bright days. It was the best place to be, thought Wilbur, this warm delicious cellar, with the garrulous geese, the changing seasons, the heat of the sun, the passage of swallows, the nearness of rats, the sameness of sheep, the love of spiders, the smell of manure, and the glory of everything.

Let's give children books that affirm life, that capture the excitement of living, the joy of being alive — of being aware.

Literature and the Reading Program

Many reading teachers say to themselves, ''Yes, of course, doesn't she know that is why we are spending time teaching reading, so children can *then* read?''

And that, I'd like to suggest, is part of the problem. We don't achieve literacy and then give children literature; we achieve literacy *through* literature.

A few weeks ago I visited an alternative school that prides itself upon its return to traditional education. Our visit started in the school's new library as the principal explained their program of more homework, more emphasis upon the three ''Rs,'' and citizenship. Then we were free to visit the classrooms. I questioned the librarian aide (there was no trained librarian) on the operation of the library and who used it, when and how. I was told that the teachers scheduled their classes in it once a week in the afternoon and that after children had finished all their other work, they could use it in the morning provided they had a note from their teacher.

I visited three classrooms, staying some 45 minutes in each room. In every classroom the children were working on reading — the skills of reading, I was told. Their seat-work, and I use that old-fashioned term advisedly, consisted of individual ditto sheets containing lists of words that had to be matched with endings, and short paragraphs with questions requiring the student to complete the blanks. In groups of four, the children came to a table and read with the teacher from dull basic readers, answered her questions (all literal memory questions), and returned to their seats. I counted on a shelf about 45 old grubby children's books that no one was reading even if he or she had time. Before I visited each room, I returned to the library to see if it was being used — it never was. Obviously no one ever finished the task of learning how to read in order to have time to enjoy reading. What a waste, what an unbelievable waste of the most important resource this country has — the minds of our children.

We wouldn't think of teaching our children to swim on dry land, but these children were being asked to learn to read from a desert of materials.

If we can believe what the psycholinguists are telling us, and I have every reason to believe it from my observation of child behavior, children learn to read for meaning and for pleasure from the very beginning.

Stories are one of the best ways into literacy at the earliest stages of a child's development. In fact, Barbara Hardy (1968) suggests that all human beings' construct of reality is, in fact, a story that we tell ourselves about how the world works. She states that the narrative is the most common and effective form of ordering our world:

> We dream in narrative, day-dream in narrative, remember, antici-
> pate, hope, despair, believe, doubt, plan, revise, criticize, construct,
> gossip, learn, hate and love by narrative.

Watch young children and see the stories that they are acting out in their lives. They are naughty and sent to their rooms and they immediately begin to tell themselves a story about how mean their parents are, how they will run away and make everyone sorry. This is the reason for the tremendous appeal of Sendak's *Where the Wild Things Are;* it taps the very well-springs of all the stories children have told to themselves for years.

Teachers who know the power of these self-told stories will make them the content of children's beginning reading. After children have read their own stories, they will move to the folktales and modern tales that echo the dreams and wishes of the very young.

Children want to learn to read because they want to read stories (their own and other persons'), real stories where something happens to real persons — not nonstories of collective persons with a careful representation of each race and sex riding subways to go to something vaguely defined as work. One of our doctoral students who was studying children's concepts of reading asked a child what her book was about. She replied it wasn't about anything, it was her reading book.

Contrast that answer with my experience with Gareth, a large six-year-old child who was in a primary school in London. Gareth was teaching himself to read from the Frances stories he adored. He told me he could read two of them and that he was working on the third. I offered to read one to him if he would read one to me. He chose *Bread and Jam for Frances* by the Hobans and, when he came to the part where Frances skips rope and sings her "jam song," he literally sang it. There was no doubt in my mind that he was discovering delight in books in the process of learning to read. Joy was not delayed until *after* he had learned all 367 skills in comprehension — it was the natural reward of reading for meaning.

Increasingly psycholinguists are telling us that reading is a response to real, meaningful language. There has to be enough of it available for the reader to anticipate, expect, and predict for meaning to emerge. Of course you can learn to read biscuit, toast, sticky, or raspberry when it is part of a chant that goes

Jam on biscuits, jam on toast
Jam is the thing that I like most
Jam is sticky, jam is sweet
Jam is tasty, jam's a treat —
Raspberry, strawberry, gooseberry, I'm very
FOND OF JAM.

In order to achieve literacy through literature I would recommend that every teacher do three things.

First, read to your children, all children every single day. This will help them begin to see literature as a source of pleasure, something they will be able to continue *for the rest of their lives*. The daily story hour will provide the language of literature, the conventions of stories such as once upon a time, the three wishes, the three brothers, the climax, the ending of they lived happily ever after. This in turn will help children as they begin to read to predict the story structure, to anticipate the climax, and to imagine the ending. They will be building an understanding of how to cope with story language. Children will also see an adult enjoying reading, something which may be a new experience for them. I have a friend who was reading Arnold Lobel's delightful story *Frog and Toad Are Friends;* she got to the part where

Toad is waiting for the mail and says, "This is my sad time of day. It is the time when I wait for the mail to come and it always makes me unhappy — because I've never gotten a letter." Well, my friend burst out laughing and her six-year-old listener said, "I didn't know grownups liked books." Children need to know that adults do like books and that they like to read them.

Second, I would provide time every single day for children to read books of their own choosing. We no longer can afford to say to children you may read a book when all your other work is done or you may read a book at home. In the first place, nothing is more important in the elementary school than to have a child reading a book and enjoying it. And, if children are watching TV five hours a day, then schools must provide time for children to read books for practice and pleasure. I am convinced that a child never becomes a reader from reading short stories in a basic reader or from going through programmed materials on the Eskimo. A child becomes a reader because he falls in love with a book, a book that tells a real story and carries significant meaning for him.

Third, I would plan time for children to share books — not requiring a deadly dull book report, but time to respond to books through discussion, through drama, movement, art, block construction, making a game from the story, any activity that takes the child more deeply into the experience of the book and makes it memorable. This is why I would have teachers read and know children's literature, so they could enter into a dialogue with children about their reading. Teachers who are enthusiastic about books will foster a kind of classroom culture where they talk with their children about favorite books, authors, and illustrators. One teacher told me of a child who had arrived late for school, forgotten his lunch, and didn't have his social studies project done. He looked up at her and said, "You know I'm having a terrible, horrible, no good, very bad day," and they laughed together remembering the fun of Judith Viorst's story by that title.

One school that I know well received money for a remedial reading teacher. The teachers all decided that they didn't need a remedial teacher; they needed someone who could turn children on to reading, particularly those children who could read but who didn't. And then they followed the plan outlined above. All the teachers agreed to read to their children every day. In fact, the teacher of the eight, nine, and ten year old group makes it a point to share every day a picture book, a poem, and a chapter from a continued story with her children. The school has sustained silent reading every afternoon with the teachers reading children's books, frequently those recommended by their students. The reading motivator, as the remedial teacher was called, bought sets of four or five paperbacks of the same title for children to read together, to discuss, and interpret through games, drama, writing, and so forth. Parent aides helped children bind their own books, which were then placed in the library for everyone to read. Parents also opened a paperback bookstore to encourage individual ownership of books. Rather than concentrating on the skills of reading, everyone concentrated on helping children discover the joys of reading. Their test scores went up higher than any other school's in the district, but the teachers and the parents were the most excited because their children were becoming readers. Instead of following the lemming rush to return to the basics, this school stopped and looked at children's purposes for reading. These teachers were not teaching for tests but for life. They knew the only true test of children's ability was whether they do indeed read. They knew, too, that children would read when they found pleasure in reading. They discovered that the way to real literacy was through literature. For, through literature, children can begin to develop a sense of their humanness; they can develop new insights into the behavior of others and themselves. Literature can add a new dimension to life and create a new awareness, a greater sensitivity to people and surroundings. It can educate the heart as well as the head. We need to remember that:

> The world stands out on either side
> No wider than the heart is wide!

References

Baldwin, J. (1963, December 21). Talk to teachers. *Saturday Review,* 42–44, 60.

Chase, M.E. (1939). *A goodly fellowship.* New York: Macmillan.

Chukovsky, K. (1963). *From two to five* (Miriam Morton, Trans.). Berkeley, CA: University of California Press.

Craven, Margaret. (1973). *I heard the owl call my name.* New York: Dell.

Hardy, B. (1968). *The appropriate form, An essay on the novel.* London: The Athlone Press, University of London.

Larrick, N. (1975). "Hey Mom, who put the television in the closet?" Address given at the Elementary Section of the National Council of Teachers of English, San Diego.

Millay, E. (1917, 1945). Renascence. From *Collected poems.* New York: Harper & Row.

Turnbull, C. (1972). *The mountain people.* New York: Simon & Schuster.

References:

Children's Books

Adams, Richard. *Watership Down.* New York: Macmillan, 1974.

Adkins, Jan. *Inside: Seeing Beneath the Surface.* New York: Walker, 1975.

Adoff, Arnold. *All the Colors of the Race.* New York: Lothrop, Lee & Shepard, 1982.

The Cabbages are Chasing the Rabbits. New York: Harcourt Brace Jovanovich, 1985.

Eats: Poems. New York: Lothrop, Lee & Shepard, 1979.

comp. *I Am the Darker Brother.* New York: Macmillan, 1968.

comp. *My Black Me.* New York: Dutton, 1974.

Tornado! Poems. New York: Delacorte, 1977.

Ahlberg, Janet and Allan Ahlberg. *The Jolly Postman or Other People's Letters.* New York: Little, Brown & Co., 1986.

Alexander, Lloyd. *The Black Cauldron.* New York: Holt, Rinehart and Winston, 1965.

The Book of Three. New York: Holt, Rinehart and Winston, 1964.

The Castle of Llyr. New York: Holt, Rinehart and Winston, 1966.

The High King. New York: Holt, Rinehart and Winston, 1968.

Taran Wanderer. New York: Holt, Rinehart and Winston, 1967.

Aliki (Brandenberg). *The Medieval Feast.* New York: Crowell, 1983.

The Two of Them. New York: Greenwillow, 1979.

Anno, Mitsumasa. *Anno's Counting House.* New York: Crowell, 1982.

Anno's U.S.A. New York: Philomel, 1983.

Arkin, Alan. *The Lemming Condition.* New York: Harper & Row, 1976.

Armstrong, William. *Sounder.* New York: Harper & Row, 1969.

Arnosky, Jim. *Secrets of a Wildlife Watcher.* New York: Lothrop, Lee & Shepard, 1983.

Atwater, Richard and Florence Atwater. *Mr. Popper's Penguins.* Illustrated by Robert Lawson. Boston: Little, Brown & Co., 1938.

Babbitt, Natalie. *The Devil's Storybook.* New York: Farrar, Straus & Giroux, 1974.

Dick Foote and the Shark. New York: Farrar, Straus & Giroux, 1967.

The Eyes of the Amaryllis. New York: Farrar, Straus & Giroux, 1977.

Goody Hall. New York: Farrar, Straus & Giroux, 1971.

Knee-Knock Rise. New York: Farrar, Straus & Giroux, 1970.

Phoebe's Revolt. New York: Farrar, Straus & Giroux, 1968.

The Search for Delicious. New York: Farrar, Straus & Giroux, 1969.

The Something. New York: Dell, 1970.

Tuck Everlasting. New York: Farrar, Straus & Giroux, 1975.

Bang, Molly. *The Grey Lady and the Strawberry Snatcher.* New York: Four Winds, 1980.

Banks, Lynne Reid. *The Indian in the Cupboard.* Illustrated by Brock Cole. New York: Doubleday, 1981.

Barrett, Judi. *Animals Should Definitely Not Wear Clothing.* Illustrated by Ron Barrett. New York: Atheneum, 1970.

A Snake Is Totally Tail. Illustrated by Lonni Johnson. New York: Macmillan, 1983.

Baylor, Byrd. *Everybody Needs a Rock.* Illustrated by Peter Parnall. Scribner's, 1974.

I'm in Charge of Celebrations. Illustrated by Peter Parnall. New York: Scribner's, 1986.

Behn, Harry. *Crickets & Bullfrogs & Whispers of Thunder: Poems and Pictures by Harry Behn.* Edited by Lee Bennett Hopkins. San Diego: Harcourt Brace Jovanovich, 1984.

Bemelmans, Ludwig. *Madeline.* New York: Viking, 1939.

Blos, Joan. *A Gathering of Days.* New York: Scribner's, 1979.

Old Henry. Illustrated by Stephen Gammell. New York: Morrow, 1987.

Boston, Lucy. *The Children of Green Knowe.* Illustrated by Peter Boston. San Diego: Harcourt Brace Jovanovich, 1955.

Brady, Irene. *Wild Mouse.* New York: Scribner's, 1976.

Brandis, Marianne. *The Tinder Box.* Original wood engravings by G. Brender a Brandis. Toronto: Porcupine's Quill, 1982.

Brown, Marcia. *Once a Mouse.* New York: Scribner's, 1961.

Shadow. New York: Scribner's, 1982.

Brown, Margaret Wise. *Goodnight, Moon.* Illustrated by Clement Hurd. New York: Harper & Row, 1947.

Browne, Anthony. *Gorilla.* New York: Knopf, 1983.

Bunting, Eve. *Ghost's Hour, Spook's Hour.* Illustrated by Donald Carrick. Boston: Clarion/Houghton Mifflin, 1987.

Burningham, John. *John Burningham's ABC*. Indianapolis: Bobbs-Merrill, 1967.

Butterworth, Oliver. *The Enormous Egg*. Illustrated by Louis Darling. Boston: Little, Brown & Co., 1956.

Byars, Betsy. *After the Goatman*. New York: Viking, 1974.

Cracker Jackson. New York: Viking, 1985.

Campbell, Rod. *Dear Zoo*. New York: Four Winds, 1984.

Carle, Eric. *The Very Hungry Caterpillar*. New York: Philomel, 1969.

Cassedy, Sylvia. *Roomrimes*. Illustrated by Michele Chessare. New York: Crowell, 1987.

Chaffin, Lillie. *We Be Warm Till Springtime Comes*. Illustrated by Lloyd Bloom. New York: Macmillan, 1980.

Ciardi, John. *Doodle Soup*. Boston: Houghton Mifflin, 1985.

You Read to Me, I'll Read to You. Philadelphia: Lippincott, 1962.

Clapp, Patricia. *Witches' Children: A Story of Salem*. New York: Lothrop, Lee & Shepard, 1982.

Clarke, Pauline. *The Return of the Twelves*. Illustrated by Bernarda Bryson. London: Gregg, 1981.

Cleary, Beverly. *Dear Mr. Henshaw*. New York: Morrow, 1983.

Ramona Quimby, Age 8. New York: Morrow, 1981.

Cleaver, Vera and Bill Cleaver. *Grover*. Philadelphia: Lippincott, 1970.

Cohen, Caron Lee. *The Mud Pony*. Illustrated by Shonto Begay. New York: Scholastic Hardcover, 1988.

Colver, Anne. *Bread-and-Butter Indian*. New York: Holt, Rinehart and Winston, 1964.

Bread-and-Butter Journey. New York: Avon Books, 1971.

Collier, James Lincoln and Christopher Collier. *My Brother Sam Is Dead*. New York: Four Winds, 1974.

Conover, Chris. *The Wizard's Daughter*. Boston: Little, Brown & Co., 1984.

Conrad, Pam. *Prairie Songs*. New York: Harper & Row, 1985.

Coolidge, Olivia E. *Hercules and Other Tales From Greek Myths*. New York: Scholastic, 1964.

Cooper, Susan. *The Dark Is Rising*. Illustrated by Alan E. Cober. New York: Atheneum, 1973.

Greenwitch. New York: Atheneum, 1974.

The Grey King. New York: Atheneum, 1975.

Over Sea, Under Stone. San Diego: Harcourt, Brace, 1966.

The Selkie Girl. Illustrated by Warwick Hutton. New York: Atheneum, 1986.

Silver on the Tree. New York: Atheneum, 1977.

Cosman, Madeleine P. *Medieval Holidays and Festivals: A Calendar of Celebrations*. New York: Scribner's, 1981.

Dahl, Roald. *James and the Giant Peach*. Illustrated by Nancy Ekholm Burkert. New York: Knopf, 1961.

deAngeli, Marguerite. *The Door in the Wall*. New York: Doubleday, 1949.

deGerez, Toni. *Louhi, Witch of North Farm*. Illustrated by Barbara Cooney. New York: Viking Kestrel, 1986.

de la Mare, Walter. *Bells and Grass*. New York: Viking, 1942.

dePaola, Tomie. *The Popcorn Book*. New York: Holiday House, 1978.

The Quicksand Book. New York: Holiday House, 1977.

Strega Nona. Englewood Cliffs, NJ: Prentice-Hall, 1975.

Dole, Bob, illustrator. *The Lion and the Mouse*. Mahwah, NJ: Troll, 1981.

Edwards, Sally. *When the World's on Fire*. New York: Coward, McCann and Geoghegan, 1973.

Esbensen, Barbara J. *Words with Wrinkled Knees*. Illustrated by John Stadler. New York: Crowell, 1986.

Falls, C.B. *ABC Book*. New York: Doubleday, 1939.

Farber, Norma. *Mercy Short: A Winter Journal, North Boston, 1692-93*. New York: Dutton, 1982.

Never Say Ugh to a Bug. New York: Greenwillow, 1979.

Fisher, Aileen. *I Stood Upon a Mountain*. New York: Crowell, 1979.

In the Middle of the Night. New York: Crowell, 1979.

Listen, Rabbit. New York: Crowell, 1964.

Out in the Dark and Daylight. New York: Harper & Row, 1980.

Fleischman, Sid. *The Whipping Boy*. Illustrated by Peter Sis. New York: Greenwillow, 1986.

Forbes, Esther. *Johnny Tremain*. Boston: Houghton Mifflin, 1943. Reprinted 1987.

Forman, James. *The Survivor*. New York: Farrar, Straus & Giroux, 1976.

Fox, Paula. *The Slave Dancer*. New York: Bradbury, 1973.

Francis, Robert. "Summons," in Stephen Dunning, *et al.*, *Reflections on a Gift of Watermelon Pickle. . .* New York: Scholastic Book Services, 1966.

Fritz, Jean. *Can't You Make Them Behave, King George?* Illustrated by Tomie dePaola. New York: Coward, McCann & Geoghegan, 1977.

Frost, Robert. *Stopping by Woods on a Snowy Evening*. Illustrated by Susan Jeffers. New York: Dutton, 1987.

Gag, Wanda. *Millions of Cats*. New York: Coward-McCann, 1928.

Galdone, Paul. *The Little Red Hen*. New York: Scholastic, 1973.

Little Red Riding Hood. New York: McGraw Hill, 1974.

The Teeny-Tiny Woman. New York: Clarion, 1984.

The Three Bears, New York: Clarion, 1971.

The Three Billy Goats Gruff. New York: Clarion, 1973.

Garner, Alan. *The Owl Service*. New York: Walck, 1968.

Gehrts, Barbara. *Don't Say a Word*. Translated by Elizabeth D. Crawford. New York: Macmillan, 1986.

George, Jean Craighead. *My Side of the Mountain*. New York: Dutton, 1959.

One Day in the Alpine Tundra. Illustrated by Walter Gaffney-Kessell. New York: Crowell, 1984.

Water Sky. New York: Harper & Row, 1987.

Gerstein, Mordicai. *The Seal Mother.* New York: Dial, 1986.

Gilson, Jamie. *4B Goes Wild.* Illustrated by Linda Edwards. New York: Lothrop, Lee & Shepard, 1983.

Glubok, Shirley. *The Art of Colonial America.* New York: Macmillan, 1970.

Goffstein, M.B. *A Little Schubert.* Boston: David R. Godine, 1985.

Goodall, John. *The Story of an English Village.* New York: Atheneum, 1979.

Greenfield, Eloise. *She Come Bringing Me that Little Baby Girl.* Illustrated by John Steptoe. Philadelphia: Lippincott, 1974.

Greenwood, Barbara. *A Question of Loyalty.* New York: Scholastic TAB, 1984.

Grimm Brothers. *Cinderella.* Illustrated by Nonny Hogrogian. New York: Greenwillow, 1981.

   The Devil with the Three Golden Hairs. Illustrated by Nonny Hogrogian. New York: Knopf, 1983.

   The Glass Mountain. Illustrated by Nonny Hogrogian. New York: Knopf, 1985.

   Hansel and Gretel. Translated by Elizabeth D. Crawford. Illustrated by Lisbeth Zwerger. New York: Morrow, 1979.

   Little Red Riding Hood. Illustrated by Trina Schart Hyman. New York: Holiday House, 1983.

   Snow White. Translated by Paul Heins. Illustrated by Trina Schart Hyman. Boston: Little, Brown & Co., 1974.

Hall, Donald. *Ox-Cart Man.* Illustrated by Barbara Cooney. New York: Viking, 1979.

Hazen, Barbara Shook. *Two Homes to Live In: A Child's Eye View of Divorce.* Illustrated by Peggy Luks. New York: Human Sciences Press, 1978.

Heller, Ruth. *Chickens Aren't the Only Ones.* New York: Putnam, 1981.

Hendershot, Judith. *In Coal Country.* Illustrated by Thomas B. Allen. New York: Knopf, 1987.

Herman, Charlotte. *Our Snowman Had Olive Eyes.* New York: Dutton, 1977.

Hill, Eric. *Where's Spot?* New York: Putnam, 1980.

Hirschi, Ron. *Headgear.* Photos by Galen Burrell. New York: Dodd, Mead, 1986.

Hoban, Russell. *A Baby Sister for Frances.* Illustrated by Lillian Hoban. New York: Harper & Row, 1964.

   Bread and Jam for Frances. Illustrated by Lillian Hoban. New York: Harper & Row, 1964.

Hoberman, Mary Ann. *Bugs: Poems.* New York: Viking Press, 1976.

Hodges, Margaret. *Saint George and the Dragon.* Illustrated by Trina Schart Hyman. Boston: Little, Brown & Co., 1984.

Holling, Holling C. *Paddle-to-the-Sea.* Boston: Houghton Mifflin, 1941.

Hooks, William H. *Moss Gown.* Illustrated by Donald Carrick. New York: Clarion, 1987.

Hopkins, Lee Bennett (ed.). *I Am the Cat.* Illustrated by Linda R. Richards. San Diego: Harcourt Brace, 1981.

Horwitz, Elinor Lander. *When the Sky is Like Lace.* Illustrated by Barbara Cooney. Philadelphia: Lippincott, 1975.

Houston, Jeanne Wakatsuki and James D. Houston. *Farewell to Manzanar.* Boston: Houghton Mifflin, 1973.

Hughes, Monica. *Hunter in the Dark.* New York: Atheneum, 1983.

The Keeper of the Isis Light. New York: Atheneum, 1981.

Hunt, Irene. *Across Five Aprils.* New York: Follett, 1964.

Hunter, Mollie. *Cat, Herself.* New York: Harper & Row, 1975.

A Furl of Fairy Wind. New York: Harper & Row, 1977.

The Haunted Mountain. New York: Harper & Row, 1972.

Hold On To Love. Harper & Row, 1984.

Knight of the Golden Plain. New York: Harper & Row, 1983.

The Mermaid Summer. New York: Harper & Row, 1988.

A Sound of Chariots. New York: Harper & Row, 1972.

A Stranger Came Ashore. New York: Harper & Row, 1975.

The Stronghold. New York: Harper & Row, 1974.

The Third Eye. New York: Harper & Row, 1979.

Three Day Enchantment. New York: Harper & Row, 1985.

The Walking Stones. New York: Harper & Row, 1970.

The Wicked One. New York: Harper & Row, 1977.

You Never Knew Her As I Did. New York: Harper & Row, 1981.

Hurmence, Belinda. *A Girl Called Boy.* New York: Clarion, 1982.

Hutchins, Pat. *Rosie's Walk.* New York: Macmillan, 1968.

Innocenti, Roberto. *Rose Blanche.* Text by Christophe Gallaz and Roberto Innocenti. Mankato, MN: Creative Education, 1985.

Jacques, Brian. *Redwall.* New York: Philomel, 1986.

Johnson, Sylvia. *Animals of the Mountains.* Illustrated by Alcuin C. Dornisch. Minneapolis: Lerner, 1976.

Keats, Ezra Jack. *Over in the Meadow.* New York: Scholastic, 1971.

Kennedy, Richard. *Amy's Eyes.* Illustrated by Richard Egielski. New York: Harper & Row, 1985.

Song of the Horse. Illustrated by Marcia Sewall. New York: Dutton, 1981.

Kerr, Judith. *When Hitler Stole Pink Rabbit.* New York: Coward-McCann, 1972.

Kerr, M.E. *Gentlehands.* New York: Harper & Row, 1978.

Konigsburg, E.L. *From the Mixed-Up Files of Mrs. Basil E. Frankweiler.* New York: Atheneum, 1967.

Kraus, Robert. *Whose Mouse Are You?* Illustrated by José Aruego. New York: Macmillan, 1970.

Kuklin, Susan. *Thinking Big.* New York: Lothrop, Lee & Shepard, 1986.

Kuskin, Karla. *Dogs & Dragons, Trees & Dreams.* New York: Harper & Row, 1980.

Near the Window Tree. New York: Harper & Row, 1975.

A Space Story. Illustrated by Marc Simont. New York: Harper & Row, 1978.

Lasker, David. *The Boy Who Loved Music.* Illustrated by Joe Lasker. New York: Viking, 1979.

Lasky, Kathryn. *Beyond the Divide.* New York: Macmillan, 1983.

Night Journey. New York: Macmillan, 1982.

Lee, Dennis. *Jelly Belly.* Illustrated by Juan Wijngaard. New York: Bedrick Books/ Harper & Row, 1985.

Lizzy's Lion. Illustrated by Marie-Louise Gay. Stoddart, 1984.

Le Guin, Ursula K. *Very Far Away from Anywhere Else.* New York: Atheneum, 1976.

A Wizard of Earthsea. Illustrated by Ruth Robbins. Berkeley: Parnassus, 1968.

L'Engle, Madeleine. *Many Waters.* New York: Farrar, Straus & Giroux, 1986.

A Swiftly Tilting Planet. New York: Farrar, Straus & Giroux, 1978.

A Wrinkle in Time. New York: Farrar, Straus & Giroux, 1962.

Lester, Julius. *To Be a Slave.* Illustrated by Tom Feelings. New York: Dial, 1968.

Lewin, Betty. *Cat Count.* New York: Dodd, Mead, 1981.

Lewis, C.S. *The Lion, the Witch and the Wardrobe.* Illustrated by Pauline Baynes. New York: Macmillan, 1961.

The Voyage of the Dawn Treader. Illustrated by Pauline Baynes. New York: Macmillan, 1962.

Lionni, Leo. *Swimmy.* New York: Pantheon, 1963.

Little, Jean. *Mama's Going to Buy You a Mockingbird.* New York: Viking Kestrel, 1985.

Lively, Penelope. *The Ghost of Thomas Kempe.* Illustrated by Anthony Maitland. New York: Dutton, 1973.

Livingston, Myra Cohn, comp. *Cat Poems.* Illustrated by Trina Schart Hyman. New York: Holiday House, 1987.

Celebrations. Illustrations by Leonard Everett Fisher. New York: Holiday House, 1985.

A Circle of Seasons. Illustrated by Leonard Everett Fisher. New York: Holiday House, 1982.

Earth Songs. Illustrated by Leonard Everett Fisher. New York: Holiday House, 1986.

Sea Songs. Illustrated by Leonard Everett Fisher. New York: Holiday House, 1986.

Sky Songs. Illustrated by Leonard Everett Fisher. New York: Holiday House, 1984.

A Song I Sang To You. Illustrated by Margot Tomes. New York: Harcourt Brace Jovanovich, 1984.

Worlds I Know and Other Poems. Illustrated by Tim Arnold. New York: Atheneum, 1985.

Lobel, Arnold. *Fables.* New York: Harper & Row, 1980.

Frog and Toad are Friends. New York: Harper & Row, 1985.

Lord, Athena. *A Spirit to Ride the Whirlwind.* New York: Macmillan, 1981.

Lord, Bette Bao. *In the Year of the Boar and Jackie Robinson.* Illustrated by Marc Simont. New York: Harper & Row, 1984.

Lowry, Lois. *Anastasia Krupnik.* Boston: Houghton Mifflin, 1979.

Rabble Starkey. Boston: Houghton Mifflin, 1987.

Lunn, Janet. *The Root Cellar.* New York: Scribner's, 1981.

Shadow in Hawthorn Bay. New York: Scribner's, 1987.

Macaulay, David. *Castle.* Boston: Houghton Mifflin, 1977.

Mill. Boston: Houghton Mifflin, 1983.

McCord, David. *All Small*. Illustrated by Madelaine Linden. Boston: Little, Brown & Co., 1986.

One At A Time. Illustrated by Henry B. Kane. Boston: Little, Brown, & Co., 1980.

MacLachlan, Patricia. *Sarah, Plain and Tall*. New York: Harper & Row, 1985.

Through Grandpa's Eyes. Illustrated by Deborah Ray. New York: Harper & Row, 1980.

McNulty, Faith. *How to Dig a Hole to the Other Side of the World*. Illustrated by Marc Simont. New York: Harper & Row, 1979.

Mouse and Tim. Illustrated by Marc Simont. New York: Harper & Row, 1978.

Magorian, Michelle. *Goodnight Mr. Tom*. New York: Harper & Row, 1983.

Major, Kevin. *Holdfast*. New York: Delacorte, 1980.

Malory, Thomas. *The Book of King Arthur and His Noble Knights*. Philadelphia: Lippincott, 1949.

Marzollo, Jean. *Halfway Down Paddy Lane*. New York: Dial, 1981.

Maruki, Toshi. *Hiroshima No Pika*. New York: Lothrop, Lee & Shepard, 1980.

Matsutani, Miyoko. *The Crane Maiden*. Illustrated by Chihiro Iwasaki. New York: Parents, 1968.

Merriam, Eve. *Blackberry Ink*. Illustrated by Hans Wilhelm. New York: Morrow, 1985.

Fresh Paint. Illustrated by David Frampton. New York: Macmillan, 1986.

It Doesn't Always Have to Rhyme. Illustrated by Malcolm Spooner. New York: Atheneum, 1964.

Jamboree: Rhymes for All Times. New York: Dell, 1984.

A Sky Full of Poems. Illustrated by Walter Gaffney-Kessell. New York: Dell, 1986.

Mohr, Nicholasa. *Going Home*. New York: Dial, 1986.

Moore, Lilian. *I Feel the Same Way*. Illustrated by Robert Quackenbush. New York: Atheneum, 1967.

See My Lovely Poison Ivy, and Other Verses About Witches, Ghosts and Things. Illustrated by Diane Dawson. New York: Atheneum, 1975.

Something New Begins. Illustrated by Mary J. Dunton. New York: Atheneum, 1982.

Think of Shadows. Illustrated by Deborah Robison. New York: Atheneum, 1980.

Morrison, Lillian. *Overheard in a Bubble Chamber & Other Science Poems*. Illustrated by Eyre DeLanux. New York: Lothrop, Lee & Shepard, 1981.

Munsch, Robert. *Love You Forever*. Illustrated by Sheila McGraw. Firefly Books Ltd., 1986.

Naidoo, Beverly. *Journey to Jo'Burg: A South African Story*. New York: Harper & Row, 1986.

North, Sterling. *Little Rascal*. New York: Dutton, 1965.

Norton, Mary. *The Borrowers*. Illustrated by Beth and Joe Krush. San Diego: Harcourt Brace, 1953.

O'Brien, Robert C. *Mrs. Frisby and the Rats of NIMH*. New York: Atheneum, 1971.

O'Dell, Scott. *Island of the Blue Dolphins*. Boston: Houghton Mifflin, 1960.

Sarah Bishop. Boston: Houghton Mifflin, 1980.

O'Neill, Mary. *Hailstones and Halibut Bones: Adventures in Color.* Illustrated by Leonard Weisgard. New York: Doubleday, 1961.

Park, Ruth. *Playing Beatie Bow.* New York: Atheneum, 1982.

Parnall, Peter. *The Mountain.* New York: Doubleday, 1971.

Paterson, Katherine. *Bridge to Terabithia.* Illustrated by Donna Diamond. New York: Crowell, 1977.

The Great Gilly Hopkins. New York: Crowell, 1978.

Pearce, Philippa. *Tom's Midnight Garden.* Illustrated by Susan Einzig. Philadelphia: Lippincott, 1959.

Peck, Robert Newton. *A Day No Pigs Would Die.* New York: Knopf, 1972.

Peet, Bill. *The Wump World.* Boston: Houghton Mifflin, 1970.

Perrault, Charles. *Cinderella.* Illustrated by Marcia Brown. New York: Scribner's, 1954.

Pevear, Richard, reteller. *Our King Has Horns.* Illustrated by Robert Rayevsky. New York: Macmillan, 1987.

Pinkwater, Daniel. *Lizard Music.* New York: Dodd, Mead, 1976.

Powers, Mary Ellen. *Our Teacher's in a Wheelchair.* Chicago: Albert Whitman & Co., 1986.

Prelutsky, Jack. *The Headless Horseman Rides Tonight.* Illustrated by Arnold Lobel. New York: Greenwillow, 1980.

Pryor, Bonnie. *The House on Maple Street.* Illustrated by Beth Peck. Morrow, 1987.

Raskin, Ellen. *The Westing Game.* New York: Dutton, 1978.

Rawls, Wilson. *Where the Red Fern Grows.* New York: Doubleday, 1986.

Rendall, J. *When Goldilocks Went to the House of the Bears.* New York: Scholastic, 1986.

Richter, Hans Peter. *Friedrich.* New York: Holt, Rinehart and Winston, 1970.

I Was There. New York: Holt, Rinehart and Winston, 1972.

Riley, James Whitcomb. *Little Orphant Annie.* Illustrated by Diane Stanley. New York: Putnam, 1983.

Sachs, Marilyn. *The Bears' House.* Illustrated by Louis Glanzman. New York: Doubleday, 1971.

Saint-Exupery, Antoine de. *The Little Prince.* Translated by Katherine Woods. San Diego: Harcourt Brace, 1943.

Sancha, Sheila. *The Luttrell Village: Country Life in the Middle Ages.* New York: Crowell, 1982.

Sandburg, Carl. *Rainbows are Made.* Selected by Lee Bennett Hopkins. Engravings by Fritz Eichenberg. San Diego: Harcourt Brace Jovanovich, 1982.

Schwartz, David M. *How Much Is a Million?* Illustrated by Steven Kellogg. Lothrop, Lee, & Shepard, 1985.

Sebestyen, Ouida. *On Fire.* Boston: Atlantic Monthly Press, 1985.

Selden, George. *The Cricket in Times Square.* Illustrated by Garth Williams. New York: Farrar, Straus & Giroux, 1960.

Selsam, Millicent. *Where Do They Go? Insects in Winter.* Illustrated by Arabelle Wheatley. New York: Four Winds, 1982.

Sendak, Maurice. *Chicken Soup with Rice.* New York: Harper & Row, 1962.

Outside Over There. New York: Harper & Row, 1981.

Where the Wild Things Are. New York: Harper & Row, 1963.

Sharmat, Marjorie. *Getting Something on Maggie Marmelstein.* New York: Harper & Row, 1971.

Shulevitz, Uri. *Dawn.* New York: Farrar, Straus & Giroux, 1974.

Silverstein, Shel. *Where the Sidewalk Ends.* New York: Harper & Row, 1974.

Simon, Seymour. *Animal Fact/Animal Fable.* Illustrated by Diane DeGroat. New York: Crown, 1979.

Discovering What Crickets Do. New York: McGraw-Hill, 1973.

Skinner, C.L. *Becky Landers Frontier Warrior.* New York: Macmillan, 1926.

Slepian, Jan. *The Alfred Summer.* New York: Macmillan, 1980.

Slote, Alfred. *Hang Tough, Paul Mather.* Philadelphia: Lippincott, 1973.

My Robot Buddy. Philadelphia: Lippincott, 1975.

Smith, Doris Buchanan. *A Taste of Blackberries.* Illustrated by Charles Robinson. New York: Crowell, 1973.

Smith, William Jay. "The Toaster" in Dunning, Stephen, *et al., Reflections on a Gift of Watermelon Pickle. . .* Glenview, Ill.: Scott, Foresman, 1966.

Smucker, Barbara. *Underground to Canada.* Toronto: Clarke Irwin, 1977.

Southgate, Vera. *The Little Red Hen,* A Ladybird Book. Loughborough, Eng.: Wills and Hepworth, 1966.

Speare, Elizabeth George. *The Sign of the Beaver.* Boston: Houghton Mifflin, 1984.

The Witch of Blackbird Pond. Boston: Houghton Mifflin, 1958.

Spier, Peter. *Tin Lizzie.* New York: Doubleday, 1975.

Steele, Flora Annie. *Tattercoats.* Illustrated by Diane Goode. New York: Bradbury, 1976.

Steig, William. *Abel's Island.* New York: Farrar, Straus & Giroux, 1976.

Amos and Boris. New York: Farrar, Straus & Giroux, 1976.

Steptoe, John. *Mufaro's Beautiful Daughters.* New York: Lothrop, Lee & Shepard, 1987.

Stevenson, Robert Louis. *A Child's Garden of Verses.* New York: Platt and Munk, 1932.

Stinson, Kathy. *Mom and Dad Don't Live Together Anymore.* Illustrated by Nancy Lou Reynolds. Toronto: Annick Press, 1984.

Stone, Harris. *The Last Free Bird.* Illustrated by Sheila Heins. Englewood Cliffs, NJ: Prentice-Hall, 1967.

Taylor, Mildred. *Roll of Thunder, Hear My Cry.* New York: Dial, 1976.

Thayer, Ernest. *Casey at the Bat.* Illustrated by Paul Frame. Englewood Cliffs, NJ: Prentice-Hall, 1964.

Thomas, Jane Resh. *The Comeback Dog.* Illustrated by Troy Howell. Boston: Houghton Mifflin, 1981.

Tolkien, J.R.R. *The Hobbit.* Boston: Houghton Mifflin, 1938.

Tolstoy, Alexei. *The Great Big Enormous Turnip.* Illustrated by Helen Oxenbury. New York: Watts, 1968.

Tomaino, Sarah F. *Persephone, Bringer of Spring*. Illustrated by Ati Forberg. New York: Crowell, 1971.

Tunis, Edwin. *Colonial Living*. New York: Crowell, 1957.

The Tavern at the Ferry. New York: Crowell, 1973.

Turner, Ann. *Dakota Dugout*. Illustrated by Ronald Himler. New York: Macmillan, 1985.

Nettie's Trip South. New York: Macmillan, 1987.

Uchida, Yoshiko. *Journey Home*. New York: Atheneum, 1978.

Journey to Topaz. New York: Atheneum, 1976.

Van Allsburg, Chris. *Ben's Dream*. Boston: Houghton Mifflin, 1982.

The Garden of Abdul Gasazi. Boston: Houghton Mifflin, 1979.

Jumanji. Boston: Houghton Mifflin, 1981.

The Mysteries of Harris Burdick. Boston: Houghton Mifflin, 1984.

The Polar Express. Boston: Houghton Mifflin, 1985.

The Stranger. Boston: Houghton Mifflin, 1986.

The Wreck of the Zephyr. Boston: Houghton Mifflin, 1983.

Viorst, Judith. *Alexander and the Terrible, Horrible, No Good, Very Bad Day*. Illustrated by Ray Cruz. New York: Atheneum, 1972.

Voigt, Cynthia. *Dicey's Song*. New York: Atheneum, 1983.

Homecoming. Atheneum, 1981.

Walsh, Jill Paton. *The Green Book*. Illustrated by Lloyd Bloom. New York: Farrar, Straus & Giroux, 1982.

White, E.B. *Charlotte's Web*. Illustrated by Garth Williams. New York: Harper & Row, 1952.

Whitney, Thomas P. *Vasilisa the Beautiful*. Illustrated by Nonny Hogrogian. New York: Macmillan, 1970.

Wildsmith, Brian. *Brian Wildsmith's ABC*. New York: Watts, 1963.

Wild Animals. New York: Oxford University Press, 1976.

Willard, Nancy. *A Visit to William Blake's Inn*. Illustrated by Alice and Martin Provensen. San Diego: Harcourt Brace Jovanovich, 1981.

Williams, Jay. *Everyone Knows What a Dragon Looks Like*. Illustrated by Mercer Mayer. New York: Four Winds, 1976.

Wojciechowska, Maia. *Shadow of a Bull*. New York: Atheneum, 1964.

Wolf, Bernard. *Don't Feel Sorry for Paul*. Philadelphia: Lippincott, 1974.

Worth, Valerie. *Small Poems*. Illustrated by Natalie Babbitt. New York: Farrar, Straus & Giroux, 1972.

Yagawa, Sumiko (reteller). *The Crane Wife*. Translated by Katherine Paterson. Illustrated by Suekichi Akaba. New York: Morrow, 1981.

Yamaguchi, Tohr. *The Golden Crane*. Illustrated by Marianne Yamaguchi. New York: Holt, Rinehart and Winston, 1963.

Yep, Lawrence. *Sweetwater*. New York: Harper & Row, 1973.

Yolen, Jane. *Owl Moon*. Illustrated by John Schoenherr. New York: Philomel, 1987.

Picnic with Piggins. Illustrated by Jane Dyer. San Diego: Harcourt Brace Jovanovich, 1988.

Piggins. Illustrated by Jane Dyer. San Diego: Harcourt Brace Jovanovich, 1987.

Ring of Earth: A Child's Book of Seasons. Illustrated by John Wallner. San Diego: Harcourt Brace Jovanovich, 1986.

Yorinks, Arthur. *Hey, Al.* Illustrated by Richard Egielski. New York: Farrar, Straus & Giroux, 1986.

Ziefert, Harriet. *Zippety Zap! A Book about Dressing.* Photos by Rudi Tesa. New York: Viking, 1984.

Zola, Meguido. *Gretzky! Gretzky! Gretzky!* Toronto: Grolier, 1982.

Zolotow, Charlotte. *Someday.* Illustrated by Arnold Lobel. Harper & Row, 1965.